Finding
the Old Testament
in the New

BOOKS BY HENRY M. SHIRES
Published by The Westminster Press

Finding the Old Testament
  in the New

The Eschatology of Paul
  in the Light of Modern Scholarship

Finding the Old Testament in the New

by HENRY M. SHIRES

THE WESTMINSTER PRESS

Philadelphia

Book design by Dorothy Alden Smith

Published by The Westminster Press ®
Philadelphia, Pennsylvania

PRINTED IN THE UNITED STATES OF AMERICA

Library of Congress Cataloging in Publication Data

Shires, Henry M.
  Finding the Old Testament in the New.

  Bibliography: p.
  1. Bible. N.T.—Relation to O.T. I. Title.
BS2387.S54   220.6′6   73–19600
ISBN 0–664–20993–9

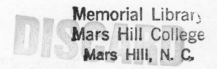
Contents

Foreword

The following study of the relationship between the two Testaments of the Bible began with the preparation of a master list of significant cross-references. Every such reference printed in the Reference Edition of the Revised Standard Version was carefully examined, and those which were judged to be insignificant or doubtful were rejected. Lists of quotations or allusions that appear in three Greek New Testaments—Westcott and Hort, Nestle, and the Bible Society edition of 1966—were similarly reviewed. Attention was also paid to the references suggested by H. B. Swete in his *Introduction to the Old Testament in Greek*. Additional instances of correspondence were gathered from standard commentaries on selected books of the Bible. Altogether, thousands of suggestions were considered, but only those which were believed to be relevant and probable were retained. The final listing is the result first of a consideration of the Old Testament passages which seem to have been cited in the New and then of a study of all those New Testament passages which appear to draw upon the Old Testament.

The references that were retained on the master list were next entered in the margins of a working Bible, keyed according to the nature of the correspondence. Thus, the qualitative and topical treatments of the citations that this book attempts are based directly upon these marginal notations and can, for this reason at least, lay some claim to freshness and originality. Obviously, the author's subjective judgment has been involved in the decisions as to which specific references were to be used; and the listing cannot in any way be regarded as exhaustive. Of necessity, there has been careful selection among many possibilities.

The author has attempted to provide material that will be of interest and help for every serious student of the Bible, whether clerical or lay. For the Christian the Old Testament, which is apt to be less well known and less often read or studied, takes on an entirely new significance when it is understood as a foundation stone for the New Testament. Jewish Scripture is seen in a completely new light when there is an appreciation of the degree to which Christian authors are indebted to it. The proper perspective for both Testaments is supplied by the understanding that together they tell one unfolding story of God's work of salvation for all his people. In similar manner, the New Testament comes to be seen as the fulfillment of the Old and as fundamentally growing out of it. Jewish Scripture is authoritatively invoked at almost every turn. The Christian writings do not stand on their own, but the two divisions of the Bible are highly interdependent. The following study is designed to make these points clear.

The reader is invited to determine for himself the frequency of citation of Old Testament passages, the many purposes that are served in the making of the citations, and the wide variety of ways in which the older material is employed by the later writers. It is instructive to discover that the convictions of the writers of Jewish Scripture are largely shared by the early Christian authors. A large part of Christianity has its origins in Judaism. A comparative study of the Testaments reveals how great is the indebtedness.

The purpose of the present writer will not have been met unless the reader, having acquired some knowledge of how the two parts of the Bible are joined by citation, is challenged to work through the particulars of further correspondences. Tables are appended so that such additional study may be easily undertaken. When it is realized that any particular passage of the Bible is a citation of an earlier writing or is itself cited later, it is at once seen in a new light and takes on a different meaning. The author hopes that his readers may be assisted to look for such passages and to recognize them when they are encountered. The indexes of passages that are directly cited and of those which are based on citations should indicate which verses are discussed in some detail.

In order to appeal to the widest possible circle of readers the text of the Revised Standard Version of the Bible has been used throughout. Definitive study of the correspondences between the Testaments must, of course, involve constant consideration of the original Hebrew of the Old Testament and the original Greek of the New. However, since the RSV is a relatively literal translation, it may be satisfactorily employed for the kind of comparative study that is undertaken here. This is all the more true because the Bible was written in two entirely different languages, and in assessing the dependence of the New Testament upon the Old we are never concerned with identical words. We have to do, rather, with verbal equivalents, and these are apparent in the English text.

The Old Testament is referred to as the O.T. and the New Testament as the N.T. The names of the books of the Bible are abbreviated in accordance with the usage of the RSV. The Septuagint is referred to with the symbol LXX.

I wish to thank the Dean and the Trustees of the Episcopal Theological School for their grant of the sabbatical leave that made possible the writing of this book.

H.M.S.

Cambridge, Massachusetts

Chapter 1

The New Testament View
of the Old Testament

THE CENTRALITY OF THE OLD TESTAMENT

In many ways the O.T. was an embarrassment for early
Christianity. The latter was presumably far removed from the
primitive thoughts and expressions of some parts of the former.
The God of the Christians seemed to have little in common
with the vengeful, angry, and changeable God of some of the
early Hebrew writings. The moral standards of the followers
of Christ could not easily be reconciled with a code of conduct
that demanded repayment in kind of "an eye for an eye." To
Christians who were making their way in the strange if not hos-
tile conditions of the Roman Empire much of the O.T. appeared to be outdated. It was the product of another day and of
different circumstances. The O.T. had been written in Hebrew,
with a few surviving sections in the closely related Aramaic
language. On the other hand, all extant early Christian writings
are in Greek. As Christianity moved from Jewish to Gentile
lands, there was much more involved than simply a new language. Adjustment had to be made to a whole new manner of
life, a decidedly different way of expressing religious experience and religious truth. The result was a specifically Christian
body of literature composed in the common language of the
eastern part of the Roman Empire. Logically, a complete break
with the O.T. seemed inescapable if not highly to be desired.

At a very early date the hostility of many Jews to the growing Christian movement led to active persecution. The Jewish
Scriptures were interpreted so as to condemn Christianity, and
certain Gnostic Christian sects repudiated the O.T. altogether,
as did especially the heretic Marcion, ca. A.D. 140–150. The
God of hate whom he saw in the O.T. had nothing to do with
the God of love as preached by Paul. Even the mainstream of
Christianity, under attack from Jew and pagan alike, was
forced to consider and defend its uniqueness. Its writings were
known as those of the *New* Testament, and the implication
was strong that the *Old* was superseded. Moreover, as soon as
Christianity moved out of Palestine, its new adherents were,
with few exceptions, Gentiles to whom the O.T. could be little
known. On the other hand, the Greek influence on the early
church constantly increased.

However, the strong and deep Jewish roots of Christianity
could not be pulled up. It could not be forgotten that Jesus
was a Jew. His teaching grew out of the religion into which he
had been born and in which he had been reared. Likewise,
with one or two possible exceptions, all the writers of the N.T.
were also Jews. Their Christian experience and convictions
were inevitably described and interpreted in well-established
Jewish terminology and thought patterns. The essence of
Christianity was to be preserved only by retaining the original
very close relationship with Judaism. If that relationship had
been lost, Christianity would have been helpless against the
currents of the prevailing religious syncretism of the time and
would have lost its distinctive character altogether. There is
much evidence to suggest that for a while, at least, the influence of Jewish tradition increased. As Christianity struggled
to establish itself in the Roman world, it utilized ideas and
ways of life that Judaism, forced to live in Gentile lands, had
already developed. Thus, the Christians made large use of the
Greek translation of the O.T. that the Jews had made to support their religious life in Greek-speaking countries.

Gerhard von Rad in *Old Testament Theology* has correctly

noted that "the strongest resistance to any idea of abandoning the Old Testament comes from the New Testament itself." (Vol. II, p. 387.) Its writers never question the Scriptural nature of the O.T. and they make constant and infinitely varied use of it as they set forth Christian truths and practices. In view of the Jewish origins of Christianity it is not surprising that Christian writings of the early period would show some reflections of the O.T., but the extent to which the O.T. is actually employed as a foundation for Christian literature is remarkable and unexpected. Of the twenty-seven books of the N.T. only the one-chapter letter to Philemon shows no direct relationship to the O.T. The remaining twenty-six contain some acknowledged O.T. quotation, or unacknowledged quotation, or a quotation that has been rephrased, or an allusion in thought or language, or at least the borrowing of an O.T. phrase. As we shall see, some of the N.T. books are heavily indebted to the O.T., while others may contain only a few reflections of it. However, its influence is pervasive. If all the O.T. influences were to be removed from the N.T., the latter would in many areas consist of little but meaningless shreds. Where the O.T. is not actually quoted, its content and ideas provide subject matter and structure for the Christian author.

A careful, detailed study of the Bible provides statistical support for these generalizations. Acknowledged O.T. quotations, always introduced by some kind of formula, are found in 239 instances in the N.T. and are drawn from 185 different passages in the O.T. Quotations that are unacknowledged and not introduced by any formula total 198 and are taken from 147 O.T. passages. In addition, 944 O.T. passages are reworded or directly referred to in 1,167 instances in the N.T. In these three categories there are at least 1,604 N.T. citations of 1,276 different O.T. passages. To this total could be added several thousand more N.T. passages that clearly allude to or reflect O.T. verses. There are also well over 100 O.T. phrases that reappear in the N.T. and that testify to the incalculable literary influence which the Old has exerted on the New. This evidence is all the more remarkable since the N.T. was written in a different language, on Gentile soil, and almost exclusively for Gentiles.

There are, of course, fundamental differences between the two Testaments. There is no uniformity between the two as there is no uniformity within either one. Yet there is much continuity in recurring concepts and ideas. Thus Paul speaks (Col. 1:25) of his commission "to make the word of God fully known." Hebrews (Heb. 4:12) also refers to "the word of God." (Cf. also Eph. 6:17 and Heb. 13:7.) In these cases it is impossible to say whether the reference is to the old covenant of Judaism or to the early Christian message. For the Christians the truth of God in the O.T. is one with the truth revealed in Christ. Most properly then "the word of God" is a comprehensive term that applies equally to both Testaments. It is paradoxically the very diversity of the Bible, arising from the variety of recorded religious experience, that points to its unity. In the primitive church the first authority was the tradition of the words and deeds of Jesus and the second was the Holy Spirit, often mentioned in the O.T. and now believed to be a present guide and source of strength. The third authority was shared with Judaism, the O.T. Thus, Christian writings were regarded as entirely consistent with it and could not be held to replace it.

FREEDOM OF CITATION

An investigation into the dependence of the N.T. on the Old involves numerous problems and difficulties. There are few explicit quotations in the O.T., but there are many in the N.T., and most of them are straightforward and clear. It is unlikely that a Christian writer would have had a copy of an O.T. book available for checking his reference to it or would have taken the time and trouble to unroll the scroll if one were at hand. Therefore, it can be assumed that generally quotations were made by memory, which was often faulty. This fact helps to explain why some of the quotations are reproduced with exactness, whereas others depart considerably from the original. In both cases the intent may have been to make a faithful quotation. It should be remembered, however, that classical Greek authors demonstrate a wide degree of freedom in their deliberate quotations. Faulty memory is to blame for some wrong ascriptions of quoted verses to named authors. In Mk. 1:2–3 there is a quotation of a verse from Malachi (Mal. 3:1) joined with a verse from Isaiah (Is. 40:3), and both are introduced by a single reference to Isaiah. Some later copyists have tried to correct the inaccuracy by changing the introduction to the general reading, "As it is written in the prophets." Likewise, in Mt. 27:9 a quotation from Zechariah (Zech. 11:12–13) is wrongly attributed to Jeremiah.

It is often very difficult to determine whether a passage taken from the O.T. is a quotation or an allusion. Moreover, the Christian author may have been so familiar with large portions of the O.T. that its influence upon his writing may often be unconscious. As Robert Gundry has noted: "Recent researches in the Qumran scrolls have shown that in the New Testament period the interweaving of scriptural phraseology and one's own words was a conscious literary method." (*The Use of the Old Testament in St. Matthew's Gospel*, p. 3.) The N.T. reveals much of this form of literary blending. Further, verbal parallelism may be accidental and no proof of any dependence. Even close similarity between two passages may be only independent literary expressions of an ongoing tradition. Not every possible instance of literary borrowing can be proved to be such. It is admittedly possible to pursue an extreme course and to see O.T. reflections everywhere in the N.T. Some of the suggestions must remain only unverified possibilities, but the evidence is cumulative. Conclusions regarding the nature of the relationship between the two Testaments in no way depend upon the establishment of all the probabilities.

COMPOSITE QUOTATIONS

Many of the quotations are clearly composite; they are drawn from more than a single source and often involve changes that are necessary to weave together material from two or three different sections of the O.T. According to Mk. 1:11 (= Mt. 3:17 and Lk. 3:22), the heavenly voice at the baptism of Jesus proclaimed, "Thou art my beloved Son; with thee I am well pleased." The words "You are my son" are found in Ps. 2:7. God's words to Abraham regarding Isaac in Gen. 22:2 refer to "your only son . . . , whom you love." Ascribed to God in Is. 42:1 is the reference to "my chosen, in whom my soul delights." Thus, the proclamation of Mk. 1:11 seems to be based upon three widely scattered O.T. verses that have been skillfully combined. Likewise, the words of Jesus given in Mk. 11:17 (= Mt. 21:13 and Lk. 19:46), " 'My house shall be called a house of prayer for all the nations.' But you have made it a den of robbers," are a quotation of Is. 56:7 and Jer. 7:11 with only the added general introduction, "Is it not written?" Occasionally a composite quotation will be drawn from two different parts of the same O.T. book. Thus, in Rom. 9:33 what is apparently a single quotation is introduced by the words "As it is written," and we read: "Behold, I am laying in Zion a stone that will make men stumble, a rock that will make them fall." The first source is Is. 28:16: "Behold, I am laying in Zion . . . a stone." The second source is Is. 8:14: "He will become . . . a stone of offense, and a rock of stumbling." The combination is apparently made because both Isaianic verses refer to "a stone." A similar composite quotation based on occurrences of the word "death" is found in 1 Cor. 15:54-55: "Death is swallowed up in victory. O death, where is thy victory? O death, where is thy sting?" The first source is Is. 25:8: "He will swallow up death for ever." The second is Hos. 13:14: "O Death, where are your plagues? O Sheol, where is your destruction?"

Occasionally a single O.T. verse will be quoted, but it will be modified because of an allusion to another passage as well. Thus, Peter, in Acts 3:25, describes God's promise to Abraham: "In your posterity shall all the families of the earth be blessed." The wording is drawn principally from Gen. 12:3: "By you all the families of the earth shall bless themselves." But the reference to posterity is found in Gen. 22:18: "By your descendants shall all the nations of the earth bless themselves." A faulty and confused memory may account for the wording in Acts. It is sometimes difficult, if not impossible, to tell from which of several passages a N.T. clause or verse has been taken. In some instances the language of an O.T. passage is merely paraphrased so as to express a new, specifically Christian thought. Passages that are apparently dependent upon the O.T. may be only reflections of a broad tradition. A N.T. author may have in mind an O.T. idea rather than any specific verse. Language and phrase forms of the O.T. influence every N.T. writer, even where no quotations are made.

UNIDENTIFIED QUOTATIONS

The sources of some of the apparent quotations from the O.T. can no longer be identified, even though in most cases some partial parallels can be drawn. One of the most striking of these instances is Mt. 2:23, where the Evangelist declares that Jesus lived in Nazareth "that what was spoken by the prophets might be fulfilled, 'He shall be called a Nazarene.'" No such prophetic statement can be found in the O.T. although Judg. 13:5, 7, and Is. 11:1 are often proposed as the root of Matthew's statement. The words ascribed to "the Wisdom of God" in Lk. 11:49 are partially paralleled in Jer. 7:25 and 2 Chron. 36:15–16, but a direct source cannot be discovered. According to Jn. 7:38, Jesus declared: "He who believes in me, as the scripture has said, 'Out of his heart shall flow rivers of living water.'" The basis for this apparent quotation is not to be found in the O.T., but somewhat similar words

occur in Isaiah, Jeremiah, Joel, and Zechariah. Another puz-
zling verse is Jn. 12:34: "We have heard from the law that
the Christ remains for ever." Such an explicit statement is not
made in the O.T., although Ps. 89:36 promises: "[David's]
line shall endure for ever." And Ezek. 37:25 promises: "David
my servant shall be their prince for ever." In the words of the
Fourth Evangelist (Jn. 19:28): "Jesus . . . said (to fulfill the
scripture), 'I thirst.'" What Scripture was thus fulfilled we
cannot determine. The words of Ps. 22:15 are one possibility:
"My strength is dried up like a potsherd, and my tongue
cleaves to my jaws." Or perhaps there is an indirect reference
to Ps. 63:1: "My soul thirsts for thee." No convincing suggestion of any kind can be made for the ground of John's allusion
(Jn. 20:9) to "the scripture, that he must rise from the dead."
Paul writes in 1 Cor. 2:9: "As it is written, 'What no eye has
seen, nor ear heard, nor the heart of man conceived, what God
has prepared for those who love him.'" The first eight words
of this supposed quotation can be found, in somewhat different
form, in Is. 64:4, but we cannot locate any Scriptural basis for
the remainder. James 4:5 states unequivocally: "The scripture
says, 'He yearns jealously over the spirit which he has made
to dwell in us.'" The O.T. contains no such declaration.

EXTRACANONICAL QUOTATIONS

In the foregoing instances it has been suggested that "scripture" may refer to literature that is outside the O.T. However,
we shall have occasion to point out that in the N.T. the word
"scripture" does clearly mean no more than the thirty-nine
books of the O.T. It is true that in Acts 17:28; 1 Cor. 15:33;
and Tit. 1:12 there are quotations from or reflections of such
Greek authors as Aratus, Menander, and Epimenides. In the
N.T. generally there are allusions to or reflections (often secondary) of books of the Apocrypha: Wisdom, Sirach, Baruch,
2 Esdras, and 1 Maccabees; and of some books of the Pseudepigrapha: Psalms of Solomon, Enoch, Assumption of Moses,

and 3 and 4 Maccabees. In addition, Paul may have made some use of the Testament of the Twelve Patriarchs, and Jude probably knew the Testament of Moses. Yet the only passage from any noncanonical Jewish literature that is even implicitly quoted in the whole N.T. is Enoch 1:9, which is abstracted in Jude 14. All other quotations, explicit or implicit, are drawn from the O.T. Scripture. The solution to the problem of quotations or specific references that cannot be immediately identified in the O.T. lies rather in a study of the ways in which Jewish Scripture is used by Christians.

CHAINS OF QUOTATIONS

The reader of the N.T. must notice at once the many instances in which two or more different quotations are strung together consecutively. As we have seen, this may be done with a single formula of introduction. Perhaps the most impressive example of this usage is Rom. 3:10–18, where the words "as it is written" are followed by verses from Ps. 14:1–3 (= 53:1–3); 5:9; 140:3; 10:7; Is. 59:7–8; and Ps. 36:1. This artificial combination of verses was made by Paul to support his assertion (Rom. 3:9) that "all men, both Jews and Greeks, are under the power of sin." Paul justifies his conclusion of a discussion of the Jews' rejection of Christianity (Rom., chs. 9 to 11) that the ways of God lie beyond man's understanding by joining (Rom. 11:34–35) a quotation of Is. 40:13 with one of Job 35:7; 41:11, introduced by the single word "for." The quotations in 2 Cor. 6:16–18, preceded by "as God said," are drawn from many parts of the O.T.; possibilities include Exodus, Leviticus, Deuteronomy, 2 Samuel, 1 Chronicles, Isaiah, Jeremiah, and Zechariah.

In other cases there is a bringing together of two or more quotations, each with its own introduction or identification. Thus, in Rom. 10:18–21 Paul sets forth quotations from Psalms, Deuteronomy, and Isaiah. Likewise, in Rom. 15:9–12 Paul joins verses from 2 Samuel, Deuteronomy, Psalms, and Isaiah;

and each of the four has its own formula of introduction. All
the verses relate to God's dealings with the Gentiles. The foolishness of the wise is illustrated by Paul in 1 Cor. 3:19–20,
where he lists separate quotations from Job and Psalms.
Paul's theological argument regarding justification by faith is
detailed in Gal. 3:6–14. It is almost exclusively based on a
series of quotations, with a minimum of interpretation, from
Genesis, Deuteronomy, Habakkuk, Leviticus, and Deuteronomy. A similar situation occurs in Gal. 4:21–30. Hebrews 1:5–
13 consists entirely of quotations, all introduced as the words
of God, from Psalms, 2 Samuel, and Deuteronomy. In Heb.
2:12–13 there are quotations from Psalms, 2 Samuel, and
Isaiah. Verses from two different psalms are linked in Heb.
5:5–6. In Heb. 13:5–6 words are borrowed from Deuteronomy,
Joshua, and Psalms. Many further examples might be given of
such a massing of quotations in the N.T., but the point seems
to be very clear without further elaboration.

MATTERS OF CONTEXT

We are told by Joachim Jeremias that "in the Judaism of this
period, when large parts of scripture were known . . . by
heart, it was regularly the custom to quote only the beginning
of a passage, even if its continuation were kept in mind." (New
Testament Theology: The Proclamation of Jesus, p. 54.) Thus,
most commentators suggest that the words spoken by Jesus
from the cross, "My God, my God, why hast thou forsaken
me?" (Mk. 15:34 = Mt. 27:46), which are the opening words
of Ps. 22, are evidence of the fact that Jesus recited the whole
of that psalm as a source of spiritual strength. It may well be
that any quotation of or direct allusion to a single verse of the
O.T. may be intended to recall the whole passage from which
it has been selected. Thus, in Rom. 3:4 Paul discusses both the
faithfulness of God and the sinfulness of man. He then quotes
Ps. 51:4, "That thou mayest be justified in thy words, and pre-
vail when thou art judged," as support for his first point. He

continues his argument with a further reference to human wickedness, which is in fact the subject of Ps. 51:5, "Behold, I was brought forth in iniquity," but which Paul did not feel the need to quote since it was already suggested to one familiar with the Biblical text.

On the other hand, the passages quoted in the N.T. are usually very short and are regarded as significant in themselves without reference to their context. In fact, in some instances a text may be applied in the N.T. in a manner that is quite contrary to O.T. meaning and context. Occasionally, isolated verses will be used by Christian authors for theological purposes in the manner of a proof text even though the original meaning of the verses could have no Christian significance. Verbal play and literalism are by no means unknown in the N.T. Moreover, in those cases where two or more Christian writers quote or refer to the same O.T. verse there is no necessary agreement among them as to the extent of the material quoted. In a few cases two N.T. writers will quote different parts of the same O.T. verse. Thus, different parts of Ps. 11:4 are directly reflected in 1 Cor. 3:17 and Mt. 5:34. Passages from the O.T. may be very closely described. So, in Rom. 9:17 Paul begins his quotation of Ex. 9:16 with the words, "The scripture says to Pharaoh." So also Paul in Gal. 3:8 introduces his quotation of Gen. 12:3; 18:18; 28:14 by stating, "The scripture . . . preached the gospel beforehand to Abraham, saying." The same preciseness in referring to a particular verse can be seen in Mk. 12:26, where a quotation of Ex. 3:6 is preceded by the question, "Have you not read in the book of Moses, in the passage about the bush?" In like manner a quotation in Acts 13:33 is correctly identified as from "the second psalm." A citation of 1 Kings 19:10, 14, is introduced (in Rom. 11:3) by another question: "Do you not know what the scripture says of Elijah, how he pleads with God against Israel?" In all these instances the N.T. authors have clearly in mind specific verses and their exact wording. Some allusions to the O.T. are admittedly reflections of a culture that is common to

Jews and early Christians, and some are incidental borrowings
from the only established literature which the N.T. knows.
However, the great majority of significant borrowings grow
out of deliberate reference to O.T. verses and passages that
can be immediately identified and that are used because there
is something in their wording which underlines Christian
teaching.

RECURRING CITATIONS

Christian use of the O.T. obviously began very early. In fact,
it is abundantly illustrated in the recorded teaching of Jesus,
as we shall see. Some of the central passages of the O.T. are
reflected in all the main portions of the N.T. The same citation
sometimes appears in various levels of the developing Christian tradition with such differences of wording or usage as to
make possible a reconstruction of the development. Thus, the
pessimistic words of Is. 6:9–10, " 'Hear and hear, but do not
understand; see and see, but do not perceive' . . . lest they
see with their eyes, and hear with their ears . . . and turn and
be healed," are cited in varying ways in Mt. 13:14–15; Mk.
4:12; 8:18; Lk. 8:10; Jn. 12:40; and Acts 28:26–27. Some of the
verses became so familiar and so widely used in the primitive
church that the reasons for selecting them in the first place
were forgotten.

FORMS OF ADAPTATION

Christian authors did not cite the O.T. for its own sake but
rather made such use of it as would advance the gospel. Accordingly, we are not surprised to discover that frequently an
O.T. text is altered in some manner for the sake of the interpretation which is made of it and the use to which it is put. For
example, Matthew makes use (Mt. 2:6) of the prophecy of
Mic. 5:2 to explain the birth of Jesus in Bethlehem. In the latter Bethlehem is described as "little to be among the clans of
Judah," but in Matthew, Bethlehem, which is known among

Christians as the birthplace of Jesus the Christ, is pictured as "by no means least among the rulers of Judah." Likewise, Paul uses Ps. 94:11 to corroborate his statement that "the wisdom of this world is folly with God" (1 Cor. 3:19–20). The psalm refers to all men: "The Lord knows the thoughts of man, that they are but a breath." But Paul sharpens the quotation to read: "The Lord knows that the thoughts of the wise are futile." A quotation is introduced in Eph. 5:14 with the words, "Therefore it is said," and the first part of that quotation is drawn from Is. 26:19; 52:1; and 60:1; but the second part, "and Christ shall give you light," is the author's own interpretation. The principle is the same if the author is here preserving the words of an early Christian hymn. Even as they are used, O.T. verses are often changed and given new meanings.

At first thought we may be disturbed by what may seem to be dishonest practice. So, too, we are not convinced by the occasional elaboration by Christian writers of mechanical, literalistic parallels. Cases of complete disregard in the N.T. of the context and original meaning of cited Scriptural passages may shake our confidence in the integrity of the writers who engage in such practices. Yet some shift in meaning must occur as any literary passage is utilized over a period of centuries. Futhermore, all literary practices are to be judged by the standards accepted in their own time. Christian authors exhibit many of the characteristics of their Jewish contemporaries. Although some of the verses quoted from the O.T. are given a Christian interpretation that ignores their original context, most of the passages cited are applied with a full awareness of that context and a fidelity to it. The selected verses as a whole fairly represent the religion of Israel and point to Christianity's intimate and essential relationship to that religion.

The attitude of the first Christians toward the O.T. is on the surface paradoxical. On the one hand, it is accepted and revered as the authoritative word of God; but on the other, it is criticized, reinterpreted, and even rejected. The N.T. use of the O.T. is to be explained only by these two apparently self-contradictory facts. This duality, which first appears in the teaching of Jesus, becomes the common Christian position reflected in all parts of the N.T.

Old Testament Authority and Inspiration

Jewish Scripture was viewed as authoritative for belief and practice even though there were for the Christians additional sources of authority. The ways in which appeal is made to the O.T. are evidence of the high regard in which it was held. For Christians, as for Jews, the place of Scripture was unique. The Scripture (literally, "that which is written") possesses an objective and fixed reality. This view is seen in the parenthetical words of Jesus in Jn. 10:35: "Scripture cannot be broken." According to Mt. 5:18, Jesus taught that as long as this world continues, "not an iota, not a dot, will pass from the law." Paul believed that in their Scriptures the Jews had been entrusted by God with a treasure that was of benefit for all humanity. (Rom. 3:2.) To one who is seeking God the Scriptures provide encouragement. (Rom. 15:4.) According to 2 Tim. 3:16, "All scripture is inspired by God and profitable for teaching. . . ." Paul writes in Rom. 7:12 that "the law is holy."

That the writings of the O.T. were inspired by God, even in their translation from Hebrew to Greek, is accepted without question by the Christian authors. In Mk. 7:13 Jesus refers to a quotation from Exodus, Leviticus, and Deuteronomy as "the word of God." Again, in Jn. 5:39 Jesus says of the Jews, with apparent approval: "You search the scriptures, because you think that in them you have eternal life." With reference to the O.T. it is said in Heb. 1:1: "In many and various ways God spoke of old to our fathers by the prophets." Moreover, the working of God in the O.T. authors is in many places specifically ascribed to the Holy Spirit. In Mt. 1:22 a quotation from Is. 7:14 is introduced as "what the Lord had spoken by the prophet." The same description is given of a verse of Hos.

11:1 quoted in Mt. 2:15. In Mk. 12:26 a citation of Ex. 3:6 is set forth as the very words of God as he spoke to Moses. In Mk. 12:36 (= Mt. 22:43; Lk. 20:42–43), Ps. 110:1 is attributed to David, who was himself "inspired by the Holy Spirit." An uncertain reference to Psalms is made in much the same words by Peter in Acts 1:16 when he declares: "The scripture had to be fulfilled, which the Holy Spirit spoke beforehand by the mouth of David." Likewise, the opening words of Ps. 2 are quoted in Acts 4:25 as the words of God, "who by the mouth of our father David, thy servant, didst say by the Holy Spirit." Further, in Acts 28:25 a citation of Is. 6:9–10 is prefaced by the comment: "The Holy Spirit was right in saying to your fathers through Isaiah the prophet." Words of God from Ex. 33:19 are quoted by Paul in Rom. 9:15. In Rom. 9:25 Paul states that God speaks in the book of Hosea. Words of God that are preserved in O.T. writings are also cited in 2 Cor. 6:16–17 with no mention of an intermediary author. So, too, in Heb. 3:7 the words of Ps. 95:7–11 are cited as the words of the Holy Spirit. Two verses of Jeremiah (Jer. 31:33–34) are also quoted as the words of the Holy Spirit in Heb. 10:15–17. In 1 Pet. 1:11 it is stated directly that the Spirit of Christ was within the prophets, and 2 Pet. 1:21 declares: "No prophecy ever came by the impulse of man, but men moved by the Holy Spirit spoke from God."

It was the recognition that the Holy Spirit was active in the writing of the O.T. which enabled Christians to accept its authority over them as over the Jews. Moses, David, Isaiah, Hosea, and other authors are looked upon as God's chosen instruments for the writing down of his words. It is the pervasiveness of God's Holy Spirit that gives an essential unity to the otherwise diverse and uneven Scriptures. Although the N.T. never discusses the ways in which the Jewish authors received or expressed their inspiration, their writings are received as a gift of God. In at least nine instances O.T. quotations are reproduced in the N.T. with the inclusion of the phrase "says the Lord." In the majority of these cases the O.T.

passage cited does not contain the phrase, but the inclusion of
the phrase in the N.T. citation amounts to a Christian interpretation of the passage as the word of God. A good example of
such usage is Rom. 12:19, which states: "It is written, 'Vengeance is mine, I will repay, says the Lord.'" In the source of
the quotation, Deut. 32:35, we find: "Vengeance is mine, and
recompense." The Greek translation is slightly different: "In
the day of vengeance I will recompense." But in neither Hebrew nor Greek does the phrase "says the Lord" occur. Verses
of Isaiah (28:11–12) are similarly interpreted in 1 Cor. 14:21.

It is significant that the N.T. refers by name far less frequently to the authors of the O.T. books than do Jewish rabbis
of the same period. The fact of inspiration of the Scriptures is
far more important than the mode of composition. In principle,
at least, inspiration extends to all the O.T. writings. Occasionally, the singular word "scripture" refers to one particular
text of the O.T. Thus, in Mk. 12:10 "this scripture" identifies
Ps. 118:22–23; and in Lk. 4:21 the same words refer back to
Is. 61:1–2. In Jn. 19:37 a quotation of Zech. 12:10 is described
as "another scripture." Early Christianity was concerned to
point out correspondences between selected O.T. texts and
many words and deeds of Jesus; but it was also aware of the
general correspondence between the O.T. as a whole and the
events of Christian history. Thus, the word "scripture" is never
used in the N.T. to indicate a single book of the O.T., whereas
the plural, "scriptures," is a designation for the body of authoritative Jewish writings. Scriptures are significant in their
unity and totality as the Word of God transmitted by the Holy
Spirit. Thus, Scripture is often personified and can be said to
"speak" or to "preach." (Cf. Rom. 9:17; Gal. 3:8, 22.)

The N.T. contains much evidence of the fact that a fairly
full knowledge of Jewish Scripture was expected of all Christians, even Gentiles converted from paganism. Thus, the theological arguments of Paul in Galatians and Romans are rooted
in selected O.T. books and cannot be understood without
knowledge of them. The Jews of Beroea were, as described in

Acts 17:11, open to Christian conversion because they were "examining the scriptures daily to see if these things were so." So, too, 2 Timothy, addressed to Gentile readers, states (2 Tim. 3:16) that "all scripture is . . . profitable for teaching, for reproof, for correction, and for training in righteousness." The first reason why Jewish Scriptures were presented to Gentile Christian converts as essential to the new faith is that they were accepted without question as the authoritative written communication of God with men. They remain in force for the duration of this age.

Yet, as we have noted, Christian writers were also able to criticize the O.T. writings and to give to them new interpretations. The O.T. can be quoted against itself. In Mk. 10:2–9 (= Mt. 19:3–9), Jesus puts aside Mosaic permission for divorce as stated in Deut. 24:1 by citing words of Gen. 1:27; 2:24; 5:2. The ancient principle of "an eye for an eye and a tooth for a tooth," which is laid down in Ex. 21:24; Lev. 24:20; and Deut. 19:21, is directly condemned by Jesus in Mt. 5:38. In Mk. 9:12 Jesus gives his own interpretation, as over against other current interpretations, of the well-known prediction (Mal. 4:5) of the return of Elijah as God's agent. The generally understood meaning of the prohibition in the law of Moses (Deut. 25:4), "You shall not muzzle an ox when it treads out the grain," was that God wanted animals to have their fair share of food. But for Paul (1 Cor. 9:9–10) the prohibition points rather to the necessity for hope in the Christian life. Christian acceptance of the authority of the O.T. was within a perspective that saw the O.T. as a necessary part of a much larger whole, namely, God's historical and continuing saving activity on earth.

CHRISTIAN INTERPRETATION

Scripture was only one authority for early Christianity. Another was Jesus Christ, and he alone is the key to the Christian understanding of all Scripture. According to Jn. 8:56, Jesus believed that Abraham had seen him in some form of visionary experience. The real meaning of the O.T. is Jesus, and it is to him that all the Scriptures point. Accordingly, Jesus can say of the O.T. (Lk. 16:16) that "the law and the prophets were until John." For Paul, too, the law and the exposition of the law are transcended by Christ because it is to him that law and prophecy point. He is their only reason for being. In Jn. 5:39 Jesus proclaims: "The scriptures . . . bear witness to me." (Cf. also Jn. 5:46.) In more than one instance the O.T. is declared to have been written for Christians. Paul, writing to the Christians at Rome, affirms (Rom. 15:4): "Whatever was written in former days was written for our instruction." With regard to the events of the exodus Paul declares (1 Cor. 10:11) that "they were written down for our instruction." Likewise, in 1 Pet. 1:12 it is said of the O.T. prophets that "it was revealed to them that they were serving not themselves but you."

Moreover, it could be claimed that the meaning of the Jewish Scriptures was hidden from the Jews themselves. Paul writes of the Jews in 2 Cor. 3:15: "Whenever Moses is read a veil lies over their minds." A hardness of heart with regard to the acceptance of Jesus as the Messiah has obscured the real significance of the Scriptures. On the other hand, the early Christians believed that the full significance of Jewish Scripture was understood by them alone. Paul states of the veil present in the reading of the O.T. (2 Cor. 3:14) that "only through Christ is it taken away." When the Scriptures are thus properly understood both their permanent value and their dependent nature are seen.

Paul announces (Gal. 3:24): "The law was our custodian until Christ came." Now that Christ has come, the law is no longer absolute. He adds (2 Cor. 3:6) that, compared with the life available in Christ, "the written code kills." Jesus had declared (Lk. 16:16 = Mt. 11:13): "The law and the prophets were until John." Now that John the Baptist has played his part in the beginning of the decisive events of the final salvation, the Law and the Prophets of the O.T. are viewed in a new light by which they are seen as pointing to Christ. Paul is sure (Gal. 3:21) that no law can bring the gift of life. Now that Christ has come, the *Old* Testament stands in relationship to a *New*. Thus, what the O.T. may have meant before the Christian era is no longer of great importance to the Christian authors. Henceforth all Scripture is to be interpreted by the fact of Christ. It is only because Paul has known and accepted the "new covenant" established by Jesus Christ that he can call Jewish Scripture "the old covenant" (2 Cor. 3:14). In the Sermon on the Mount, Jesus' words possess the same kind of authority that had hitherto belonged only to Jewish Scripture. Words and commands of Jesus are given such authority by Paul. (Cf. 1 Cor. 7:10; 9:14; 11:23.) And already in one of the late books of the N.T. (2 Pet. 3:16–17) the Pauline epistles are referred to as "scriptures."

THE CONCEPT OF FULFILLMENT

Both Jews and Christians recognized that because the Scriptures were inspired writings their unfulfilled prophecies demanded some kind of fulfillment. The O.T. everywhere looks toward a future in which God will reign over all mankind and there will be peace and happiness on earth. There is in the Jewish Scriptures an inescapable incompleteness and a deep longing for the coming of God in power and right to correct man's evils and failings. At the heart of the first Christian proclamation was the conviction that Jesus is the fulfillment of the unfulfilled prophecies and hopes of the O.T. The whole story of God's plans and purposes for Israel as developed in all the Jewish writings is now said to reach its climax and goal in the life and work of Jesus of Nazareth. In this manner Christian authors are governed by a belief in an essential continuity between the Jewish Scriptures and their own compositions. The God whose words and deeds are recorded in the O.T. is the same God who is revealed in Jesus. Summaries of Biblical history, such as those of Acts, ch. 7, and Heb., ch. 11, are designed to connect the long story told in the O.T. with the relatively few years of the Christian events. Continuity is also seen as development along an ascending line. The Christian climax is inconceivable without the groundwork that is both described in and laid by the O.T. From the perspective of Christian conviction Jewish writings inevitably take on a new meaning that could not have been understood before the life of Jesus.

According to Mt. 5:17, Jesus did not do away with the Law and the Prophets, but he said: "I have come not to abolish them but to fulfil them." Elsewhere, Jesus views his own life as a series of events that have been predicted in the Scriptures. (Cf. Mt. 26:54, 56; Mk. 9:12; 14:21, 49; Lk. 4:21; 18:31; 21:22; 22:37.) Moreover, the conviction of the early Christians that the Jewish Scriptures did contain many predictions regarding the manner of Jesus' life and death is abundantly illustrated in the N.T. Thus, in speaking to Nathanael, Philip testifies (Jn. 1:45): "We have found him of whom Moses in the law and also the prophets wrote." In Acts 3:18 Peter declares: "What God foretold by the mouth of all the prophets, that his Christ should suffer, he thus fulfilled." Other very similar instances are Acts 3:21, 24; 13:27, 29; 17:2; 18:28; 24:14; 26:22; 28:23. Paul writes (Rom. 1:2–3) of "the gospel of God which he promised beforehand through his prophets in the holy scriptures, the gospel concerning his Son." (Cf. also Rom. 3:21.) The central place of the O.T. in primitive Christian creedal affirmation is shown in 1 Cor. 15:3–4: "That Christ died for our sins in accordance with the scriptures, that he was buried, that he was raised on the third day in accordance with the scriptures." A. G. Hebert has summarized: "It is scarcely an exaggeration to say that whenever a New Testament writer quotes or alludes to the Old Testament, it is in order to exhibit some aspect or other of the Divine Purpose that had been fulfilled in Jesus." (*The Authority of the Old Testament*, p. 200.)

Dependence on Jewish Scripture in the N.T. involves far more than combinations of words or single ideas. Every quotation or allusion may presuppose both its immediate context and its relation to the entire Hebrew tradition. Christians believed that all parts of the O.T. testified to the coming of Christ. They were thus convinced that the true meaning of the O.T. is Jesus Christ and that he alone provides the means of understanding it. In 2 Tim. 3:15–16 there is reference to "the sacred writings which are able to instruct you for salvation through faith in Christ Jesus." But the Scriptures have no saving power in themselves; faith in Christ is the essential element.

The third authority for early Christianity, along with the Jewish Scriptures and Jesus, was the Holy Spirit, who was somehow to be closely related to Jesus. In 1 Pet. 1:10–11 it is written: "The prophets . . . inquired what person or time was indicated by the Spirit of Christ within them." The words of Jesus are described (Jn. 6:63) as "spirit and life." In the same Gospel (Jn. 14:26), Jesus promises to his disciples: "The Holy Spirit, whom the Father will send in my name, he will teach you all things." According to Lk. 24:27, it is the risen Jesus, who cannot be essentially distinguished from the Spirit, of whom it can be said: "Beginning with Moses and all the prophets, he interpreted to them in all the scriptures the things concerning himself." In Lk. 24:45 it is added: "He opened their minds to understand the scriptures." According to Jn. 12:16, the disciples did not understand that Jesus' entry into Jerusalem had been foretold in Scripture, "but when Jesus was glorified, then they remembered that this had been written of him." The story of Emmaus (Lk. 24:13–35) conveys the teaching that the spirit of the risen Jesus will interpret to all Christian readers the truths regarding himself that are to be found in all the Scriptures.

Paul asks the relevant question (Rom. 3:31): "Do we then overthrow the law by this faith? By no means! On the contrary, we uphold the law." In the Christian view the O.T. cannot be fully understood without the N.T. But the reverse is equally true. The Christian writings do not stand by themselves but draw much of their substance from the Jewish Scriptures. Furthermore, without the O.T. Christians would have found it almost impossible to explain the person of Jesus or the meaning of his acts, especially of his death and resurrection. It was the O.T. that enabled the Christian community to identify itself as the New Israel. It was the O.T. that alone could provide the perspective in which the Christian events could be seen as the culmination of God's continuing plan of salvation. There are, of course, very important differences between the two Testaments; but there is a common theological base. In the N.T. the O.T. is brought to a sharp focus by which its diverse parts find their proper place.

The authority that the early Christian writers ascribed to Jewish Scripture was not such that it prevented all alteration of the O.T. text. Rather, as E. D. Freed has noted, in his book *Old Testament Quotations in the Gospel of John* (p. 27), "All the New Testament and early Christian writers frequently altered the passages quoted to support the theological view of the writer which was responsible for the use of the quotation in the first place." At times it appears that the O.T. is being rejected as no longer in force. Yet support for this type of judgment is sought in the O.T. itself. Even within Jewish Scripture we discover the same kind of freedom in the treatment of inherited traditions that we see in the way in which N.T. authors make use, for their own purposes, of O.T. material. Jewish writers had already demonstrated that, in order to discover God's unfolding purpose in the often strange and unexpected developments in Jewish history, it was sometimes necessary to adapt old traditions to meet new situations. Christians had no doubts about the newness brought by Jesus, and they made such use of the traditions of Scripture as would clarify that newness.

Chapter 2

How the Old Testament
Is Used

WAYS OF JEWISH INTERPRETATION

The N.T. makes use of the O.T. in a wide variety of ways and for many different reasons. It should be recognized at the outset that early Christian writers were influenced, both consciously and unconsciously, by the presuppositions and the practices of their contemporaries; N.T. authors are to be understood and assessed only when full allowance has been made for the ideas, purposes, and methods of rabbinical writers and of the authors of the Dead Sea Scrolls, which are not much earlier than the rise of Christianity. Thus, in the first Christian century the rabbis were already developing an elaborate scheme for interpreting the O.T. Scriptures, and it was inevitable that the writers of the N.T. books would make such use of that scheme as suited them for their own purposes. As the the rabbis held that the O.T. had various levels of meaning, so the first Christian writers also discovered different hidden truths in Jewish Scripture. As the rabbis often disregarded the context of an O.T. passage and concerned themselves rather with a study of individual letters or syllables and the relationship of words to each other, so N.T. authors occasionally interpret Scripture in a mechanical, literalistic manner that leaves the modern reader quite unconvinced. A dramatic example of the emulation of this rabbinical usage is Paul's treatment of Deut. 30:12, 14 in Rom. 10:6, 8. In Deuteronomy it is stated that God's commandment is not in heaven, so that men should ask, "Who will go up for us to heaven, and bring it to us . . . ?" Rather, the commandment "is very near you; it is in your mouth and in your heart." Paul, however, refers these words to "the righteousness based on faith"; and he identifies the commandment or the word with Christ. Another illustration is provided by Paul in Gal. 3:16, where he quotes Gen. 12:7. Although the Hebrew text of the latter reads the plural "descendants," the Greek translation (LXX) uses a word that is singular in form and plural in meaning, translated as "seed." In any case, Paul's interpretation is based simply upon the form of an O.T. word, and he concludes that God's promise to Abraham is really a reference to Christ. To us this type of argument seems to miss the true significance of Scripture. However, the N.T. writers ought not to be judged unfairly. The scholarship available to them was that of their own time and place.

The Dead Sea Scrolls, produced at Qumran, were also influenced by rabbinical ideas and usage; but they in turn have indicated that at Qumran there were some new types of Biblical interpretation. The authors of the Scrolls were particularly given to explaining contemporary events as the fulfillment of O.T. prophecies. However, they did feel free to introduce whatever minor alterations and modifications of the O.T. text they felt necessary in order to support their application of that text. Moreover, the Qumran interpretation of the O.T. was neither systematic nor consistent. A single text of Scripture was not always interpreted in the same way, and an O.T. quotation or reference is made for the admitted purpose of providing support for a belief already held. The Scrolls often reveal a kind of proof-text approach to the O.T. In all these descriptions we find a similarity to the situation in the N.T. Early Christian writers are not greatly different from the writers at Qumran. In fact, there is a small group of O.T. texts that are used in both the Scrolls and the N.T. These include verses from Leviticus, Isaiah, and Ezekiel.

Christian writers, rabbis, and the Qumran authors all share the view that behind the literal and the historical meaning of Scripture there is a deeper spiritual meaning. They all agree in addition that the external and obvious aspects of Jewish history point to a divine reality that continues to work itself out on earth. In the N.T., as also among the rabbis and the Qumran authors, O.T. texts are treated with a large degree of freedom. The literal, historical meaning of Scripture is frequently overlooked or transcended. There is, of course, no observance of the modern rules of literary criticism by any first-century author. Yet within the rabbinical writings, the Dead Sea Scrolls, and the N.T., Jewish Scripture occupies a most prominent place. In the three areas the words and phrases of the O.T. are material from which the later authors construct their own compositions. Writers of all three types of literature make regular appeals to the O.T. for support for their own ideological positions and arguments.

The N.T. contains some examples of doubtful, unnatural, and forced interpretation of the Old Testament. This is especially true in Hebrews, where (Heb. 1:5–13) the author artificially combines seven different O.T. passages from Deuteronomy, 2 Samuel, and Psalms and treats them all as the words of God to or about his Son, Jesus Christ. Another interesting case is the description of Jesus in 1 Pet. 2:4 as the stone that has been rejected by men. The author first (1 Pet. 2:6) quotes Is. 28:16, which refers to a cornerstone that God is laying for his redemptive purpose in Zion. Next (1 Pet. 2:7) he cites Ps. 118:22, which states that the stone which the builders rejected has become the cornerstone. Finally (1 Pet. 2:8), the author quotes Is. 8:14, which refers to a stone that will make men stumble. These diverse citations have a common reference to a stone, and for that reason they are joined in 1 Peter. Furthermore, they are all arbitrarily interpreted as referring to Jesus

Christ and belief or unbelief in him. In another example, the humanitarian provision of Deut. 21:23 for the removing before nightfall of the body of one who had been crucified on a tree "for a hanged man is accursed by God" is made by Paul (Gal. 3:13) the basis of the statement that Christ became a curse on our behalf and so freed us from the curse of the law.

On the other hand, such instances of strained interpretation are the exception rather than the rule. Use of the O.T. in the N.T. is generally consistent and reasonably established. It is grounded in a thoroughly defensible view of God's saving activity in Jewish history. Sometimes the N.T. makes an alteration in a Scriptural verse or ignores its context in applying it to a first-century situation, but on the whole early Christian writers employ Jewish Scripture in a literal manner. The great bulk of the quotations are careful reproductions or translations of the original Scripture. In most instances the historical sense is carefully preserved, and often the source of the quotation is accurately acknowledged even though such reference was not the normal practice at the time. Moreover, what may appear to be peculiarities of Christian interpretation of the O.T. become understandable and logical when the presuppositions of Christian usage are examined.

THE CHRISTIAN PERSPECTIVE

The N.T. usage of the O.T. was in part influenced by earlier Jewish tradition, but for the most part it was something essentially new and productive. It involved a highly selective employment of certain Scriptural passages that would clarify or confirm Christian beliefs. Authors of the N.T. were well aware of the fact that in citing the O.T. they were invoking an authority that was respected by all Jews and many Gentiles as well. For the early Christians, Christ was seen as the goal of all Jewish history, and thus the O.T. as the primary record of that history is viewed in the light of Christian belief. The first Christians were all Jews who had been trained in Jewish traditions. They could understand the newness of Christianity only over against the background of their inherited faith. The significance of the coming of Jesus could be portrayed at first only in direct relationship to the Scriptures. There was no other framework in which he could be placed. Yet at the same time Jesus could not be fully comprehended by the O.T. because in his appearance a new element had been introduced. His Messiahship both fulfilled and transcended Scriptural prophecies and popular hopes. A great deal of light could be thrown on the meaning of his life and death from the Scriptures, but Christian belief could not be proved by any combination of O.T. verses. Scripture was a primary resource for N.T. authors, but it could not be a source.

The moving force of the N.T. is the experience of Jesus— first, by those who knew him in his earthly life and, second, by those who knew him only spiritually or through the reports of others. But in every instance Jesus comes first. His transmitted teaching, the traditions of his acts and his death and resurrection, the doctrines of his person and character, formed the core of Christian preaching. It was this gospel which determined how and to what extent the O.T. would be employed for argument and clarification. In fact, the decisive revelation of God in the life and death of Jesus Christ gave new and deeper meaning to the O.T., which the disciples had never found in it before. The whole story of God's dealings with his chosen people from the calling of Abraham was now viewed as the preparation for the climactic birth of Jesus. It is quite possible, and even probable, that in a few instances the wording of an O.T. passage cited by a Christian writer may explain the form of a particular tradition about Jesus' words or deeds. Thus, Matthew (Mt. 21:1-11) recounts the story of Jesus' triumphal entry into Jerusalem by quoting Zech. 9:9, which, in the normal manner of Hebrew poetic parallelism, refers to one animal as "an ass, . . . a colt the foal of an ass." The Evangelist, either through ignorance of the form of Hebrew poetry, or, as is more likely, in a desire to present a completely literal fulfillment of O.T. prophecy, describes Jesus as sitting simultaneously on both an ass and a colt! However, such cases are rare, and on the whole the independently formed gospel tradition about Jesus carefully controls and directs N.T. usage of Scripture, which is thus kept in a subordinate place. It is the gospel, with its record of key events and their basic interpretation, that determines the selection of supporting Scriptural passages. But Christian usage of the O.T. was itself creative as new selections and groupings and interpretations were made of Scriptural verses. Authors of the N.T. were convinced that through Christ God had given to them the same Spirit that had earlier inspired the O.T. writers. They further believed that it was this Spirit which enabled them to utilize Scriptural passages in ways that could not have been foreseen or imagined by the O.T. authors themselves.

Just as the experience of Christ was not limited to those who had seen or heard Jesus of Nazareth during his earthly life but was available also through the Spirit to Christians of succeeding generations, so too Christians began to discover the presence of a preexistent Christ in many of the events of O.T. history. In 1 Cor. 10:4 Paul declares that all those who were with Moses in the wilderness wanderings experienced the supernatural Rock which followed them, and he adds that this Rock was really Christ. Moreover, in Jn. 12:38–40 two sections of Isaiah are quoted (Is. 53:1; 6:9–10) and applied to the general unbelief that greeted Jesus' ministry. The Evangelist concludes (Jn. 12:41) that Isaiah wrote as he did long ago because he did see even then the glory of Jesus and so referred to him. Even within the O.T., traditional history is rewritten in the light of later insight and interpretation. This is what has happened in 1 and 2 Chronicles, and it is largely the case with Deuteronomy. The same is true, in very much briefer scope, of Ps. 78. In the N.T. Jewish history is constantly being reinterpreted in the light of the truth that Jesus has disclosed. The most notable example of such an interpretive review is the speech before the Sanhedrin in Jerusalem attributed to Stephen in Acts, ch. 7. More than any other section in the whole New Testament this chapter is almost entirely a patch-work of Old Testament quotations and references. There are 29 references to Genesis, 28 to Exodus, 2 to Leviticus, 1 to Numbers, 5 to Deuteronomy, 6 to Joshua, 3 to 1 Kings, 1 to 2 Kings, 4 to 2 Chronicles, 1 to Job, 17 to Psalms, 4 to Isaiah, 3 to Jeremiah, 3 to Ezekiel, and 1 to Amos. Of the thirty-nine books of the O.T. fifteen are appealed to, and within the sixty verses of Acts, ch. 7, there are at least 108 references to O.T. passages. The selection of the Scriptural material is obviously arbitrary, but the whole chapter is governed by the idea that since the Jews always in their history had rejected the gracious dealings of God, it was only to be expected that they should also have refused and killed Jesus, the final expression of God's love.

The New Testament refers to the Old Testament in diverse ways and for varied purposes. Sometimes more than one category may be involved. Occasionally a quotation will have no apparent purpose. On the other hand, most of the O.T. references in the N.T. can be assigned to one of a small number of major classifications.

HISTORICAL UNDERSTANDING

As we have already noted, the O.T. is most often cited in the direct, historical, and literal sense. Its authority is recognized as binding upon Christians as well as upon Jews. In this usage we are reminded of the fact that the Scripture was employed as an important means of strengthening faith and giving in-struction within the Christian community. Where its literal sense is retained, care is usually taken to reproduce the O.T. text with as much exactness as possible. Often Scriptural commands are quoted as still valid for the members of the new covenant. Thus, when Jesus is asked what he thinks is the great commandment in the Law (Mt. 22:36), he replies by quoting Deut. 6:5 and Lev. 19:18. According to Paul (Rom. 13:8–10), the Christian is under obligation to keep the com-

mandments, of which four are quoted from Ex. 20:13–17 and
Deut. 5:17–21. Paul suggests that this duty is discharged by
the love of neighbor commanded in Lev. 19:18. The necessity
to observe all of the Decalogue is stressed also in Jas. 2:11.
Marriage among Christians as well as among Jews is to be
based upon the order of Gen. 2:24 that a man, leaving his
parents, shall be so joined to his wife that the two become one
(Eph. 5:31). All the quotations in Mark from the books
of the Law (Genesis to Deuteronomy) are of this type of legal
citation. In this and in other ways the O.T. is not superseded
in the N.T. but is presupposed as one of its foundations.

Christianity accepted without question the fundamental belief of Judaism that it is in history, including both man and
nature, that God most clearly reveals himself. Events in time
and place rather than mental speculations or mystical trances
are for the Biblical writers the raw material of theology. At the
center is the story of God's active guidance of his people
Israel and his purpose for them and through them for the
whole world. Thus, Christians saw the critical events of their
time as the culmination of all that had gone before in Israel.
The N.T. authors are necessarily aware of the historical perspective and they make constant reference to the past, both
recent and ancient. Summaries of Jewish history are to be
found not only in Acts, ch. 7, but also in Acts, ch. 13, and
Heb., ch. 11.

Among the earliest Christian writers there is relatively little
concern about who Jesus was, but there are many statements
about what God did for humanity in the life of Jesus. This final
action of God is frequently tied through O.T. citation and reference to earlier actions of God. Such quotations are often vital
to the argument of the N.T. authors, who attempt to draw theological conclusions from their references. In any case, it is
this historical understanding which lies behind some of the
central N.T. proclamations. In his speech in Jerusalem at Pentecost (Acts 2:14–36), Peter describes "Jesus of Nazareth, a
man attested to you by God with mighty works and wonders

and signs which God did through him in your midst," and he declares further that after Jesus had been crucified "God raised him up, having loosed the pangs of death." Elsewhere in the same speech other actions of God are pictured in words taken from Psalms and the prophet Joel. Since the Christian gospel tells of what God has done in the history of Israel as well as in the life of Jesus, it is essential that the record of his deeds in the O.T. be accurately transmitted.

OLD TESTAMENT PREDICTIONS OF CHRIST

One of the most widespread N.T. uses of the O.T. is to see it as a series of predictions that have been realized, especially in the life of Jesus and also in the experiences of the young church. The Major and Minor Prophets are naturally drawn upon most heavily for predictions that are believed to have come to pass, but Psalms and many other parts of the O.T. are treated in a similar manner. From this point of view the O.T. is necessarily incomplete as it looks forward to a future time when its hopes can be attained. Scripture awaits the coming of a leader who will on God's behalf deliver the Jewish people from their evils and who will also be a servant. Such longing reaches a climax in the Suffering Servant passage, Is. 52:13 to 53:12. It is highly significant that the N.T., with its belief that Jesus is this long-expected leader and servant, utilizes this Isaianic passage by quotation and reference more than any other O.T. passage of similar length. Ten N.T. books reflect it directly in approximately fifty-eight verses. Whether or not Jesus ever thought of himself as the Suffering Servant, it is absolutely certain that his early followers did so. Although the Messiah as such is not represented in the O.T. as suffering, N.T. writers do make the link through direct and indirect use of Isaianic prophecy. It is only in this manner that we can explain the words of the risen Jesus, spoken on the road to Emmaus (Lk. 24:26): "Was it not necessary that the Christ should suffer these things and enter into his glory?" In the

O.T., which is the collection of the authoritative writings of the old covenant, there is the promise of a new covenant (Jer. 31:31–34): "Behold, the days are coming, says the Lord, when I will make a new covenant with the house of Israel and the house of Judah." From the beginning, Christianity, following the lead of Jesus, saw itself as that new covenant, and its writings were so named. Likewise, in Joel (Joel 2:28–29) there is a prophecy of a time when God would give his Spirit to all rather than simply to the few prophets. Again, it was the contention of early Christianity, starting with Pentecost (Acts 2:14–21), that through Christ, God's Spirit was available to all who would receive it. Thus, the N.T. insists that the admitted incompleteness of the O.T. with regard to the coming of a leader sent by God, the promise of a new (and better) covenant to replace the one made with Moses, and the expectation of a time when the hitherto severely restricted gift of God's Spirit would be extended to all has been filled up by the life and death of Jesus.

Prophecies take on new meaning and relevance when their fulfillment is in view, and in turn there can be no thought of fulfillment without some earlier promise or prediction. The first Christian writers believed that the O.T. had foretold the whole life of Jesus, including his words and deeds, as well as the events of the initial stages of the church. The Scriptural accounts of the calling of Abraham, the exodus, the reign of David, and the preaching of Isaiah are seen as preliminaries to the decisive event of Jesus' birth. In the N.T. it becomes equally true that the most important role of the O.T. is to point forward to the events of the N.T. and that it is Jesus who for the first time makes clear the significance of the O.T. It should be noted further that in the early Christian view Moses not only served as mediator in the giving of the law to Israel but also prophesied the coming of Jesus Christ. The resurrection story of the journey to Emmaus says of Jesus (Lk. 24:27) that "beginning with Moses and all the prophets, he interpreted to them in all the scriptures the things concerning himself."

Philip's testimony to Nathanael is found in Jn. 1:45: "We have found him of whom Moses in the law and also the prophets wrote, Jesus of Nazareth." Even more direct are the words of Jesus in Jn. 5:46: "If you believed Moses, you would believe me, for he wrote of me." The same conviction lies behind the claim of Paul (Acts 26:22) that in his speech before King Agrippa he is "saying nothing but what the prophets and Moses said would come to pass."

Just as in the Dead Sea Scrolls it is suggested that the O.T. prophet can have only a partial understanding of the meaning of his predictions because the end time has not yet come, so Christian writers maintain that the prophets had predicted far more than they knew. As the Habakkuk Commentary of Qumran painstakingly relates the words of that prophet to the figure and times of the Teacher of Righteousness, so Matthew supports as many of Jesus' teachings and deeds as possible by O.T. quotations. However, there is a unique concentration on the concept of realization in almost all early Christian writings. Thus, C. F. D. Moule has written: "It is very striking that, with all the parallels between the New Testament use of scripture and its use in the Qumran writings and in other Jewish literature, the note of *fulfillment* seems to be peculiar to the New Testament." (*The Birth of the New Testament,* p. 57, n.1.) Christians are very much aware of living in that new era which had long been expected. Jesus' own description of his ministry (Mt. 11:5), to be reported to the imprisoned John the Baptist, is a compilation of material from Is. 26:19; 29:18–19; 35:5–6; and 61:1: "The blind receive their sight and the lame walk, lepers are cleansed and the deaf hear, and the dead are raised up, and the poor have good news preached to them." According to Lk. 4:21, when Jesus had finished reading Is. 61:1–2 in the synagogue service at Nazareth, he added: "Today this scripture has been fulfilled in your hearing."

Writers of the N.T. generally accept without question the belief that all the Jewish prophets had witnessed in definite and recognizable ways to the saving activity of Jesus. So

Zechariah declares (Lk. 1:68–79) that God has acted in send-
ing his Son into the world "as he spoke by the mouth of his
holy prophets from of old." In another speech in the Temple at
Jerusalem, Peter presents the life and death of Jesus (Acts
3:22–24) as foretold by words of Moses (Deut. 18:15, 19)
and by "all the prophets who have spoken, from Samuel and
those who came afterwards." Paul asserts (Rom. 1:2) this good
news of Jesus' work of salvation God had "promised beforehand through his prophets in the holy scriptures." Jesus and
his disciples are everywhere said to have brought into realization all the half-realized hopes of Scripture.

Specific claims that the O.T. has been fulfilled are limited
to the Gospels and Acts and in each case to the event of Jesus.
The only exception is a single reference to Abraham in Jas.
2:23. Jesus himself suggests (Mt. 26:53–54) that he might
have summoned legions of angels to his defense against his
armed enemies in Gethsemane, but if he had, "how then
should the scriptures be fulfilled, that it must be so?" Jesus
declares to the Father in his "high priestly prayer" (Jn. 17:12)
that he has guarded his disciples carefully, with none lost except Judas, "the son of perdition, that the scripture might be
fulfilled." According to John (Jn. 19:28), Jesus' word from the
cross, "I thirst," was said "to fulfil the scripture." The concept of the direct relationship between O.T. prediction and
its N.T. realization is especially prominent in the story of Jesus'
death and resurrection. The account of Paul's preaching in
Thessalonica given in Acts (Acts 17:2–3) illustrates this concentration: "He argued with them from the scriptures, explaining and proving that it was necessary for the Christ to suffer
and to rise from the dead, and saying, 'This Jesus, whom I
proclaim to you, is the Christ.'" Paul writes in precisely the
same manner in 1 Cor. 15:3–4: "I delivered to you as of first
importance . . . that Christ died for our sins in accordance
with the scriptures, that he was buried, that he was raised on
the third day in accordance with the scriptures."

In a large number of cases it is the Scriptures in their totality that are regarded as bearing a witness to Christ rather than specific verses or portions, and a general knowledge of the O.T. on the part of both writer and reader seems presupposed. A single verse or a whole segment of Scripture may lie behind the statement of Mt. 26:24: "The Son of man goes as it is written of him." In Mt. 26:56 Jesus explains his arrest in Gethsemane with a general reference: "All this has taken place, that the scriptures of the prophets might be fulfilled." So, too, in Mk. 9:12 Jesus asks: "How is it written of the Son of man, that he should suffer many things and be treated with contempt?" Another unspecified reference is made by Jesus in Lk. 21:22: "These are days of vengeance, to fulfil all that is written." Jesus rebukes the apostles who were walking to Emmaus (Lk. 24:25) for their failure "to believe all that the prophets have spoken." According to Jn. 5:39, it is the Scriptures in their entirety that bear witness to him. The comprehensiveness of such a reference is made even clearer in Lk. 18:31, where Jesus informs the Twelve that in Jerusalem "everything that is written of the Son of man by the prophets will be accomplished." The words of the resurrected Jesus in Lk. 24:44 take in the whole sweep of Scripture: "Everything written about me in the law of Moses and the prophets and the psalms must be fulfilled."

The words of Peter in Acts 3:18 are unique in the N.T.: "What God foretold by the mouth of all the prophets, that his Christ should suffer, he [God] thus fulfilled." Nowhere else is it stated that God directly causes the fulfillment, nor is there any suggestion of a fatalistic or mechanical necessity that has produced these results. Rather, the N.T. writers are so impressed with the facts of fulfillment that they have no interest in their causes or modes. So many instances of fulfillment are set forth in the Gospels that they are usually introduced by set formulas, such as, "This took place so that what was spoken by the prophet [or "Isaiah," or "Jeremiah," or "the Lord"] might be fulfilled." Sometimes the formulas are placed on Jesus' lips, and sometimes they are introduced by the Evangelists. Twice, in Jn. 18:9 and 32, such a formula is used regarding the fulfillment in the passion events of words previously spoken by Jesus; and the effect is to give to the teaching of Jesus the same validity granted the words of God in the O.T.

In their apparent desire to discover as many instances of fulfillment of prophecy in the life of Jesus as possible, the Evangelists occasionally exceed the limits of credibility. Thus, according to Mt. 2:14–15, the residence of Joseph and Mary and the infant Jesus in Egypt until the death of Herod was to fulfill the words of Hos. 11:1: "Out of Egypt have I called my son." Those words in Hosea, however, are not predictive. They describe, rather, the depth of God's love for Israel that caused him to bring the Jewish people out of their Egyptian bondage. So, too, the treatment (Mt. 2:17–18) of Jeremiah's reference (Jer. 31:15) to Rachel's mourning for her children as a prediction of the mourning that followed the slaughter of the babes at Bethlehem is unconvincing. Although there are a few cases where a slight similarity between an O.T. statement and a N.T. event is viewed as the fulfillment of prophecy, most of the time the claim to fulfillment has some reasonable basis in fact. Moreover, early Christian authors normally concern themselves with the principal elements of their proclamation and their relationship to the overall course of the O.T. They are not impressed with mere coincidences of similarity. C. H. Dodd has noted: "The N.T. writers do not, in the main, treat the prophecies of the O.T. as a kind of pious fortune-telling, and seek to impress their readers with the exactness of correspondence between forecast and event." (*According to the Scriptures*, p. 127.) Furthermore, there is no reason to conclude that stories of N.T. happenings have been created in order to agree with an earlier Scriptural passage. The influence of the older writing upon a N.T. account that is viewed as its fulfillment is limited almost entirely to the deliberate or unconscious borrowing of language.

The resurrection is that aspect of Jesus' life which in the N.T. is most frequently represented as a literal fulfillment of

O.T. prophecy. There are many references to Hos. 6:2: "On the third day he will raise us up, that we may live before him." Jesus predicts (Mt. 16:21 = Lk. 9:22) that, after he has suffered and been killed, he will, in accordance with this prophecy, rise from the dead on the third day. This prediction is mentioned two more times (Lk. 24:7 and 46) after the resurrection has taken place. The prophecy of Hosea is also the basis of Paul's statement in 1 Cor. 15:4 that "Christ . . . was raised on the third day in accordance with the scriptures." However, the N.T. makes little use of the argument from a literal fulfillment of the O.T. compared with its listing of similarities between N.T. events and Scriptural antecedents. The most common form of the Christian interpretation of the O.T. is typology, a kind of comparison in which the older events are seen as helping to explain and make understandable the later events but not in any way to control them.

TYPOLOGICAL INTERPRETATION

The typological interpretation of the O.T. grows out of the view that Scripture describes all the principal forms of the purpose and activity of God and that the persons and events of the O.T. therefore help to explain what has happened in the life and death of Jesus. Occurrences in the O.T. are frequently seen as foreshadowing the later Christian developments. A "type" in this sense is a comparison or an illustration, but it is not an identification. At most, N.T. events, which are recognized as essentially unique, are related as the final projection of Scriptural incidents and institutions. An example is provided by the prediction of Jesus (Mt. 12:40): "As Jonah was three days and three nights in the belly of the whale, so will the Son of man be three days and three nights in the heart of the earth." In this case Jonah, certainly not to be identified with Jesus, has nevertheless become the "type" of Jesus. In Ex. 34:28 it is stated that Moses was with the Lord on Mt. Sinai for forty days and forty nights and that during this time he fasted. So, too, in the Synoptic Gospels (Mt. 4:2 = Mk. 1:13 = Lk. 4:2) it is written that Jesus fasted in the wilderness for forty days and forty nights. Here Moses is seen as the "type" of Jesus. In Jn. 3:14 the lifting up of the serpent by Moses in the wilderness (Num. 21:9) is the "type" of the crucifixion of the Son of man.

Thus, Christian authors often refer to the O.T. not for logical support of an argument but for illustration. It is not the Biblical way to present theological truths as philosophical formulas. That is the manner of Greek writers. Biblical writers have to do for the most part with concrete imagery. Accordingly, in the N.T. we find dependence on the O.T. largely through word pictures. A statement that can be accepted as true on other grounds may be supported or clarified by the citation of an O.T. passage.

There is in the N.T. some allegorical interpretation of the O.T. in which the details of the older account are presented as essential for the understanding of the Christian event. Probably the most extended allegorical treatment in the N.T. is to be found in Gal. 4:21–31, where the story of the birth of Ishmael to Hagar and of Isaac to Sarah (Gen. 21:1–12) is made the foundation for Paul's teaching regarding the freedom of the Christian. Another such instance is the elaboration in Heb. 7:1–10 of the brief account of Melchizedek in Gen. 14:17–20. Yet such allegory is rare in the N.T. and is used for illustration rather than for proof. Where it is present, it probably reflects the influence of rabbinical usage, the writings of Philo, and contemporary Greek Stoicism. It is not a natural part of N.T. thought.

It is doubtful that early Christianity would have retained its close relationship to the O.T. if it had not been able to engage in some reinterpretation that was held to be consistent with the nature of Scripture. Many of the circumstances of the primitive church were new, especially after the mainstream of Christianity had left Jewish soil and Greek, rather than Hebrew or Aramaic, had become the language of preaching and writing. With this freedom to reinterpret, however, the N.T. could preserve the general meaning of the O.T. while applying selected passages to contemporary experiences. Thus, the O.T. was updated and modernized. Paul's review of the Hebrew wanderings in the wilderness (1 Cor. 10:1–5) is followed (1 Cor. 10:6) by his affirmation that "these things are warnings [literally, "types"] for us." That all human beings are sinful even in his own day, Jews and Gentiles alike, Paul concludes from his long series of O.T. quotations in Rom. 3:9–18. Paul can write to fellow Christians (Rom. 15:4): "Whatever was written in former days was written for our instruction." So, too, the words of God in Deut. 25:4, Paul says (1 Cor. 9:10), were "written for our sake." He adds (1 Cor. 10:11) that the accounts of the wilderness wanderings "were written down for our instruction." Paul holds that even in his day Jews can read the O.T. only with a veil over their faces, whereas Christians may read it with the full and unveiled light of Christ (2 Cor. 3:12–16). In brief, Christians have made the O.T., rooted though it is in the ancient past of the Jews, their own special possession whose meaning relates directly to their particular situation. Its typological interpretation, broadly conceived, is thus required.

LITERARY INFLUENCE OF THE OLD TESTAMENT

For the N.T. writers the O.T. was the best known body of literature of any then in existence. The influence of Scripture upon Christian literary composition was not confined to the areas that have been described. It was inevitable that O.T. language would reappear throughout the N.T. The familiarity of its authors with the words, phrases, and literary forms of Scripture is reflected throughout all early Christian writings. The language of the O.T. is an integral part of the intellectual heritage of the apostolic authors, and they employ it freely to express their own ideas. Moreover, the literary influence of

Jewish Scripture is often exerted even when there is no awareness of it on the part of the N.T. writer.

Particularly notable are the very brief phrases, idiomatic
expressions, and metaphors that are to be found in the O.T.
and that occur again in the N.T. without any acknowledgment
of their presumed source. Of course, some of the parallels are
to be accounted for as simply the effect of a common tradition
and culture, and a few may be only accidental. Yet the evidence for a literary borrowing, whether deliberate or unconscious, is overwhelming. Almost all portions of the O.T. are
reflected in this way in virtually every section of the N.T. In a
few instances the literary dependence is essential to the argument of the apostolic writer, but in most cases it is purely
coincidental.

The preceding discussion of the ways in which the N.T.
uses and interprets Jewish Scripture has been in general terms.
We have tried to set forth those assumptions and interpretations
which are shared by all the primitive Christian writings. We
have seen that there is a remarkable degree of uniformity in
the N.T. approach to the O.T. However, there is also a significant amount of variety in the treatment of Scripture among
the various authors of the N.T., and the picture would be
neither clear nor accurate if we did not pay some attention to
the characteristic usages of the different apostolic writers.

The only book of the N.T. that provides no certain evidence
of a dependence on the O.T. is Philemon, but there is relatively
little borrowing from the O.T. in the pastoral epistles and in 2
and 3 John. Moreover, there are no formula-quotations in the
Johannine epistles and in the book of Revelation. In the remaining twenty-one books of the N.T. the degree of direct and
indirect borrowing from the O.T. ranges from considerable to
heavy. Furthermore, among the authors who refer most often
to the O.T. there is no agreement as to the preferred types of
interpretation. Most of the writers have their decidedly individual methods and procedures, which can be observed beyond the large areas of agreement.

Paul's Use of the Old Testament

Among all the N.T. writers the most extensive use of the O.T. is made by Paul. In the ten epistles traditionally ascribed to him there are approximately 78 direct quotations from the O.T. (H. B. Swete, *Introduction to the Old Testament in Greek*, p. 392.) Of these, 71 are found in the central group of his epistles—Romans, 42; 1 and 2 Corinthians, 19; and Galatians, 10. The later "epistles of the captivity" thus contain few direct citations. It is clear that Paul's quotations occur in his solidly theological works. Moreover, his quotations are much more accurate and faithful to the original when they are taken from the Law and Psalms than when they are drawn from the historical books and the Prophets. It is probable that Paul, with his Pharisaic training, usually quotes from memory rather than with immediate access to the text. His style of writing and his choice of words are so influenced by his detailed knowledge of Scripture that it is often difficult to determine when Paul is quoting and when he is merely alluding to the O.T. Sometimes Paul's citations are somewhat inexact, and the reason may be a faulty memory or else a desire merely to paraphrase. The direct quotations are often introduced by a formula that acknowledges their source, but such a formula is no guarantee of an exact quotation and may in fact be followed by an adapted reference only. On the other hand, an accurate quotation may have no introductory formula. There are two O.T. verses that are cited two times each by Paul. Jeremiah 9:24 is quoted somewhat loosely with an introductory formula, "As it is written," in 1 Cor. 1:31 and again in 2 Cor. 10:17, this time with no introduction. So, too, Hab. 2:4, "The righteous shall live by his faith," is cited with a full formula in Rom. 1:17 and again in Gal. 3:11 with only the one-word introduction "for." The great bulk of Paul's quotations are drawn from the books of the Law, Isaiah, and Psalms. However,

Paul's numerous allusions represent most of the books of the O.T.

Paul had a very high regard for the O.T. and had no wish to reject its authority. It was of fundamental importance in the shaping and expressing of his theology. He can describe Scripture (Rom. 3:2) as "the oracles of God." For him (Rom. 7:12) "the law is holy, and the commandment is holy and just and good." Furthermore, the meaning of Christ cannot be understood apart from the narrative of the O.T. The redeeming work of Jesus presupposes (Rom. 5:12–15) the fall of man and its effects (Gen. 3:6, 19). The faith of Abraham (Gal. 3:6) and the giving of the law through Moses (Gal. 3:19) are a part of the necessary background of Christian salvation. The concept of the sovereignty of God is derived (Rom. 9:14–21) from Exodus and Isaiah.

Usually Paul refers to the O.T. as a whole as "the law" (e.g., 1 Cor. 14:21, where a quotation of Is. 28:11–12 is so identified) or simply as "the scripture" (or "the scriptures"). However it is described, Paul reveres the O.T. as the revealed word of God. At the same time Paul was convinced that the Jews, because they lacked the Holy Spirit, could not discover the truth that was contained in Scripture. In his view (2 Cor. 3:14–15) "a veil lies over their minds" whenever they try to read the Old Testament. The words of Is. 6:9, "Go, and say to this people: 'Hear and hear, but do not understand; see and see, but do not perceive,'" are cited six times within the New Testament (Mt. 13:14–15; Mk. 4:12; 8:18; Lk. 8:10; Jn. 12:40; and Acts 28:26–27). This widespread early Christian belief is a part of Paul's thinking. In Rom. 11:8 Paul supports such a view by blending words from Deut. 29:4 and Is. 29:10: "God gave them a spirit of stupor, eyes that should not see and ears that should not hear, down to this very day." Paul's argument concludes that because the Jews were thus incapable of a true understanding of the O.T. they misused it as if it were only a legal document and an end in itself. In Rom. 2:27 Paul pictures the Jews as those "who have the written code and circumcision but break the law." The misunderstood O.T. is categorized (Rom. 7:6) as "the old written code." Paul adds (2 Cor. 3:6): "The written code kills."

Paul was inevitably influenced by his Pharisaic training and continues to make use of some of the well-known Jewish literary methods in his utilization of the O.T. Current rabbinical interpretation of the O.T. appears in instances where Paul discusses the form of a single word (Gal. 3:16) or is otherwise captured by an extreme literalism. Also rabbinic is Paul's use of the Deuteronomic prohibition (Deut. 25:4) of muzzling an ox when it is treading grain to support his conclusion (1 Cor. 9:9–10) that "the plowman should plow in hope and the thresher thresh in hope of a share in the crop." Belonging also to Paul's earlier Jewish training is his custom of combining two or more different O.T. verses in either (*a*) an eclectic quotation or (*b*) a chain of citations. A clear example of the first type is provided by Rom. 9:33: "Behold, I am laying in Zion a stone that will make men stumble, a rock that will make them fall; and he who believes in him will not be put to shame." From Is. 8:14–15 Paul has drawn the words, "A stone that will make men stumble, a rock that will make them fall"; and from Is. 28:16 (LXX) he has taken both the beginning and the ending of his quotation, which is introduced by the formula "as it is written." Illustrations of the second type are also numerous in Paul, especially in Romans. Sometimes the separate citations in the chain are distinguished by formulas, which usually identify the O.T. author of the source. In Rom. 9:12–13 a citation of Gen. 25:23 is immediately followed by one from Mal. 1:2–3. So also in Rom. 9:25–29 we find quotations joined from Hos. 2:23 and 1:10; Is. 10:22–23 and 1:9. In Rom. 10:18–21 there are quotations, separated only by formulas of introduction, from Ps. 19:4; Deut. 32:21; and Is. 65:1–2. Deuteronomy 29:4 and Ps. 69:22–23 are joined in the same way in Rom. 11:8–10. In Rom. 15:9–12 Paul cites, in order, 2 Sam. 22:50 (= Ps. 18:49); Deut. 32:43; Ps. 117:1; and Is. 11:10 (LXX). Occasionally, such a chain quotation will be

introduced by only a single formula. Romans 3:10–18 is an example and has already been noted as combining citations of
five different psalms and one passage of Isaiah. In Rom.
11:34–35 quotations from Is. 40:13 and Job 35:7 are joined
after the word "for." Finally, in 2 Cor. 6:16–18, following the
words "as God said" there are quotations from Exodus (= Leviticus), Jeremiah, Isaiah, and Deuteronomy. These group citations, which suggest artificiality and arbitrariness, are no
longer convincing; but they can be understood only in the light
of contemporary rabbinical practice. Paul was influenced by
his Jewish training.

On the other hand, there is good reason to believe that the
determining factor in Paul's use of Scripture was his belief in
Jesus as the Messiah. Since Paul gives us the earliest extant
Christian writings, it is very difficult to distinguish between
Paul's own contributions to the interpretation of the O.T. and
what he has received and transmitted from those who were
Christians before him. In any case, however, his treatment of
the O.T. is pervasively Christocentric. At times Paul seems to
think of Christ as the speaker or else as spoken to in various
O.T. passages. This is especially true of Paul's use of the word
"Lord," which in the O.T. always means "God" but which
with Paul (and all later Christians) often signifies "Christ."
Paul's handling of the O.T. will often appear to the outsider
to be radical and capricious. Especially in Galatians and Romans he uses selected texts from the law for proof that the
Mosaic commandments cannot provide a way of salvation. At
other times he applies to the calling of the Gentiles some O.T.
texts that were written to describe God's calling of the people
of Israel. But basic to Paul's idea of the O.T. is the conviction
that Jesus Christ has fulfilled its prophecies and brought its
true meaning to light. So he writes in 2 Cor. 1:20: "All the
promises of God find their Yes in him [Jesus Christ]." Consistently, Paul discovers Christ to be preexistently active in
O.T. history. Thus, he affirms (1 Cor. 10:4) that the Rock
which followed Moses and the Israelites in the wilderness and

from which they drank water was Christ. Paul makes this interpretation even though there is no following rock in the O.T.
narrative, according to which water is given the Israelites at
three different places. The effect of Paul's use of O.T. citations
in Rom., ch. 10, is to suggest that Christ proclaimed the truth
about himself to Moses, David, and Isaiah. In Rom. 10:5–10
Paul completely reinterprets the discussion in Deuteronomy
(Deut. 30:11–14) of God's commandment as immediately at
hand for every Israelite. The law has become Christ, who does
not have to be brought down from heaven because he is close
to everyone who will accept him. The O.T. text itself has no
basis for Paul's conclusion, but he can easily transfer its
thought to the truth that he has already known in Christ.

On many occasions Paul utilizes the O.T. in its literal and
historical sense, but just as often he may pay no attention to
the context of a cited passage. He may discover in an O.T. text
ideas that were not present in the mind of the author of that
text, and he may make an entirely new interpretation, even
while carefully retaining the words of the original passage.
The good news of God's saving act in Christ was, according to
Paul (Gal. 3:8), preached to Abraham. The coming of Christ
had been promised in the O.T. (Rom. 1:2). The obedience
and sufferings of Christ Paul finds (Rom. 15:3) foretold in
Ps. 69:9. The death and resurrection of Jesus were in accordance with the Scriptures (1 Cor. 15:3–4). His resulting Lordship and dominion have earlier been described in Ps. 110:1
and 8:6 (1 Cor. 15:25, 27). Even his triumphant and final return have been set forth (2 Thess. 1:10) in Zechariah (Zech.
14:5) and Isaiah (Is. 49:3).

Thus, Paul finds incompleteness in the O.T. and a prediction
of greater things to come in Christianity. The true faith of
Abraham was tragically followed by the curse of trying to find
salvation through literal obedience to the law. In removing
that curse Christ has made available to all the saving faith
previously found only in Abraham (Gal. 3:6–14). As Moses,
returning to his people from God's presence on Mt. Sinai, was

forced to veil his face, so the Jewish people read the O.T. with
a veil over their minds. But from those who come to him Christ
removes that veil, and the truth of the O.T. can be known (2
Cor. 3:7–18). Only with the help of the Holy Spirit can Scripture be understood; and Paul is certain that through Christ
the Holy Spirit has come to all Christians.

For Paul, therefore (Rom. 15:4), the O.T. was really written
for the followers of Jesus Christ. The events of the wilderness
wandering, which Paul describes in 1 Cor. 10:1–10, he concludes (v. 11) "happened to them as a warning, but they were
written down for our instruction." Paul notes (Gal. 3:13) that
in fulfilling the curse put by Deut. 21:23 on everyone who
hangs on a tree, Christ became "a curse *for us*." The defects of
the O.T. have been corrected and its prophecies fulfilled in
Christ. Paul holds that the words of God in the O.T. are therefore of great value and help to the disciple of Christ as he
seeks to appropriate in his own life the reality of the new
covenant.

THE SYNOPTIC GOSPELS

The Synoptic Gospels—Matthew, Mark, and Luke—follow
the same pattern and have much in common. To a large degree they share the same tradition about the life and words of
Jesus, which antedates all of them. Matthew and Luke use a
second type of tradition, and there are significant amounts of
material found only in Matthew and only in Luke. In any
study of the use of the O.T. in the Synoptic Gospels, therefore,
it is necessary to distinguish between the usage of Jesus and
that of the earliest church. Thus, there are many O.T. quotations that appear in all three Synoptic Gospels and a number
of others that occur in two of them. Those which are found in
only one Gospel may reveal something of the interests and
methods of the particular Evangelist. That each Gospel writer,
in spite of his dependence on earlier traditions both oral and

written, has his own characteristics and contributions cannot be denied.

Mark as the earliest Gospel presumably stands closest in time to the common Synoptic tradition, and we cannot easily separate what belongs to that tradition and what is original with Mark. The situation is further complicated by the fact that almost all the Markan material reappears in Matthew and/or Luke. In any case, however, Mark's employment of the O.T. seems to follow the established pattern.

Matthew pays far more attention to the O.T. than does Mark, and there are in his Gospel at least 16 O.T. quotations that are not found in Mark or Luke. He quotes the O.T. mainly to indicate the ways in which Jesus has in the details of his life fulfilled O.T. prophecies. Specific O.T. verses are connected by Matthew with the following ten events: the annunciation to Joseph (Mt. 1:22–23), the birth of Jesus in Bethlehem (Mt. 2:5–6), the return from Egypt (Mt. 2:15), the killing of the babies in Bethlehem (Mt. 2:17–18), the preaching of John the Baptist (Mt. 3:3), Jesus' residence in Capernaum (Mt. 4:14–16), his healing of the sick (Mt. 8:17), his teaching in parables (Mt. 13:14–15), his entry into Jerusalem (Mt. 21:4–5) and the thirty pieces of silver given for Jesus' betrayal (Mt. 27:9). The many O.T. citations in Matthew are often loosely appended and interpreted in accordance with the theological views and purpose of the Evangelist. He writes his Gospel to show that Jesus was the Messiah, and his O.T. quotations are used to support that goal. It is significant that chapters 1 and 2, whose material is essentially unique among the Gospels, are heavily dependent on the Jewish Scripture.

In the tradition that Luke shares with Matthew he does not always retain the O.T. quotations and references. Moreover, since he is writing primarily for Gentiles, he plays down the idea that O.T. prophecy has been fulfilled in specific aspects of Jesus' life. He is much more concerned to establish the fact that the O.T. as a whole witnesses to Jesus as the Messiah. The first two chapters in Luke, which are also virtually unique, are filled with O.T. references and appear to be a form of tradition incorporated by the Evangelist into his later work. The canticles—the angel's message to Zechariah (Lk. 1:14–17), the Magnificat (Lk. 1:46–55), the Benedictus (Lk. 1:68–79), and the Nunc Dimittis (Lk. 2:29–32)—are little else than a patchwork of O.T. citations and allusions.

The book of Acts, written by the author of the Gospel of Luke, contains only one O.T. quotation other than those which are found in the speeches of Peter, Stephen, and Paul. Moreover, in the speeches recorded in the second half of Acts the influence of the O.T. is far less evident because, presumably, the author no longer had available the previously prepared source that he followed in the first half of Acts and that did refer often to the O.T.

THE GOSPEL OF JOHN

In the Gospel of John we meet with a somewhat independent use of the O.T. The Fourth Evangelist does not feel in any way restricted by what earlier writers may have done. He shows himself free to refer to the O.T. in his own way and for his own ends. Compared with those of the Synoptic authors, John's quotations of the O.T. are few. Only three of his O.T. citations are to be found also in the other Gospels. Yet John's Gospel is closely related to Jewish Scripture. In addition to the quotations there are numerous Biblical allusions and indirect references. The Evangelist is primarily influenced by his theological convictions, and he sees the O.T. as a resource that he may use in the effective formulation of his views. But for Christians the meaning of the O.T. is prophetic. Jesus is the Messiah promised in Scripture. Thus, according to Jn. 5:39, Jesus says to the Jews: "You search the scriptures . . . ; and it is they that bear witness to me." Since "scripture cannot be broken" (Jn. 10:35) because it has come from God, it can only be fulfilled.

John is particularly interested in the relation of the passion of Jesus to Scripture. The serious problem of the refusal of the Jews generally to believe in Jesus is related (Jn. 12:37–40) to Is. 53:1 and Is. 6:9–10. The same theme is taken up again in Jn. 15:24–25 and this time referred to Ps. 35:19 (= Ps. 69:4). John is disturbed by the figure of Judas, who is for him the symbol of the aggressive unbeliever. According to Jn. 13:18, his defection was predicted in Ps. 41:9. Details of the crucifixion narrative are referred to the O.T. The clothing of the crucified Jesus is distributed (Jn. 19:23–24) so as to agree with Ps. 22:18. Jesus utters from the cross (Jn. 19:28) the words "I thirst" to fulfill Ps. 69:21. After Jesus' death his side was pierced and his legs were left unbroken (Jn. 19:32–37) so as to conform to Ex. 12:10 (LXX) and 46 (= Num. 9:12 and Ps. 34:20) and also Zech. 12:10.

In addition, John contains many indirect quotations and some general allusions to Scripture. In Jn. 20:9 we are told that Peter and the other disciple who ran to Jesus' tomb on Easter morning "did not know the scripture, that he must rise from the dead." We can only guess as to what portion of Scripture the writer means. Old Testament themes, not limited to specific verses but firmly implied in many portions of Scripture, are taken over by John to support his views of Jesus as the Christ. Examples are the Johannine allegories of the good shepherd (Jn. 10:1–16) and the true vine (Jn. 15:1–10).

THE INDEBTEDNESS OF HEBREWS

Hebrews displays a marked reverence for the words of the O.T. It is the author's firm belief that Scripture has been written by God and that its words are those which God has spoken in the past and still speaks. In Heb. 1:6–9 citations of Deut. 32:43 (LXX) and Ps. 104:4; 45:6–8 are introduced by a single formula, "God says," even though the verse from Deuteronomy is in the song of Moses and the verses from Psalms are not ascribed to God. The third-person description in Gen.

2:2 of God's rest on the seventh day from his work of Creation is in Heb. 4:4 presented as God's own speech. Because he regards the words of Scripture as the utterance of God, the author of Hebrews can occasionally attribute personal attributes to an O.T. verse. In some cases the Greek can be equally well translated: "it [the scripture] says," or "he [God] says." In Heb. 2:11–13 the words of Ps. 22:22; 2 Sam. 22:3 (LXX); and Is. 8:18 are attributed to Christ. Likewise, in Heb. 10:5–7, Ps. 40:6–8 is repeated as the speech of Christ when he came into the world. In Heb. 3:7–11, also, Ps. 95:7–11 (LXX) is cited as the utterance of the Holy Spirit. And in Heb. 10:15–17 two verses of Jeremiah (Jer. 31:33–34) are quoted as the words of the Holy Spirit. Yet these expressions of Christ and the Holy Spirit are also those of God himself. (Cf. Heb. 4:7; 8:8.) In all these cases the present tense is employed because the divine speech is timeless in its relevance. In the introductory formulas that precede O.T. quotations in Hebrews there are two references to Moses and one to David, as God's servants; but otherwise all O.T. citations are thought of as God's words and so make no reference to any Jewish author, contrary to N.T. usage generally. The unity of Scripture is thus maintained. All the O.T. books that are cited in Hebrews are treated as Law and so are viewed as of the same authority and position.

Some sections of Hebrews are mainly a series of O.T. quotations with a minimum of interpretation or discussion. In chapter 1, seven O.T. passages are quoted in order to describe the person of Jesus Christ, God's Son. In chapter 11 a review of Jewish history is built upon references to about 30 sections of historical narrative from Genesis to 2 Chronicles; and Abraham and Moses emerge as the most important leaders. Altogether, at least 28 O.T. passages are cited, and 21 of these are not quoted elsewhere in the N.T. Dependence on the O.T. is extremely heavy throughout, and its interpretation involves ingenuity and creativity.

Even though the O.T. is revered as the continuing word of

God, it is nevertheless seen as a record of incomplete revelation. The contrast between the old and the new is presented at the start (Heb. 1:1–2): "In many and various ways God spoke of old to our fathers by the prophets; but in these last days he has spoken to us by a Son." In fact, the O.T. cannot present the full truth (Heb. 10:1), "since the law has but a shadow of the good things to come instead of the true form of these realities." The function of the O.T., therefore, is to predict and prepare for the coming of Christ, who is seen as in preexistent form active in O.T. history. Moses' acceptance of his role as leader of the oppressed Jews in Egypt entailed (Heb. 11:26) "abuse suffered for the Christ." For the author of Hebrews the O.T. is filled with symbols and types of the Son, in whom alone O.T. beginnings reach their successful conclusion.

THE BOOK OF REVELATION

Among the major books of the N.T. only Revelation contains no explicit or argumentative quotation of the O.T., but it constantly cites O.T. verses or phrases without any acknowledgment of the borrowing. Thus, in Rev. 7:16 we find a description of the saints in heaven: "They shall hunger no more, neither thirst any more; the sun shall not strike them, nor any scorching heat." The words are taken directly from the picture of the future condition of God's people drawn by Is. 49:10: "They shall not hunger or thirst, neither scorching wind nor sun shall smite them." Such quotations, which are introduced casually and without formula and which are used for descriptive purposes rather than for theological argument, are frequent. Moreover, direct and indirect references of all kinds to O.T. language and phrases and ideas occur in almost every verse. With only a few unimportant exceptions all the books of the O.T. are utilized. No N.T. author shows a greater influence by the words and thought of Scripture. Since he is writing an apocalypse, a literary image of the coming triumph of God over his enemies and the rewarding of his faithful followers, the writer of Revelation draws most heavily on the O.T. prophets and Daniel, but other parts of the O.T. are not neglected as he searches everywhere for instructive images with which to portray the imminent victory of God and Christ.

Chapter 3

What Was Chosen for Citation

The almost limitless literary parallels between the O.T. and the N.T. can be studied under four major headings. Class one includes all the N.T. quotations of the O.T. that are prefaced by a formula of introduction that clearly designates that which follows as a quotation and that often names the original author. Material in this class is objectively definable and usually represents careful and accurate reproduction of the O.T. text. Class two is also made up of O.T. quotations, but they are without any introduction or acknowledgment and are somewhat fewer in number than the citations in the first class. Class-two quotations cannot therefore always be determined with the same objectivity and accuracy. Sometimes they may be less faithful to the form and wording of the Hebrew original, but in every case their character as intended quotations is unmistakable. As a subheading of this second class we must include those more than 100 distinctive O.T. phrases which reappear unpredictably throughout the N.T. Class three consists of large numbers of N.T. verses in which O.T. material has been distinctly utilized. There is direct borrowing, but at the same time the O.T. has been treated with a greater degree of freedom. The author may have wanted to make a quotation, but if so, he has altered his source. Material in the O.T. may have been inaccurately remembered, or the argument of the N.T. author may have required some adaptation. Dependence on the O.T. may be real but unconscious. In dealing with verses assigned to class three the critic must admit the necessity for some subjective judgment. Yet the characteristics of this class are distinct. It is possible to speak also of a fourth class in which there is indirect or probable dependence upon the O.T. The uncertainties are such, however, that verses placed in this class may represent only the influence of a general tradition of thought and expression that forms part of the background of the O.T. also. Such parallel expressions of a common influence become too numerous and too lacking in real significance to make possible or worthwhile their identification and examination. Thus, in this study we will limit ourselves to the first three classes, with particular attention to the first class.

FORMULA-QUOTATION

The formula-quotations of class one provide the most satisfactory means available for investigating in detail the whole subject of the N.T. use of Scripture. As previously noted, there are 239 instances of citations of this type in the N.T., and they are absent only from Philemon, Colossians, 1 and 2 Thessalonians, Titus, Philemon, 1, 2, and 3 John, Jude, and Revelation. Common to all three Synoptic Gospels 8 such quotations occur; 4 more are found in both Matthew and Mark; and an additional 5 appear in both Matthew and Luke. Furthermore, there are 22 citations of this class unique to Matthew and 4 that are unique to Luke. John contains 13 and Acts, 25. In his four major epistles (Romans, 1 and 2 Corinthians, Galatians), Paul includes 76 of these citations, of which more than one half are found in Romans. Also notable are the 37 formula-quotations that appear in Hebrews. The instances of citations of the first class can thus be isolated and counted and their manner of introduction and use analyzed. Furthermore, in each case there can be no doubt about the Christian author's studied intent to quote the O.T. as a central part of his argument. The authority of a Scriptural passage cited by a Christian writer did not, of course, depend upon the presence of an introductory formula; but in almost every instance where the formula is used the question of Scriptural authority is regarded by the author as important.

Such formulas were in current use by both the rabbis and the unknown writers of the Dead Sea Scrolls; and N.T. practice must be weighed against that fact. As much as possible the Christian authors retained the usage of their earlier counterparts. Parallels between Christian and Jewish expressions are to be expected and are indeed found. Jews and Christians alike are convinced that even though there are human instruments as authors, it is really God who speaks in Scripture. This is true where the words of God are preserved in the O.T., as in Ex. 3:6: "I am the God of Abraham, and the God of Isaac, and the God of Jacob." When these same words appear in Mt. 22:32, they are easily prefaced by the question, "Have you not read what was said to you by God?" So, too, the words of God to Abraham that are preserved in Gen. 12:3, "By you all the families of the earth shall bless themselves," are correctly reported in Acts 3:25 as the promise of God. Entirely consistent with Jewish understanding and use is the N.T. custom of ascribing the words of O.T. writers directly to God or indirectly to God through human agents. Thus, God speaks by a prophet (Mt. 1:22) or by David through the Holy Spirit (Acts 4:25) or in Hosea (Rom. 9:25). As spokesmen for God, mention is also made of Moses, Isaiah, Jeremiah, Joel, and Daniel. Moreover, formulas that speak of human authors of Scripture are applied without change to passages that are attributed directly to God. Although the idea of "the word of God" often suggests Scripture in its totality, the same phrase can also mean some particular verse or Scriptural passage. This is true of the reference of Jesus in Mk. 7:10 to God's commandment to honor parents (Ex. 20:12 and 21:17 = Deut. 5:16 and Lev. 20:9). The same may be said of Jesus' reference to Is. 41:23 in Jn. 10:34–35. God speaks not only in the course of

the Bible as a whole but also in the particularities and con-
creteness of individual verses. This truth is in no way affected
by the fact that, as we have noted in a few instances, an introductory formula is followed by a passage that in whole or in
part cannot be identified in the O.T. Such is the case in Mt.
2:23; 1 Cor. 2:9; 1 Tim. 5:18b; and Jas. 4:5; but otherwise the
citation that is prefaced by a formula is always positively lo-
cated in the O.T.

Although there is a great variety of different formulas used
in rabbinical writings and also at Qumran, the variations in
form are far more numerous in the N.T. Thus, in the latter we
discover great differences in the one believed to be speaking
in cited passages. In 35 of the 239 introductory formulas God
(or the Lord) is held to be the speaker. At least 2 times Christ
is described as the one who speaks. The Holy Spirit is said to
make his own pronouncements 3 times, and on other occasions
the Holy Spirit is mentioned as the agent of Scriptural utterance. On the other hand, the passive voice is employed frequently, with no reference to any speaker. Or we often find
that the speaker is said to be Scripture itself. Human speakers
referred to in the formulas include "the prophet" (3), Moses
(5), David (7), Isaiah (14), Jeremiah (2), and Joel (1). The
apparent attribution of Scripture to a human author may only
be the writer's way of fixing the place of the O.T. citation.
The words "what is said in the prophets" (Acts 13:40) refer
to the Hebrew Book of the Twelve (prophets), and the quotation that follows is properly from Habakkuk, one of these
minor prophets. In similar fashion two quotations from Hosea
are prefaced (Rom. 9:25) by the words, "As indeed he [God]
says in Hosea." In 1 Cor. 9:9 a citation of Deut. 25:4 is introduced by the formula, "For it is written in the law of Moses."
The source of a quotation is even more narrowly fixed in Mk.
12:26 (= Lk. 20:37), where Ex. 3:6 is cited after the question,
"Have you not read in the book of Moses, in the passage about
the bush, how God said to him . . . ?" On the other hand,
there are two O.T. quotations in Hebrews that are introduced

by words which are either intentionally vague or necessarily so because the author cannot identify the source of remembered Scripture. In Heb. 4:4 words from Gen. 2:2 are preceded by the statement, "For he [God] has somewhere spoken of the seventh day in this way." In Heb. 2:6 a quotation of Ps. 8:4–6 is prefaced by a similarly general declaration, "It has been testified somewhere." Whether the Scriptural citation is specifically identified or simply quoted as Scripture and whether it is attributed directly to God or described as the words of a human writer, in all cases it is utilized just because it is held to possess divine authority and timeless relevance.

There are 169 different formulas among the total of 239. In fact, few of the formulas occur more than once; but many of the differences are slight and of no real significance. The words "It is written" appear 5 times; and the slightly altered formula "For it is written" is used in 13 instances. The essentially same words "as it is written" are found in 15 places. With minor additions at the beginning or the end, this basic formula "it is written" is utilized 55 times, nearly one fourth of the N.T. total. The second major type of formula refers to what is said in Scripture or to what God says. There are 70 examples of this type of usage. On 22 occasions we discover references to the words or writings of the prophets or of one of them by name. There are 12 references to the Psalms, of which 9 mention David, their traditional author. The fulfillment of Scripture or of prophecy is the basis of 17 of the formulas, of which only 1 stands outside the four Gospels. The remaining formula types are unimportant and few in number and so need not be detailed here.

The wording of the formulas reveals some of the presuppositions that underlie the N.T. use of Scripture. The majority of them strongly imply, even if they do not directly affirm, the divine origin and the resulting authority of Scripture. But the formulas also suggest some of the ways in which the Christians made use of the O.T. for their own purposes. In 36 cases formulas consist of only one word each, and in 5 more instances there are only two words each. Altogether 8 forms are involved; they consist of the words "and," "but," "for," "no," "and again," "or again," "thus," and "as." When these words are considered together, they strongly call to mind literary and even oral argument. It seems probable, therefore, that at the least many of these one- or two-word formulas point to the often bitter controversy that quickly arose between the infant Christian church and its Jewish parent. In this struggle O.T. quotations became an integral part of the Christian theological position, and Scripture was quoted against the very people among whom it had originated. This tentative conclusion is made all the more probable when we note that in 2 cases an O.T. citation is introduced by the rhetorical question, "Have you never read?" and that in 4 more instances the formula is the substantially identical: "Have you not read?" Moreover, among the major types of formula already surveyed we find 8 more rhetorical questions and 61 cases where initial words are those often used in argument and conflict. These include "while," "since," "therefore," "hence," and "consequently." The continuing importance of Scripture for Christians in their own peculiar situation is also indicated by the fact that the past tense, as in "said," "spoke," and "promised," is found in only 45 of the N.T. formulas. The dominant idea is that Scripture speaks in the Christian present.

Since there is a large measure of preciseness about the formula-quotations, it is profitable to study their origins. Again we discover that there are notable differences among the various N.T. writers as to which O.T. books are utilized most often. Matthew, with his interest in law, has 18 quotations from the Law. He has also 8 from Isaiah, and 2 from Jeremiah, 8 from the Minor Prophets, 6 from Psalms, and no other. In Mark we find 6 citations of the Law, 3 of Isaiah, 1 of Jeremiah, 2 of the Minor Prophets and 2 of Psalms. Luke contains 8 quotations from the Law, 4 from Isaiah, 1 from Jeremiah, 1 from the Twelve, and 4 from Psalms. John has only 1 citation of the Law, 4 of Isaiah, 2 of Zechariah, and 6 of Psalms. Thus, in the four Gospels as a whole we find that out of a total of 87 class-one quotations 33 are taken from the Law; 19 from Isaiah and 4 from Jeremiah; 13 from the Minor Prophets; and 18 from Psalms. Since there are no other quotations of this class in the Gospels, they belong entirely to the Law, the Prophets, and the Psalms, the very same listing that occurs in Lk. 24:44. Notable by their absence are the historical books (known as "the earlier prophets") and all the other Writings, which were the last to be included in the Hebrew canon of Scripture.

In the book of Acts we find 9 formula-quotations from the Law, 5 from Isaiah, 4 from the Twelve, and 2 from Psalms. Of the 83 class-one quotations in Paul (apart from the three in Ephesians) 52 appear in Romans. In all his epistles Paul quotes, with formula, the Law 29 times, Isaiah 29 times, Jeremiah once, the Twelve 6 times, and Psalms 19 times. In addition, we find 2 such quotations from 1 Kings and 1 each from 2 Samuel, Job, and Proverbs. The author of Hebrews uses 8 such quotations from the Law, 1 from Isaiah, 3 from Jeremiah, 2 from the Twelve, 19 from Psalms, and only 4 others.

In the entire N.T. there are 239 class-one quotations. More than 35 percent of these are from the Law, and 24 percent are drawn from Isaiah and Jeremiah. Eight of the twelve Minor Prophets furnish another 10 percent of the total, while Psalms are quoted in this way in 24 percent of the cases. The final 7 percent of these quotations are provided by 5 more O.T. books. Thus, 16 of the 39 books of the O.T. account for 90 percent of the class-one quotations, and there is not even 1 such quotation from 18 of the O.T. books.

When the unacknowledged quotations of class two and the indirect or altered citations of class three are studied, the general picture is not much changed. In the second class there are 198 quotations, and of these 16½ percent are derived from the Law. Another 30 percent come from the three Major Prophets —Isaiah, Jeremiah, and Ezekiel. The Minor Prophets furnish 6½ percent, and Psalms accounts for more than 23 percent. Thus, 15 books of the O.T. provide 76 percent of the class-two quotations, and 11 more books are used for the remaining 24 percent. Finally, 13 O.T. books are not quoted in this way in the N.T.

The citations of the third class are by their nature much more numerous and total 1,167. Almost 30 percent of these are drawn from the Law. The Major Prophets provide 24 percent, and 10 percent more come from the Minor Prophets. Psalms contributes an additional 18 percent. Thus, 82 percent of class-three material is taken from 21 O.T. books, and 18 percent is drawn from 18 more books.

When the citations of O.T. passages of all three classes are considered together, it can be seen that we are dealing with 1,604 N.T. passages that are directly dependent upon the O.T. The Law is cited in 342 of these instances, amounting to more than 20 percent of the whole. The three Major Prophets provide 405 of the citations, 25 percent of the total. The twelve Minor Prophets provide 142 citations, another 9 percent. The 311 uses of Psalms are 19 percent of the passages under study. These 21 O.T. books furnish 81 percent of all the direct citations, and 19 percent are derived from the remainder. No O.T. book is completely ignored, and the use of the O.T. is especially widespread in class three. On the other hand, the great preponderance of borrowings from the Law, the Prophets, and the Psalms can be clearly seen.

COLLECTIONS OF OLD TESTAMENT TEXTS

The Dead Sea Scrolls point to the probability that the members of the Qumran Community brought together in a formal collection passages of Scripture that were regarded as Messianic prophecies. There is also reason to believe that other Jews had even earlier attempted such a collection. If a chain of Messianic texts was in existence in the first century A.D., Christians could have made good use of it and might even have altered or added to it. The utilization by N.T. writers of a Book of Testimonies containing a grouping of O.T. proof texts that could support the claim of Jesus' Messiahship would explain why some passages have been quoted in Christian writings and why others have been disregarded. However, there is no evidence that any generally recognized collection of O.T. texts ever circulated in the early church. It is more than likely that certain verses and passages of the O.T. were employed in primitive Christian preaching and teaching and that they became so increasingly familiar that N.T. writers may have quoted them from memory and so at times unintentionally departed from the form of the original text. Yet the manner in which the citations are employed often indicates that the Christian author has in mind not only the words but also their context, which could not have been a part of a Book of Testimonies. A grouping of some O.T. passages may have been transmitted orally in the first years of Christianity, but we cannot conclude that there ever was a written collection available for N.T. authors. There is no objective way to determine which of the O.T. citations might have belonged to such a book, and its only reality may lie in later listings of O.T. quotations that were, for whatever reason, actually used in the N.T.

A Selective Use

Early Christian writers found some portions of the O.T. to be of more immediate value to them than others. A closer study of the individual O.T. books discloses that some chapters or sections have been quite heavily employed by several N.T. writers, whereas other areas are entirely overlooked or cited only sparsely.

In Genesis the narratives of Creation and the Fall (Gen., chs. 1 to 5) are directly reflected in eighteen of the twenty-seven N.T. books. The story of Abraham (Gen., chs. 12 to 25) is also very influential. Other N.T. citations of Genesis are scattered except for approximately 30 N.T. references to the story of Joseph (Gen., chs. 37 to 50). Citations of Exodus in the N.T.

are numerous and are drawn rather evenly, mostly from the first thirty-four chapters. God's calling of Moses and the Decalogue are of the greatest interest to the N.T. authors. Leviticus is used relatively little except for some unimportant references to ritual law and practice; citations of Numbers are even less numerous. Deuteronomy, on the other hand, is cited more often than any other book of the Law. Almost every chapter of it is directly reflected in the N.T., and only seven N.T. books, which contain no more than twenty-one chapters, have no citation of it.

The situation is very different in the six historical books from Joshua through 2 Kings. They comprise about 20 percent of the total material in the O.T. but contribute only 6 percent of the N.T. citations. They contain only a single passage that is of fundamental importance for N.T. writers and that is cited or reflected in six N.T. books: 2 Sam. 7:12–14, God's promise of a Davidic savior. This evidence necessitates the conclusion that whereas Jewish history from Abraham through the death of Moses was of primary significance for the early Christians, subsequent history had relatively little interest until the coming of Jesus.

The whole N.T. is under a heavy debt to the three Major Prophets, and of these Isaiah is most influential by far, furnishing 248 of the 405 N.T. citations of these prophets. The sixth chapter of Isaiah, the narrative of the prophet's call, is cited by all four Gospels, Acts, and Revelation. Seven of its thirteen verses are thus reflected, and it is probable that the whole of the chapter may have been in the mind of each N.T. writer when he quoted any part of it, as is surely the case with some other chapters in Scripture that are widely quoted. The second part of Isaiah (Is., chs. 40 to 66) is more frequently cited than is the first. Thus, the prophecy of a voice crying in the wilderness (Is. 40:3–5) is quoted, with a formula of introduction, in all four Gospels. In the description of the Suffering Servant (Is. 52:13 to 53:12) there are only two verses that are not reproduced in whole or in part somewhere among the

N.T. books. Yet only one of the nine or ten writers citing this section quotes as many as two successive verses of it. It is the figure of the vicarious and freely accepted suffering of an innocent victim that is in the thought of all nine or ten authors. This Isaianic passage is influential not only in its particular wording but also in its underlying image. With the single exception of Psalms, Isaiah is more often cited in the N.T. than any other portion of Scripture. (The book of Psalms will be discussed in Chapter 6.)

Jeremiah and Ezekiel are used in much the same way as is Isaiah, but the citations of both together are fewer than those of Isaiah alone. The influence on the N.T. of the prophecy of the new covenant (Jer. 31:31–34) is major, and five N.T. authors cite it directly. All twelve Minor Prophets are utilized in at least one of the three classes of usage. Hosea and Zechariah are the ones most widely quoted, the latter furnishing language and figures for N.T. apocalyptic writing.

Daniel is also a major source for much N.T. apocalyptic expression. The four Gospels, the Pauline epistles, and Revelation all exhibit knowledge of its seventh chapter. Citations of the Wisdom literature in the N.T. are mostly taken from Proverbs, and total 44. They are well dispersed throughout the thirty-one chapters and have little theological significance as they are almost entirely moral precepts and maxims.

Examination of the use of the O.T. in the N.T. must, logically, include some attention to those sections of Scripture which are not directly reproduced in the N.T. Careful study indicates that of the 187 chapters in the Law only 33, mostly from Genesis and Numbers, are not directly reflected in some way in the N.T. In the six historical books (Joshua to 2 Kings) 75 of the 146 chapters are unused in the N.T. About the same degree of nonuse is discovered in the cycle of 1 and 2 Chronicles, Ezra, and Nehemiah. No N.T. use is apparently made of 39 of the 166 chapters in the three Major Prophets, and almost the same percentage applies to the Minor Prophets as well. Only 19 of the 150 Psalms are not directly reproduced in some way in the N.T. There are 26 of the 85 chapters in the Wisdom literature that are unused. There is no observable pattern in those chapters of the O.T. which are not cited in the N.T., and the explanation must be that of a deliberate choice exercised by the early Christian authors. Once again it is evident that primary attention was given to the Law, the Prophets, and the Psalms. The historical books and the Wisdom literature show a significantly smaller N.T. use.

Consideration of the Jewish writings that lie outside the O.T., the books of the Apocrypha and the Pseudepigrapha, suggests that N.T. authors referred to this literature in only a very limited way. There are no N.T. quotations from the Apocrypha or the Pseudepigrapha, and it is significant that there are not. There are some indirect references to these non-canonical books, but few cases are certain because often the apocryphal verse in question is paralleled by an O.T. statement, from which the N.T. writer is more likely to have borrowed. Jude 14 may be influenced by the Book of Enoch 1:9 and 60:8, but it may be explained equally well as the result of the influence of passages in Genesis, Deuteronomy, 1 Chronicles, Daniel, and Zechariah. Among the books of the Apocrypha, 1 Maccabees, The Wisdom of Solomon, and Sirach seem most likely to have been utilized indirectly in the N.T.; and of the pseudepigraphical writings the Psalms of Solomon, the Martyrdom of Isaiah, and the Assumption of Moses may have played some part. In any case, however, these later Jewish writings were not held in the same regard as the books of the O.T. by the N.T. authors, and they are nowhere referred to by name (except possibly in Jude 14). The early Christian writers regarded the O.T. as authoritative and so appealed to it directly to support their theological views; but if they consciously employed these later Jewish books at all, they did so with great freedom and complete informality. The books of the O.T. were obviously regarded as having a unique status. There are actual quotations of class one and class two from

twenty-nine of the thirty-nine books of the O.T. The remaining
ten O.T. books are included in class three, but there are no
sure examples even of class-three citations from any Jewish
writing outside of the O.T.

THE STATE OF THE OLD TESTAMENT CANON

The precise limits of the Jewish canon of Scripture, the official listing of authoritative books, during the N.T. period cannot be precisely determined. In fact, the knowledge that we
possess indicates that Christian use of Jewish writings preceded any final Jewish action in closing that canon. No attempt
was made to limit the extent of Scripture until several decades
after the fall of Jerusalem in A.D. 70. Moreover, the real decisions about which books belonged to Scripture and which
books did not were made by the constant use of the synagogues and not by any formal councils, whose role was restricted to placing a final seal of approval on the choices that
many generations of Jews had already made in practice. The
Jewish view of Scripture in this respect, as in so many others,
passed over into early Christianity; and thus the canon of the
N.T. was arrived at in the Christian church in a very similar
manner. However, both for Jews and Christians the criterion of
use involved acceptance and rejection. A passage in 2 Peter
(2 Pet. 3:15–16), probably the latest of the N.T. books, provides some interesting evidence. The author refers positively
to the letters of Paul and relates them to "the other scriptures."
By this wording, apostolic epistles are apparently being viewed
in the same light as the O.T. books. Furthermore, this same
author reproduces, in chapter 2, the brief epistle of Jude but
deliberately excludes those several portions which may be references to apocryphal books. For him, Scripture means the
O.T. and also Paul's letters, but nothing else.

The five books from Genesis to Deuteronomy formed the beginning of Jewish Scripture and were usually referred to as the

books of the Law, or the books of Moses. Although the word
"law" is used in the N.T. with a variety of meanings, it frequently is a designation for the first five books of the O.T., the
Pentateuch; and conversely the Pentateuch is always described
in the N.T. as "the law." This first division of the Jewish O.T.
canon was also central for early Christianity. Its authority is
seen even in the exceptional reference in 1 Cor. 14:21 to a quotation from Isaiah (Is. 28:11–12) with the prefatory statement,
"In the law it is written."

At some time in the period after the Babylonian exile the
books of the Prophets were added to the growing O.T. canon.
They included the historical books of Joshua, Judges, Samuel,
and Kings, the three Major Prophets (Isaiah, Jeremiah, and
Ezekiel) and the Minor Prophets (gathered into one book and
known as The Twelve). The latter may be mentioned in Sirach
49:10: "Of the twelve prophets let the memorial be blessed."
In Acts 7:42 a quotation from Amos (Amos 5:25–27), one of
the Twelve, is introduced with the formula, "As it is written
in the book of the prophets." Again, in Acts 13:40 a quotation
from Hab. 1:5 is prefaced by similar words, "What is said in
the prophets." Another such instance occurs in Acts 15:15,
where the citation of Amos 9:11–12 is preceded by the statement that "with this the words of the prophets agree, as it is
written." On the other hand, the prophets were also thought of
as individuals, and two of the Minor Prophets (Joel and Hosea)
are quoted by name. Only once (Jn. 6:45) is Isaiah quoted
anonymously as among "the prophets." On fourteen occasions
Isaiah is called the prophet or is described as prophesying.
Six more times Isaiah is named but without reference to his
prophetic status. Twice Jeremiah is quoted by name as a
prophet. Once (Mt. 13:35) a quotation from Psalms is described as "what was spoken by the prophet," and there is one
reference (Mt. 24:15) to the words of "the prophet Daniel."
Traditional prophecy, along with the Law, was held to be
authoritative by N.T. writers.

Officially, in the time of Jesus the O.T. consisted only of

these two collections and so a convenient designation of Scripture was the phrase "the law and the prophets." The authority that at first had belonged to the Law alone was now believed to have been extended to include the Prophets. This assumption is apparent in the words of Jesus found in Mt. 5:17–18: "Think not that I have come to abolish the law and the prophets; . . . not an iota, not a dot, will pass from the law." The final reference to the Law alone is held to cover the Prophets also. The phrase "the law and the prophets" is common in the Gospels and in Acts. Luke, in his Gospel and in Acts, also uses 5 times the phrase with identical meaning, "Moses and the Prophets." In all these cases the intent of the author is to refer to the totality of the officially accepted Scripture. So for Jesus, in Mt. 7:12, the Golden Rule "is the law and the prophets." Similarly, Jesus' summary of the law, selected from Leviticus and Deuteronomy, is described (Mt. 22:40) as the substance of "all the law and the prophets." In Lk. 16:16 Jesus speaks of the transcendent quality of the new order that he brings and says in contrast: "The law and the prophets were until John." In Jn. 1:45 Philip's testimony to Jesus is: "We have found him of whom Moses in the law and also the prophets wrote." In his defense before Felix (Acts 24:14) Paul claims that as a Christian he worships God, "believing everything laid down by the law or written in the prophets." In Jesus' parable of the rich man and Lazarus (Lk. 16:19–31) Abraham answers Lazarus' request for special treatment of his brothers by stating: "They have Moses and the prophets." According to Acts 28:23, Paul spent his time while under house arrest and awaiting his trial in Rome arguing with the Jews and "trying to convince them about Jesus both from the law of Moses and from the prophets."

The two parts of the O.T. were believed to belong together and to constitute a unity. Just as the authority of the Law was ascribed also to the Prophets, so the predictive quality of the Prophets was also applied to the Law. This development lies behind the words of Jesus in Mt. 11:13: "All the prophets and the law prophesied until John." In his defense before Agrippa, Paul asserts (Acts 26:22) that in his preaching he has said "nothing but what the prophets and Moses said would come to pass." The use by N.T. authors of citations of the Law and the Prophets rests upon their authority, belonging originally to the Law, and their predictive aspect, belonging originally to the Prophets. In the synagogue services of the first Christian century there were regularly readings from both the Law and the Prophets, as is indicated by Acts 13:15.

The content of the two parts of Scripture was fixed by this time, but some additional books were recognized in practice as also having the force of the written Word of God. These were separate works which at first circulated independently, but which gradually were accepted as authoritative by the use to which they were put. The prologue to Ecclesiasticus (ca. 130 B.C.) states: "Whereas many and great things have been delivered unto us by the law and the prophets, and by others that have followed in their steps, . . . my grandfather Jesus, when he had much given himself to the reading of the law, and the prophets, and other books of our fathers. . . ." A few lines later there is another reference to "the law itself, and the prophets, and the rest of the books." Philo, writing close to the time of Jesus' birth, quotes from Psalms, Proverbs, Job, Ezra, and Nehemiah as if they were a part of Scripture. Almost unconsciously a third part, composed of miscellaneous works that became known as "the Writings," was being added to the O.T. Although this third division was not officially recognized and defined until the Council of Jamnia in A.D. 90, its authoritative quality and its content were already a part of the tradition taken over by the N.T. writers.

In Rom. 15:10–12 there are quotations from Deuteronomy (the Law), Isaiah (the Prophets), and Psalms (the Writings). This combination may, of course, be accidental and therefore insignificant; but it is in accord with the specific listing in the words of Jesus in Lk. 24:44: "These are my words which I spoke to you, . . . that everything written about me in the law

of Moses and the prophets and the psalms must be fulfilled."
The Scripture that was used by Jesus did contain the Psalms
and other books beyond the Law and the Prophets. A threefold division seems to lie behind the comment of Luke in the
resurrection story of Jesus' walk to Emmaus (Lk. 24:27): "Beginning with Moses and all the prophets, he interpreted to
them in all the scriptures the things concerning himself." The
order is significant. The O.T. began with the law of Moses and
was expanded with the Prophets and completed with the Writings, which are implied in the phrase "all the scriptures."
Words of Jesus in Mt. 23:35 refer to "all the righteous blood
shed on earth, from the blood of innocent Abel [Gen. 4:8] to
the blood of Zechariah the son of Barachiah, whom you mur-
dered between the sanctuary and the altar [2 Chron. 24:21]."
For the Evangelist, the historical narrative of Scripture starts
with Genesis (the Law), continues in the Joshua-Kings cycle
(the Prophets), and now includes Chronicles (the Writings).
Although many of the Writings are scarcely used in the N.T.
(Ruth, Ezra, Nehemiah, Esther, Ecclesiastes, Song of Solomon,
Lamentations), none is without some direct relationship to the
N.T. Equally important is the fact that there is no certain N.T.
use of any books outside of the threefold division of the O.T.
Their status as Scripture is the most important single factor in
the choice made for citation by the early Christian authors.

THE ROLE OF THE GREEK OLD TESTAMENT

Although the N.T. makes use of only those books which are
held to be Scripture, it does not consider their exact wording
to be unchangeable. As we have noted, the O.T. is often
treated freely with alterations, substitutions, omissions, additions, and new interpretations. The text need not be handled in
a completely literalistic manner. This same freedom is exercised in the choice of the form of language in which the O.T.
is set forth. The original language of all the O.T. books is Hebrew, with a few sections appearing in the cognate Aramaic.

However, the O.T. books were all translated into Greek before the beginning of the first century B.C., and the collection of these Greek translations, accompanied by the apocryphal books in Greek, circulated as the Septuagint (LXX).

By the time of Jesus the Greek language was rather widely known and used in Palestine, and the LXX was present alongside the Hebrew O.T. The Septuagint contained a Greek theological vocabulary that was immediately available for the N.T. authors, all of whom wrote for Greek-speaking Christian congregations. The LXX was without question one of the most creative factors in the emergence of the N.T. No problem was raised for the Christian writers in citing O.T. passages from the translated Greek version rather than from the original Hebrew. Thus, an overwhelming majority of the O.T. citations are drawn from the LXX. The situation has been pointedly summarized by Krister Stendahl that the N.T. in general gives the impression of a conscious desire to reproduce the LXX text correctly. (*The School of St. Matthew,* 2d ed., p. 158.) Moreover, every part of the N.T. shows some knowledge and use of the Septuagint, and no book depends solely upon the original Hebrew form of the O.T.

Sometimes the O.T. citations will differ both from any known Hebrew form of the text and from any known Greek translation, and it is always a possibility that the N.T. writers have in any instance made their own new and direct Greek translations from the Hebrew. In many cases, of course, citation is from the Hebrew with no regard to the Greek. The Hebrew (or Aramaic) wording is preserved, by transliteration, in Mt. 27:46 (Mk. 15:34), where Ps. 22:1 is quoted. In some instances the desired meaning would have been lost if the quotation had been from the Greek rather than from the Hebrew. Yet it is the use of the LXX at all that is most surprising.

Of all the major N.T. writers Matthew shows the least influence of the Septuagint. His quotations are usually from the Hebrew except where its use would not serve his argument. In these cases he turns to the LXX. Perhaps the clearest illustration of this practice is Mt. 1:23, where Matthew cites Is. 7:14 as a prophecy of the virgin birth, which he narrates in Mt. 1:18–25. The Hebrew form of this verse is: "Behold, a young woman shall conceive and bear a son"; but the LXX reads: "Behold, a virgin shall conceive and shall bring forth a son." Only four of the formal quotations in Mark do not agree with the LXX. In the account of the conflict between Jesus and the Pharisees over the issue of the ritual washing of hands before meals as presented by Mk. 7:1–8 (= Mt. 15:1–9), Jesus uses a formula-quotation of Is. 29:13. In the Hebrew the last part of the verse states: "Their fear of me is a commandment of men learned by rote." In the LXX form, which is used by both Matthew and Mark, we find: "In vain do they worship me, teaching the commandments and doctrines of men." The concluding words of Jesus (Mk. 7:8), which contrast the commandment of God and the tradition of men, are supported by the LXX but not by the Hebrew form of Is. 29:13, and so it is clearly the Greek version that is used.

In Luke's Gospel there is little dependence upon the Hebrew O.T., whereas in Acts the quotations are entirely from the Greek. In Acts 15:16–18 James, presiding over the Council of Jerusalem and giving his decision that the Christian mission to the Gentiles, as well as to the Jews, should be continued, quotes Amos 9:11–12. And again the LXX is employed, for in the Hebrew the role of the Gentiles in the promised restoration of Israel is vague, whereas in the LXX the purpose of that restoration is "that the remnant of men, and all the Gentiles upon whom my name is called, may earnestly seek me, says the Lord." In John and in the Pauline epistles likewise, the LXX is normally utilized. Revelation, although without any formula-quotations, contains class-two and class-three citations that appear to be the author's own Greek translation and that are often influenced by the LXX.

Hebrews, which is on the surface so concerned with things Jewish as to give rise to its title, but which is actually heavily influenced by Greek concepts and terms, depends more upon the Septuagintal form of the O.T. than does any other N.T. book. In chapter 1 the author of Hebrews supports his opening declaration of the exalted and unique status of Jesus as God's Son by a series of O.T. quotations. In Heb. 1:6 the author applies to Jesus the words of Deut. 32:43 (LXX): "Let all God's angels worship him." The Hebrew form is quite different and would not have been helpful: "Praise his people, O you nations; for he avenges the blood of his servants."

In approximately 50 instances N.T. citations differ notably from their original Hebrew form, and in only a few cases does a passage from the LXX represent entirely new material not found in the Hebrew. However, the N.T. shows the same kind of freedom in its use of verses from the LXX as it displays in its citation of the Hebrew, and in neither case do N.T. writers treat the O.T. text as something that is to be received literally. An examination of 39 verses of the LXX, cited in the N.T., that differ significantly from their Hebrew counterpart provides some further understanding. (Cf. Table 4. A similar examination of the Greek version of the Psalms is presented in Chapter 6.) The 39 passages occur in 14 O.T. books. Of these, 9 are found in the Law and 23 in the Prophets with only 7 coming from the Writings. Perhaps N.T. writers felt more free to use passages of the LXX that differed decisively from the Hebrew in the case of the Law and the Prophets, about whose Scriptural status there were no doubts, than they did in the case of the Writings, which had not yet been officially accepted as part of the O.T. Of the 39 verses, 14 are from Isaiah, which, along with Psalms, is the O.T. book most commonly cited in the N.T. The 39 passages are cited in more than half of the N.T. books, further evidence that the use of the LXX is found throughout the N.T. As we would expect, 9 of the instances occur in Hebrews. Finally, 8 of the citations are of class three, where the borrowing is less direct than quotation, and all but one of these are drawn from the firmly established Law and the Prophets, whose content was so well known that they could be cited without the necessity of quotation. On the other hand, 30 of the instances are quotations, mostly with formula. For the N.T. authors the authority of the LXX was no less than that of the Hebrew O.T., for they were both seen as the Word of God.

Chapter 4

Jesus and the Old Testament

The complex N.T. attitude toward the O.T. must have its principal roots in the thought and practice of Jesus. He must have been the powerful example and the creative influence that enabled the early Christian writers to handle the O.T. with both respect and freedom and to interpret it as basically the record of the expectation of Jesus Christ, in whom alone it finds its true meaning. The views of Jesus must lie behind the fact that the N.T. authors in their use of the O.T. in part retain their Jewish heritage and in part reject or transform it. The new and unique position of the N.T. with regard to Scripture requires an explanation as to how it came to be, a sufficient cause, and Jesus must provide the answer. How he viewed the O.T. and how he used it in his teaching were naturally matters of great concern to all his followers and were highly influential throughout the N.T.

Our knowledge of Jesus' relationship to the O.T. is limited almost entirely to the four Gospels; and although they contain a relatively large amount of material, they are in their present form the products of a time some decades after the death of Jesus. During the period of the oral transmission of the tradition regarding Jesus' words and deeds the authentic information has in some instances been lost, in others changed to meet the emerging needs of the Christian community, and in still others supplemented. Thus, the Gospels preserve in written form virtually all that we can know of the historic Jesus; but they also contain much tradition that came into being between the time of Jesus' death and the writing of the Gospels. Furthermore, the original and unique contribution of each Evangelist cannot be overlooked. However, the attempt to distinguish precisely each of these three elements is often no more than the exercise of subjective judgment. All three factors are so intricately intertwined that only with the greatest difficulty and lingering uncertainty can any verse be tentatively assigned to one source. On the other hand, some characteristics and tendencies of each element can be discovered, and in general there is agreement that in the Gospels the authentic tradition about Jesus' life has been modified by the many ways in which it was employed in the early church. In this study we must be concerned primarily with the content of the Gospels as they have come to us, but at the same time we will give some attention to what seem to have been the views of Jesus himself in the use of Scripture.

The parallels between the teachings that the Gospels attribute to Jesus and the O.T. are notable for their great number and their pervasiveness. (Table 5 sets forth the particulars. For obvious reasons, not every possible parallel has been included. Identical phrases that could have been part of a common heritage and that do not prove direct literary dependence have not been listed.) The material has been examined according to the usual analysis of Gospel sources. The first division consists of 30 teachings that have identifiable O.T. parallels and occur in Mark as well as in Matthew or Luke, or in both Matthew and Luke. Only 3 such sayings occur uniquely in Mark. Matthew and Luke, presumably drawing upon a second common source, usually known as Q, contain 29 separate teachings with O.T. parallels. Matthew, which emphasizes Jesus' teaching ministry far more than the other Gospels, includes 37 instances of teaching with O.T. parallels that belong exclusively to that Gospel. Luke has 17 such instances that are uniquely his, and the same number is true of John. Thus, teachings with O.T. parallels are ascribed to Jesus in significant numbers in all the sources of the Gospels, i.e., Mark, Q, M (special source used by Matthew), L (special source used by Luke), and John. The tradition that in his speech Jesus drew heavily upon the O.T. is deeply rooted and everywhere attested.

Old Testament books that are apparently reflected in these teachings show about the same usage that we have found for the N.T. as a whole. In the first category, Mark with equivalents occurring in Matthew and/or in Luke, there are 14 references to the Law, 17 to the Major Prophets, 6 to the Minor Prophets and 6 to the Writings. In the material common to Matthew and Luke but not in Mark we find 15 references to the Law, 10 to the Major Prophets, 2 to the Minor Prophets and 8 to the Writings. In the largest category, material in Matthew only, there are 19 references to the Law, 13 to the Major Prophets, 8 to the Minor Prophets, and 7 to the Writings. The same proportions hold for the material unique to Luke and to John. Thus, in the teachings attributed to Jesus in all the sources the heaviest dependence is upon the Major and Minor Prophets, with the Law in second place. Within the Pentateuch, Deuteronomy is drawn upon almost two times as frequently as any other book. Among the Major Prophets, Isaiah is cited more than are Jeremiah and Ezekiel together. It should also be noted that even though Jesus showed strong preferences for a few books, he had a wide knowledge of most parts of the O.T. In the sayings attributed to him, thirty of the thirty-nine books of the O.T. are represented.

The Continuing Authority of the Old Testament

Jesus' attitude toward the O.T. was, of course, precritical. As a first-century Jew he believed that Moses was the author of the Pentateuch and that David wrote the Psalms. He stayed very close to the O.T. throughout his life. Basically he accepted its validity and permanent value. To the young man who asked what he must do to inherit eternal life Jesus replied by reviewing the Ten Commandments (Mk. 10:17–22 = Mt. 19:16–22; Lk. 18:18–23). On many occasions Jesus indicated that the fundamental requirements of men were given by God in the Law. In Mk. 7:1–13 (= Mt. 15:1–6) we see how Jesus places in sharp contrast the commandment of God and the mere tradition of men. He quotes Ex. 20:12 (= Deut. 5:16) and Ex. 21:17 (= Lev. 20:9) as examples of the former. Often in the midst of controversy with his Pharisaic opponents Jesus cites the Pentateuch and upholds its binding nature. The indissoluble nature of marriage is supported (Mk. 10:2–9 = Mt. 19:3–6) by an appeal to Gen. 1:27; 2:24; 5:2. When one of the scribes asks Jesus about the chief commandment of the Law (Mk. 12:28–31 = Mt. 22:35–40; Lk. 10:25–28), Jesus answers with his own combination of Deut. 6:5 and Lev. 19:18.

Jesus was not so much interested in proof texts from the O.T. as authoritative backing for his teaching as he was in the whole sweep of the history of God's dealings with his people, which the O.T. proclaims. In the teachings of Jesus contained in the Gospels we find references to the long line of Biblical characters and heroes. He mentions Abel, Noah, Abraham, Isaac, Jacob, Lot and his wife, Moses, Elijah, Elisha, Naaman, David, Solomon, Isaiah, Jonah, and Daniel. The first of the two authentic traditions about Jesus' relationship to the O.T. is that he upheld it. According to Mt. 5:17–18, he spoke unequivocally: "Think not that I have come to abolish the law and the prophets; I have come not to abolish them but to fulfil them. For truly, I say to you, till heaven and earth pass away, not an iota, not a dot, will pass from the law until all is accomplished." Later, in Mt. 23:2–3, Jesus tells his hearers to follow all the directions of those who carry on the role of Moses in applying God's law.

THE NEW INTERPRETATION OF JESUS

The second authentic tradition about Jesus' view of Scripture is that he directly and indirectly abrogated it as it had been literally understood. Between the two aspects of the tradition there is a marked tension and a seeming contradiction; but each is true insofar as the fact of the other will allow. Jesus upheld the O.T.; but he also became its first radical interpreter. Since, as we have seen, the authority of the O.T. is accepted throughout the N.T., it is all the more significant that the Gospel tradition should have retained Jesus' fundamental reevaluation of Scripture. In part, he made use of the methods of interpretation that were currently employed by the scribes and Pharisees. At times both the form and the content of Jesus' teaching suggest contemporary Jewish instruction. Yet his views were very different from those of other teachers of his time, and he used the O.T. with striking originality.

In the first place, Jesus taught that although the O.T. was still true, it did not go far enough. Thus, in Mt. 5:21–22 he reaffirms the prohibition of murder that was laid down in Ex. 20:13 (= Deut. 5:17), but he then adds that the sin lies not only in the act of physical violence but also in the anger that promotes it. So, too, in Mt. 5:27–28 he reviews the commandment against adultery (Ex. 20:14 = Deut. 5:18) and declares that the sin consists as much in the evil desire as in the deed.

Secondly, Jesus judges Scripture by choosing to quote some of it while deliberately omitting other parts. At times he suggests that some of the O.T. is on a lower level and that it must be assessed by those sections which are on a higher level. Thus, in Mk. 10:2–9 (= Mt. 19:3–9) Jesus declares that God's intention that marriage should be indissoluble is made clear by the words of Gen. 1:27; 2:24; and 5:2 and that therefore the Mosaic provision for divorce in Deut. 24:1 was only a recognition of human weakness and not a divine commandment. In Mt. 5:38–42 Jesus admits that the O.T. lays down the principle

of "an eye for an eye and a tooth for a tooth" (Ex. 21:24 =
Lev. 24:20; Deut. 19:21), but he states that the correct principle is absolute nonresistance. Similarly, in Mt. 5:33–37 he
points to the O.T. prohibition of swearing falsely (Lev. 19:12);
but he declares that there should be no swearing at all. For
Jesus, then, parts of the O.T. had only a limited or temporary
authority that has now disappeared.

Thirdly, Jesus feels no hesitation in giving his own interpretation to some of Scripture. In Mk. 2:23–28 (= Mt. 12:1–8; Lk.
6:1–5) he recalls the incident of David's request from a priest
for holy bread to be eaten by himself and his soldiers (1 Sam.
21:1–6) and draws from it the conclusion that the Son of Man
is Lord of the Sabbath. In Mk. 12:35–37 (= Mt. 22:41–45;
Lk. 20:41–44), Jesus argues that the words of Ps. 110:1 prove
that the Christ cannot be David's son. Testifying to this independent approach of Jesus to Scripture is the fact that in the
first part of the Sermon on the Mount (Mt., ch. 5) six times
Jesus contradicts a section of the O.T. with the words: "It was
said to the men of old . . . . But I say to you . . . ." Furthermore, in each of these six cases it is a verse from the Law, the
first part of Scripture, that is being contradicted. It is difficult
for us to understand the revolutionary nature of such an approach by a Jew and the boldness with which he spoke. Yet
Jesus regarded himself as required to make such judgments and
as possessing an authority to which even the form of Scripture
was subject.

For Jesus the events of the O.T. were real and significant,
but that history was not complete and pointed toward developments that were yet to come. Typical is the statement of Jesus
in Mt. 12:41 (= Lk. 11:32): "The men of Nineveh . . . re-
pented at the preaching of Jonah, and behold, something
greater than Jonah is here." He adds in the following verse:
"Something greater than Solomon is here." Jesus viewed his
own mission in the light of all that God had done earlier. Because the working of God is one reality and not many, Jesus
believed that the Scripture applied immediately to himself.

The command of Deut. 8:3, "Man shall not live by bread alone, but by every word that proceeds from the mouth of God," becomes (Mt. 4:4 = Lk. 4:4) Jesus' first answer to the tempter in the wilderness.

Jesus uses the O.T. freely and naturally throughout his ministry just because he knows that it does pertain to him. Furthermore, he saw his words and deeds as fulfilling what the O.T. had knowingly and unknowingly predicted. According to Mk. 1:15, Jesus began his preaching ministry by saying, "The time is fulfilled," and he must have had in mind the prophecy of Ezek. 7:7, "The time has come, the day is near." It was popularly held, on the basis of Mal. 4:5, that before the long-awaited Kingdom of God could come on earth Elijah must reappear. In Mk. 9:12–13 Jesus accepts the correctness of the expectation but points out that "Elijah has come." According to Mt. 11:14, Jesus identified him with John the Baptist. The point is that since the preliminaries are over, the day is here. In the words of Mt. 11:13 (= Lk. 16:16) Jesus declared, "All the prophets and the law prophesied until John." The new age has come with Jesus. He instructs the followers of the imprisoned and uncertain John the Baptist to tell their leader what they have seen and heard of the ministry of Jesus (Mt. 11:2–6 = Lk. 7:18–23), and he describes his ministry in words that are quoted from several sections of Isaiah (Is. 26:19; 35:5–6; 29:18; 61:1–2). Jesus sees himself as fulfilling in his words and deeds what has been prophesied in Scripture. As told in Lk. 4:16–21, when Jesus took part in the synagogue service in Nazareth, he read aloud from Isaiah (Is. 61:1–2); and after he had finished, he declared, "Today this scripture has been fulfilled in your hearing." Consistently, Luke attributes to the risen Christ (Lk. 24:44) the claim that "everything written about me in the law of Moses and the prophets must be fulfilled."

There is abundant evidence to support the belief that it is Jesus who begins the Christological interpretation of the O.T. that permeates early Christian writings. Undoubtedly, he was much influenced by the picture of the Son of man that is drawn in Dan., ch. 7, and by other apocalyptic elements of Daniel, Joel, and Zechariah. However, his greatest affinity is with Isaiah. Although he utilizes all sections of the prophet to explain and clarify his work, it is the image of the Suffering Servant of Is. 52:13 to 53:12 that most often underlies his teaching about himself as well as later N.T. thinking about Jesus. Contemporary Jewish reflection about the Messiah had not yet, as far as we know, made any connection between the Messiah and the Suffering Servant. The fact that the connection is definitely made in the N.T. as a whole is most satisfactorily explained if Jesus conceived of his own mission in terms of the prophecy. The familiar words of Jesus in Mk. 10:45 (= Mt. 20:28), "The Son of man . . . came not to be served but to serve, and to give his life as a ransom for many," are descriptive of his entire life (and death) and are plainly based on Is. 53:12: "He poured out his soul to death, and was numbered with the transgressors; yet he bore the sin of many." The fundamentally important vicarious principle that the death of an innocent person may remove the sins of others is involved in the whole passage, and we may refer particularly to Is. 53:4–6, 10–11: "Surely he has borne our griefs and carried our sorrows; . . . he was wounded for our transgressions; . . . with his stripes we are healed; . . . the Lord has laid on him the iniquity of us all. . . . He makes himself an offering for sin, . . . he shall bear their iniquities." These verses are reflected also in Matthew, John, Romans, and 1 Peter, where they are correctly applied to Jesus' death. The words that Jesus used at the Last Supper in administering the bread and the wine arise out of the new covenant prophesied in Jer. 31:31, but they also have in mind the healing self-sacrifice of the Suffering Servant. Thus, in Mk. 14:24 (= Mt. 26:28; Lk. 22:20) Jesus declares: "This is my blood of the covenant, which is poured out for many." In the form of the tradition of the Supper employed by Paul in 1 Cor. 11:23–26, Jesus says of the broken bread: "This is my body which is for you." In the mind of Jesus the new covenant that is brought into being by his death is at the same time the fulfillment of the prophecy of Isaiah. He believes that God has called him to be the Suffering Servant, through whom the world's salvation can be accomplished.

There is a wide variety in the ways in which Jesus draws upon Scripture in his teaching. He sees his whole life as the climax of the long story of God's dealings with Israel, and he regards single events or deeds as the fulfillment of particular O.T. prophecies. Scripture is regarded as the standard against which actions or attitudes are to be judged, and its statements are often the logical premises from which Jesus draws his own conclusions. Phrases and concepts of the O.T. provide much of the form of Jesus' instruction.

Formula-quotations of the O.T., other than Psalms, are ascribed to Jesus 23 times and occur in all four of the major Gospel sources. They usually set forth some aspect of God's word that Jesus' hearers have been ignoring or violating. Occasionally, they constitute a prediction that is said to have been fulfilled in Jesus' time or person. Almost as frequently, a total of 19 times, Jesus quotes the O.T. directly, without any formula or other acknowledgment of source; and in some of these instances only a phrase or a clause is cited. Again, all the Gospel sources testify to the usage. In most cases it may be assumed that the quotation was made with the understanding that the hearers would immediately recognize it without any formal preface, but in others the citation may have been unconscious and simply the result of Jesus' familiarity with Scripture.

Normally, at least 91 times, when Jesus refers directly to the O.T., the wording of the text is changed, or there is a paraphrase of the original, or there is a borrowing of an idea. In every case, however, direct dependence upon the O.T. is indicated. A few examples will illustrate this usage. Isaiah 49:24 asks: "Can the prey be taken from the mighty?" and in Mk. 3:27 (= Mt. 12:29; cf. Lk. 11:21) Jesus states: "No one can enter a strong man's house and plunder his goods." In Job

42:2, Job confesses to God: "I know that thou canst do all things"; and in Mk. 10:27 (= Mt. 19:26; Lk. 18:27) Jesus says: "All things are possible with God." The metaphorical expression, "to drink the cup," a reference to suffering, used in Jer. 49:12, is found again in Jesus' searching question addressed to James and John in Mk. 10:38 (= Mt. 20:22).

The Old Testament and Jesus' Parables

In his most characteristic parables Jesus often turns to the O.T. An example is the parable of the vineyard of Is. 5:1–7, which begins with the information that "my beloved had a vineyard . . . . He digged it, . . . and planted it; he built a watchtower in the midst of it." The similar parable of Jesus begins in Mk. 12:1 (= Mt. 21:33; Lk. 20:9): "A man planted a vineyard, . . . and dug a pit, . . . and built a tower." The theme of infidelity and its punishment is at the heart of both forms of the parable. The Lukan parable of the fig tree (Lk. 13:6–9) opens with the statement that "a man had a fig tree planted in his vineyard; and he came seeking fruit on it and found none." This experience of God is first related in Jer. 8:13: "When I would gather them, says the Lord, there are no grapes on the vine, nor figs on the fig tree." In the parable of the chief seats, in Lk. 14:8–10, Jesus says: "When you are invited by any one to a marriage feast, do not sit down in a place of honor, lest a more eminent man than you be invited by him; and he . . . will come and say to you, 'Give place to this man' . . . . But . . . go and sit in the lowest place, so that . . . your host . . . may say to you, 'Friend, go up higher.'" The source of the thought and of much of the wording of this parable is to be found in Prov. 25:6–7: "Do not put yourself forward in the king's presence or stand in the place of the great; for it is better to be told, 'Come up here,' than to be put lower in the presence of the prince." The parable of the prodigal son (Lk. 15:11–24) relates to the O.T. at various points. We may note the reference in Deut. 21:16 to "the day

when he assigns his possessions as an inheritance to his sons"
(cf. Lk. 15:12) and the statement of Prov. 29:3 that "one who
keeps company with harlots squanders his substance." (Cf.
Lk. 15:13, 30.) We observe also the description of Pharaoh's
reception of Joseph in Gen. 41:42: "Pharaoh took his signet
ring from his hand . . . and arrayed him in garments of fine
linen." (Cf. Lk. 15:22.) We are told in the parable of the
Pharisee and the publican (Lk. 18:9–14) that "the tax col-
lector . . . would not even lift up his eyes to heaven." It is
likely that the words of Ezra 9:6 have been recalled: "O my
God, I am ashamed and blush to lift my face to thee." The
parabolic reference (Mt. 7:24–25 = Lk. 6:48) to "a wise man
who built his house upon the rock," which did not fall in an
ensuing storm, may depend in part on the affirmation of Prov.
12:7: "The house of the righteous will stand."

In his teaching Jesus made constant use of the O.T. At times
he quoted it with approval. At times he interpreted it and
gave to it a new and even opposite meaning as he treated it
with his own authority. At times he drew upon the forms of
O.T. wording to provide the framework of his instruction. In
brief, the O.T. was without question constantly before him in
all that he taught. He did not follow it slavishly but used it
creatively and with a deliberate selectivity that was rooted in
his own experience of God.

Chapter 5

Christian Doctrine and the Old Testament

As Acts points out, the death and the resurrection of Jesus were followed almost immediately by the beginning of Christian preaching, which was initially designed to bring the Jewish hearers to an acceptance of Jesus of Nazareth as the Christ, God's Messiah, in whom salvation had been brought to the world. Because Jesus in his own teaching and in his concept of his mission had relied heavily upon the O.T. and because all of his earliest followers were Jews, the church from the beginning tied its teaching about Jesus closely to Scripture. The writers of the N.T. knew and believed the central truths taught by Judaism, and from the perspective of those truths they reflected on the significance of the life and death and resurrection of Jesus and formulated the initial statements of Christian theology. Christians and Jews together were convinced that God was working directly in history to accomplish his redemptive purpose. They agreed that the people of Israel were the chief agents for the divine plan. N.T. authors echo distinctly the three principal points of the basic message of the O.T. (Cf. G. von Rad, *Old Testament Theology*, Vol. II, p. 362: "The Old Testament has no focal point such as is found in the New.") It is everywhere emphasized that the story of God's salvation begins with the calling of Abraham to be his servant and the latter's faithful response to

God's promises. The next high point for both Testaments is God's deliverance of Israel from slavery in Egypt and the making of the covenant between God and Israel through Moses. The fundamental action is completed with the giving to Israel of the Promised Land along with the responsibilities that are inherent in the covenant. For the O.T. the story is substantially complete at this point. For the N.T. one more element must be added.

Writers of the N.T., indebted to Judaism and to Jesus, continued to proclaim the oneness of God. He was the Lord of Israel and also of Jesus. His purpose, declared in Israel and also in Jesus, was one and could contain no inconsistency. What God had done in Jesus was therefore the climax of all his lengthy dealings with the Jewish people for the sake of the whole world. Moreover, just as the O.T. could now be seen as preliminary, so, too, the life and person of Jesus could be understood only against the background of the story told by Scripture. On the other hand, between the O.T. and the coming of Jesus there was for N.T. authors no significant gap, nor could there be any contradiction. Although God had done something "new" in Jesus, there was no discontinuity between Jesus and the saving acts of the O.T.

The use of the O.T. by N.T. writers is necessarily somewhat different from its use by Jesus because the situation has changed. Once the life of Jesus had been completed by his death and resurrection, he was henceforth to be regarded not only as a teacher but also as a bringer of salvation. What he believed and what he taught about God and man and himself were now only part of the picture. The crucial point was what others believed and taught about him as God's servant. After his resurrection Jesus could be viewed in a new and larger perspective that was not available during his earthly life. The teaching of the N.T. about Jesus, as distinct from the teaching of Jesus, also has its roots in Scripture. It could not be otherwise since Christians proclaimed that Jesus was God's Messiah and that the O.T. was the word of the same God.

THE APOSTOLIC PREACHING

The content of primitive Christian preaching has been thoroughly studied within the past few decades. Substantial agreement has been reached among scholars as to the outlines of that preaching. (Cf. especially C. H. Dodd, *The Apostolic Preaching*.) Primary evidence is provided by the epistles of Paul and the sermons in the first half of Acts ascribed to Peter and Paul, and further substantiating information is found in the Gospels and the general epistles. The apostolic preaching included six major statements: First, the prophecies of the O.T. have been fulfilled in the new age. Second, the life of Jesus was in all its aspects in accord with the purpose of God. Third, Jesus Christ now reigns as the exalted Lord. Fourth, the Holy Spirit, possessed by all Christians, is the proof of Christ's presence and power. Fifth, Jesus Christ will return in triumph in the last time. Sixth, in order to receive the benefits of Christ's work it is necessary to repent. The meaning of all these six propositions is expounded in the N.T. primarily by citing O.T. verses. It is also true that in most of the cases where an O.T. passage is cited by two or more N.T. writers that passage is used to support one of the principal points of the apostolic proclamation, or kerygma. The relationship between the N.T. kerygma and Scripture is direct both in general terms and also in specific details. It is these particulars that must now be studied.

OLD TESTAMENT PROPHECY FULFILLED

The starting point of apostolic preaching was the declaration that in the Christian experience all God's activity in history reached its climax and that thus all the incompleteness and all the prophecies of the O.T. had been fulfilled. The theme of the exodus, which lies at the center of the second principal declaration of the O.T. kerygma, appears in many sections of the N.T. The church is pictured as reliving the deliverance of the Jews from Egypt and their subsequent tribulations in their desert wanderings. Before he led his people out of Egypt, Moses, in the name of God, commanded (Ex. 13:7): "No leaven shall be seen with you in all your territory." The fresh start that God was making for his people was thus to be symbolized. In writing to the pilgrim Christian community in Corinth, Paul orders (1 Cor. 5:7): "Cleanse out the old leaven that you may be a new lump." In 1 Cor., ch. 10, Paul likens the followers of Christ to the wandering Israelites and in the first eleven verses refers 18 times to sections of Exodus and Leviticus, which tell the story of the exodus. The admonition of Heb. 3:12, "Take care, brethren, lest there be in any of you an evil, unbelieving heart, leading you to fall away from the living God," is reminiscent of the rebellion of the Jews in the wilderness described in Num., ch. 14, and mentioned again in Heb. 3:16–18. The Passover celebration described in Ex. 12:1–11 called for a "lamb . . . without blemish," and in 1 Pet. 1:19 Christ is said to be precisely that lamb. The exodus experience is directly applied to Christians in Jude 5. In Acts 13:16–23 Paul presents in a sermon in the synagogue in Pisidian Antioch a summary review of Jewish history from the patriarchs to David and then concludes that God has most recently sent Jesus, a descendant of David, to be a Savior in fulfillment of the divine promises. The coming of Jesus is the culmination of the long story that Scripture tells. In his sermon to the people of Jerusalem on Pentecost (Acts 2:14–36) Peter states that the reception of the Holy Spirit by the disciples (Acts 2:1–4) was the realization of what God had promised long before through the prophet Joel (Joel 2:28–32). In Rom., chs. 9 to 11, Paul discusses in some depth the question of why the Jews as a race have not accepted Jesus as the Christ, and he attempts to formulate a philosophy of God's workings in history. He is particularly concerned to delineate the role of Gentile Christians in bringing the Jews to a knowledge of Christ. It is highly significant that these three chapters form one of the sections of the N.T. most heavily dependent on the O.T. through citations of and references to Genesis, Exodus, Leviticus, Numbers, Deuteronomy, Joshua, 2 Kings, 2 Chronicles, Job, Psalms, Isaiah, Jeremiah, Hosea, Joel, Habakkuk, Malachi, and Proverbs. Life in Christ is for the N.T. authors the goal of all Scripture.

God's Plan and Jesus' Life

The second element of the apostolic kerygma is that God has planned all that has happened to Jesus, and once more the O.T. has become the chief support of Christian proclamation. That Jesus should have been put to death shamefully on a cross was contrary to every Jewish Messianic expectation and was thus extremely difficult for the early Jewish Christians to understand. Explanations for this type of death were therefore sought earnestly in the O.T. and at a very early date. According to Deut. 21:23, "a hanged man is accursed by God." Yet Christians freely admitted that Jesus was crucified. In speaking to the council of the Jews in Jerusalem, Peter refers (Acts 5:30) to "Jesus whom you killed by hanging him on a tree." In speaking of Jesus to Cornelius (Acts 10:39), he declares: "They put him to death by hanging him on a tree." Paul relates this fact to Scripture in his sermon at Antioch of Pisidia by claiming (Acts 13:29): "When they had fulfilled all that was written of him, they took him down from the tree." There is a similar direct statement in 1 Pet. 2:24: "He himself bore our sins in his body on the tree." Paul admits that the manner of Jesus' death made him a curse in terms of the law of Deuteronomy, but he argues (Gal. 3:13) that for that very reason Christ vicariously "redeemed us from the curse of the law." Paul knows that this is a major hurdle for Jews and foolishness for sophisticated Gentiles, but he confesses (1 Cor. 1:23): "We preach Christ crucified."

The particular form of Jesus' death involved mental and physical suffering and also a voluntary sacrifice on behalf of others, and the O.T. is believed to provide prophecies of both. According to Lk. 24:25–26, the risen Jesus challenges his as yet unknowing companions on the walk to Emmaus: "O foolish men, and slow of heart to believe all that the prophets have spoken! Was it not necessary that the Christ should suffer these things and enter into his glory?" A short time later Jesus addresses his eleven disciples gathered in Jerusalem (Lk. 24:46): "Thus it is written, that the Christ should suffer." In one of Peter's Jerusalem sermons (Acts 3:18) he speaks in almost identical words: "What God foretold by the mouth of all the prophets, that his Christ should suffer, he thus fulfilled." In Acts 17:2–3 it is said that Paul went to the synagogue of the Jews in Thessalonica, "and for three weeks he argued with them from the scriptures, explaining and proving that it was necessary for the Christ to suffer." Paul is again reported to have claimed in his defense before Agrippa (Acts 26:22–23): "I stand here testifying both to small and great, saying nothing but what the prophets and Moses said would come to pass: that the Christ must suffer." The central theological tradition of Christianity that Paul received and then transmitted (1 Cor. 15:3–8) started with the declaration that "Christ died for our sins in accordance with the scriptures." All these unidentified and general references to the O.T. do not refer to any individual passages but have in mind, rather, the overall emphases of Scripture.

On the other hand, in connection with N.T. references to Jesus' death there are also many citations of particular verses. Paul, in Rom. 3:24–25, mentions "Christ Jesus, whom God put forward as an expiation by his blood." He probably has in mind the ritual requirements (Lev. 16:14, 16) for Aaron to "take some of the blood . . . and sprinkle it . . . before the mercy seat [expiation]. . . . Thus he shall make atonement . . . because of the uncleannesses of the people of Israel, and because of their transgressions." Paul adds (Rom. 8:32) that in all of Jesus' sacrificial suffering God "did not spare his own Son." Without doubt Paul is thinking of Abraham's willingness to sacrifice Isaac and God's commendation (Gen. 22:12): "You have not withheld your son, your only son."

However, it is the classic prophecy of the Suffering Servant (Is. 52:13 to 53:12) to which we must return. As we have seen, it was much in the mind of Jesus and helped to mold his thinking. Following the example of their Master, the N.T. writers also leaned heavily upon it. After writing that Jesus healed large numbers of sick persons at Capernaum, Matthew gives his interpretation (Mt. 8:17): "This was to fulfil what was spoken by the prophet Isaiah [Is. 53:4], 'He took our infirmities and bore our diseases.'" The vicarious effect of Jesus' deeds is directed to his daily ministry as well as to his death. The early testimony of John the Baptist to Jesus (Jn. 1:29) proclaims: "Behold, the Lamb of God, who takes away the sin of the world!" Isaiah had said of the Servant (Is. 53:10): "He makes himself an offering for sin." To the N.T. writers the life and death of Jesus are alike in their vicarious saving power, and this is so because in all things Jesus has been perfectly obedient to what he believed to be God's will for him, whether it was the conduct of his daily ministry or the acceptance of the way of the cross. Most of the comment has to do with the death of Jesus, however, because it is there that his obedience and the vicarious power of his sacrifice are centered. The Suffering Servant is likewise innocent (Is. 53:9): "He had done no violence, and there was no deceit in his mouth." Applying this passage to Jesus, 1 Pet. 2:22 reads: "He committed no sin; no guile was found on his lips." The Servant was obedient and accepted without complaint the suffering that was unjustly his but that was unavoidable if he was to remove the effects of the wrongdoing of others. Of him it is written (Is. 53:7): "He was oppressed, and he was afflicted, yet he opened not his mouth." Jesus is described in the same way in 1 Pet. 2:23: "When he was reviled, he did not revile in return; when he suffered, he did not threaten." It is said of the Servant (Is. 53:12): "He poured out his soul to death"; Paul echoes the words and writes of Jesus (Phil. 2:8), "He humbled himself and became obedient unto death." The purpose and the result of the death of Jesus were vicarious. He died for the sake of others. We are told (Is. 53:5) that the Servant "was wounded for our transgressions," and Paul writes in almost identical language (Rom. 4:25) that Jesus "was put to death for our trespasses." It is also said of the Servant (Is. 53:5): "With his stripes we are healed." The same thought is expressed regarding Jesus in 1 Pet. 2:24: "By his wounds you have been healed." Paul states of Jesus as God's son (Rom. 8:32) that God "gave him up for us all," and the dependence on Is. 53:12 (LXX) is unmistakable: "He was delivered because of their iniquities." The same compound Greek verb, translated as "gave up" and "delivered" is present in both verses. When the author of Hebrews writes (Heb. 9:28): "Christ, having been offered once to bear the sins of many," he is directly dependent on Is. 53:12, which states that the Servant "bore the sin of many." In the same verse we are told that the Servant "made intercession for the transgressors," and Heb. 7:25 declares that Jesus saves all who draw near to God through him because "he always lives to make intercession for them." Many more parallels could be given, but these should suffice to demonstrate that as the N.T. writers sought for ways of interpreting the life, and especially the death, of Jesus, they utilized almost every verse of the main Suffering Servant passage of Isaiah.

However, the authors of these early Christian writings were aware also of the other servant passages of Isaiah; and the sections of Is. 42:1–4; 49:1–6; 50:4–9; and 61:1–2 are all widely cited in the N.T.

Since the resurrection experience was the immediate cause of the rapid growth of Christianity in its initial period, it is not surprising to discover that the death and resurrection of Jesus are often treated as a single transforming reality in the N.T. Many of the verses discussed above in connection with Jesus' sacrificial death contain also a reference to his being raised from the dead, and the O.T. is regarded as prophesying both events. According to John 20:9, Peter and the other disciple, who went to the tomb of Jesus on Easter morning, "did not know the scripture, that he must rise from the dead." Paul, in the words of Acts 13:32–33, says to the Jews of Pisidian Antioch: "What God promised to the fathers, this he has fulfilled to us their children by raising Jesus." The author of Acts (Acts 17:2–3) informs us that for three weeks Paul argued with the Jews of Thessalonica "from the scriptures, explaining and proving that it was necessary for the Christ to suffer and to rise from the dead." According to Acts 26:22–23, Paul believed that Moses and the prophets foretold that Christ would be the first to rise from the dead.

Once more, no particular passages of the O.T. are cited; but the background seems to be the whole trend of Scripture. In one aspect of the resurrection of Jesus, however, the O.T. is specifically cited. In 7 instances in Matthew and Luke it is stated that Jesus would rise or had risen "on the third day." The equivalent Markan phrase is "after three days." Peter, referring to the resurrection of Jesus, says, according to Acts 10:40: "God raised him on the third day." Paul reminds the Corinthians (1 Cor. 15:4) that the primitive Christian tradition proclaimed that "he was raised on the third day in accordance with the scriptures." Exactly which O.T. verse is being cited we can't be sure, but several possibilities emerge. In 2 Kings 20:5, 8, God instructs Hezekiah through the prophet Isaiah to "go up to the house of the Lord on the third day." A more likely source is the hope of the penitent expressed in Hos. 6:2: "On the third day he will raise us up, that we may live before him." The words are immediately applicable to Jesus because as the Suffering Servant he has been completely identified with the redeemed people.

The beginnings of theological reflection on both the person and the work of Jesus as God's Son, set forth in the N.T., continue to show a marked dependence on Scripture. Jesus is known throughout the N.T. as the Servant prophesied by Isaiah. In Revelation, as also in his own teaching in the Gospels, Jesus is seen as the Son of man. As such he is the representative of the community of those who have received God's salvation. He is also the son of David, through whom the promises of God are realized, although he is far from being the kind of Davidic Messiah who was the object of popular Jewish hopes, and in some places in the N.T. his Davidic descent is denied or minimized. The writer of Acts believes (Acts 13:34) that the words of Isaiah (Is. 55:3) were first spoken to Jesus: "I will give you the holy and sure blessings of David." At the beginning of Romans, Paul declares (Rom. 1:3) that Jesus "was descended from David according to the flesh"; he may have had in mind the Messianic prophecy of Is. 11:1: "There shall come forth a shoot from the stump of Jesse." In Rev. 5:5 Jesus is called "the Root of David," as it is also written in Rev. 22:16. Revelation 3:7 states that Jesus Christ "has the key of David, who opens and no one shall shut, who shuts and no one opens." It is a direct quotation of Is. 22:22.

Closely connected with the idea of Davidic descent is the concept of a Messiah, who is often, though not always, considered a son of David. That Jesus was the promised Messiah was the belief of all the N.T. writers, and it is not thought necessary to make specific assertions of that conviction although often they do appear. However, Scripture is frequently employed to support the belief. The writers are selective in their choice of passages to cite, and many O.T. verses that formed the core of Jewish Messianic expectation were not utilized in the N.T. Some of the passages that were quoted in the N.T. may not have been understood by contemporary Judaism to refer to the Messiah. But the N.T. does refer, with Messianic implications, to Is. 9:1–6; 11:1–9; Jer. 23:5–6; Ezek. 17:22–24; 34:23–24; 37:22–25; Amos 9:11; Mic. 5:1–3; and Zech. 9:9–13. The popular Jewish idea of a conquering king is a part of the Christian interpretation only with severe modifications. As the risen Christ, Jesus has conquered and will conquer, but his victory and his reign will not be those of this present world.

The life, death, and resurrection of Jesus are clarified and interpreted in the N.T. by countless references to Scripture. The O.T. thus provides many of the basic concepts and some of the terminology of the earliest theological assessment of Jesus and his deeds. To show this development we have looked almost exclusively at relevant sections of Acts, the Epistles, and Revelation; but it should be noted that the Gospels, which do offer a form of biography of Jesus, display the same dependence on the O.T. for their theological interpretations of the story that they tell. Each Gospel contains a degree of evaluation and comment that has been added by the Evangelist or by the transmission of the basic material about Jesus' life. This interpretation may be found in the preface or conclusion of the writing, or it may be introduced into the elements of the story. In a very large number of cases the Gospel narratives describing the activities of Jesus exhibit a remarkably close relationship to Scripture. In a few instances Jesus may well have deliberately conformed his actions to familiar O.T. laws, customs, and patterns; and faithful reporting would inevitably suggest Scriptural parallels. Normally, however, the parallels are offered by the Evangelists, who have consciously or unconsciously chosen O.T. statements or phrases as the proper means for narrating their story. (See Table 6.) All four Gospels have this characteristic, and all sections of Jesus' life are involved. Within the Gospels several stories regarding John the Baptist and Herod Antipas contain descriptions which recall O.T. verses, and there are a very few similar stories in Acts regarding Peter, Stephen, Paul, Herod Agrippa I, and Eutychus. But Scriptural influence on N.T. narrative is otherwise limited to the Gospel accounts of Jesus, and there the stories of the passion are especially reminiscent of the O.T. The situation will be made clearer with some examples.

The stories of the birth and infancy of Jesus in the first two chapters of both Matthew and Luke, though differing almost completely from each other, stand apart from the rest of the Gospel narrative in their massive employment of the O.T. Of the 180 verses in the four chapters only 72 show no direct parallel with the O.T. Matthew seems to have in mind the story of the birth and infancy of Moses as related in the first several chapters of Exodus. The instruction of the angel to Joseph in Egypt (Mt. 2:20) to return to the land of Israel with the infant Jesus and Mary because "those who sought the child's life are dead" is strikingly similar to God's instruction to Moses in Midian (Ex. 4:19) to return to Egypt because "all the men who were seeking your life are dead." Luke, on the other hand, shows knowledge of the story of the birth and infancy of Samuel as narrated in the initial chapters of 1 Samuel. The Lukan section on Jesus' birth closes (Lk. 2:52) with the statement: "And Jesus increased in wisdom and stature, and in favor with God and man." The summary has been borrowed from 1 Sam. 2:26: "The boy Samuel continued to grow both in stature and in favor with the Lord and with men." Luke's story of the presentation of the infant Jesus in the Temple at Jerusalem (Lk. 2:22–24) shows many references to the Pentateuch. The occasion is given as the purification required in the Law. The regulations are given in Lev., ch. 12, including the offering of two turtledoves or two young pigeons. Luke's account also contains a quotation from Ex. 13:2, 12.

At various points the ministry of Jesus is depicted as being closely in line with the O.T. According to Mk. 1:10 (= Mt. 3:16; Lk. 3:21), Jesus saw heaven opened at his baptism, just as Ezekiel (Ezek. 1:1) describes the opening of heaven at the beginning of his prophetic ministry. All three Synoptic Evangelists also refer to the descent of the Spirit on Jesus (Mt. 3:16; Mk. 1:10; Lk. 3:22), just as the Messianic prophecy of Is. 11:2 has promised: "The Spirit of the Lord shall rest upon him." The narrative of the temptation of Jesus in the wilderness, notably in Matthew, has at least five different points of contact with the O.T. Matthew 4:2 notes that the period was "forty days and forty nights." This exact phrase is used of the duration of the flood over all the earth in Gen. 7:4, 12; and it is said to have been the length of time that Moses was with God on Mt. Sinai, fasting (Ex. 24:18; 34:28; Deut. 9:9, 11).

Finally, we are told (1 Kings 19:8) that Elijah journeyed to Mt. Horeb, fasting, also for "forty days and forty nights." Matthew writes (Mt. 4:5) that the devil took Jesus to "the holy city." Jerusalem is described as "the holy city" also in Neh. 11:1, 18. Matthew's statement (Mt. 4:8) that Jesus was taken "to a very high mountain" strongly suggests the words of Ezek. 40:1–2: "The hand of the Lord . . . set me down upon a very high mountain." Matthew further reports (Mt. 4:9) that the devil said to Jesus: "All these I will give you, if you will fall down and worship me." Four times (Dan. 3:5, 6, 10, 15) Daniel uses the phrase "fall down and worship" in connection with the image that is the symbol of all evil. Finally, Mark, in his brief account, mentions (Mk. 1:13) that Jesus "was with the wild beasts." This appears to be a reference to a well-known Messianic prophecy (Is. 11:6–9) which looks toward the new age when all the wild animals will be at peace with one another.

In the story of the transfiguration (Mk. 9:2–8 = Mt. 17:1–8; Lk. 9:28–36) a reference to booths ("tabernacles") is connected with a reference to the presence of a shadow-producing cloud. The account seems to have been directly influenced by Ex. 40:34: "The cloud covered the tent of meeting, and the glory of the Lord filled the tabernacle."

The passion narrative is dependent upon the O.T. at many points. The account of the triumphal entry of Jesus into Jerusalem (Mk. 11:1–10 = Mt. 21:1–9; Lk. 19:29–38; Jn. 12:12–15) is built upon the prophecy of Zech. 9:9, which Jesus undoubtedly saw himself as fulfilling: "Rejoice greatly, O daughter of Zion! . . . Lo, your king comes to you; . . . humble and riding on an ass." Also influential is the wording of 2 Kings 9:13, which describes the people's reception of Jehu: "Every man of them took his garment, and put it under him." The narrative of Jesus' cleansing of the Temple (Mk. 11:15–17 = Mt. 21:12–13; Lk. 19:45–46; Jn. 2:14–16) also draws upon a prophecy of Zechariah (Zech. 14:21): "There shall no longer be a trader in the house of the Lord of hosts on that day." The pronouncement of Jesus, " 'My house shall be called a house of prayer for all the nations.' But you have made it a den of robbers," is a combined formula-quotation of Is. 56:7 and Jer. 7:11. In the story there are also found references to Ex. 30:13; Lev. 1:14; 5:7; 12:8; and Mal. 3:1–3. The reader of the Gospels is told a total of 7 times (Mk. 14:61; 15:5; Mt. 26:63; 27:12, 14; Lk. 23:9; Jn. 19:9) that during the interrogation that was a part of his trial Jesus was silent and made no reply. Behind this fact we may find the description of the Suffering Servant in Is. 53:7: "He was oppressed, and he was afflicted, yet he opened not his mouth." We are told (Mk. 15:27 = Mt. 27:38; Lk. 23:33; Jn. 19:18) that Jesus was crucified between two condemned robbers, and again we may discover the influence of Isaiah's Servant, about whom it is written (Is. 53:12), "He was numbered with the transgressors." According to Mt. 27:57, 60, a rich man, Joseph of Arimathea, placed the body of Jesus in his own new tomb, and in Is. 53:9 it is said of the Servant, "They made his grave . . . with a rich man in his death."

THE LORDSHIP OF JESUS

The first of the six propositions of apostolic preaching was that in the Christian experience O.T. prophecy had been fulfilled. The second was that nothing that has happened to Jesus is contrary to God's plan and will. Both of these propositions are supported throughout the N.T. by repeated citations of the O.T. The third proposition of primitive Christian proclamation was that Jesus Christ now reigns as exalted Lord. We continue to find that the proposition is rooted in Scripture. In the O.T., and especially in its Greek translation (LXX), God is very frequently called "the Lord." Authors of the N.T., already convinced of the divinity of Jesus' origin and mission, often apply to Jesus without any awkwardness Scriptural verses in which the name "Lord" appears that were originally written of God. Thus, the words of Is. 40:3, "A voice cries: 'In the wilderness prepare the way of the Lord,' " are referred (Mk. 1:3 = Mt.

3:3; Lk. 3:4) to the activity of John the Baptist as the fore-runner of Jesus. The words of Joel 2:32, "All who call upon the name of the Lord shall be delivered," are quoted in Rom. 10:13 and in Acts 2:21. In the former they are certainly used of Jesus and in the latter possibly so. Jesus is known and wor-shiped as the Lord in the early church, and he is therefore heir to all that the O.T. says of God as the Lord. Scripture is employed to defend Christian belief. It was prophesied of the Suffering Servant (Is. 52:13): "My servant . . . shall be ex-alted and lifted up." According to Jn. 3:14 and 8:28, Jesus as the Son of man must be lifted up, physically in crucifixion and spiritually in glorification. Having in mind both the Isaianic prophecy of the Servant and its fulfillment in Jesus' death, Paul writes (Phil. 2:8–9): "[He] became obedient unto death, even death on a cross. Therefore God has highly exalted him." Jesus as the embodiment of God's Suffering Servant has been exalted and, according to the divine plan, he rules as Lord, a name given him by God himself (Phil. 2:9).

The community over which Christ rules as exalted Lord is the New Israel, which is in some respects continuous with the Israel of the O.T. and in some other respects is so superior to it that the old has been brought to an end. In the O.T. the fundamental bond between God and his people is the covenant that was drawn up on Mt. Sinai but that is reflected in other covenants earlier and later. Of this covenantal relationship the N.T. writers are also very much aware. In the song of Zechariah (Lk. 1:72) there is a reference to God's holy cove-nant, and the writer may well be thinking of God's promise to Abraham in Gen. 17:7: "I will establish my covenant be-tween me and you and your descendants after you throughout their generations for an everlasting covenant." However, the prophets recognized that Israel had not followed the terms of the covenant and had been unfaithful to God and unmindful of her obligations. They suggested that God would provide a new and entirely different and potentially more fruitful rela-tionship. For both Jesus and the N.T. authors the prophecy of a new covenant was of paramount importance, especially as set forth by Jeremiah, who writes (Jer. 31:31–34): "Behold, the days are coming, says the Lord, when I will make a new covenant with the house of Israel and the house of Judah."

It is proclaimed by all the primitive Christian preachers that in Jesus Christ the promised new covenant has come. In the words of Jer. 31:32–33, God declares that the new covenant will be "not like the covenant which I made with their fathers . . . . I will put my law within them, and I will write it upon their hearts." To the Christians of Corinth, Paul writes (2 Cor. 3:3): "You are a letter from Christ delivered by us, written not with ink but with the Spirit of the living God, not on tablets of stone but on tablets of human hearts." In his view (2 Cor. 3:6) the followers of Christ are "ministers of a new covenant." Hebrews describes Jesus (Heb. 7:22) as "the surety of a better covenant," and adds concerning God (Heb. 8:13): "In speaking of a new covenant he treats the first as obsolete. And what is becoming obsolete and growing old is ready to vanish away."

Especially in Matthew, John, Acts, and Hebrews we can discover evidence of the increasingly stern struggle between Judaism and Christianity; and Christians occasionally cite the O.T. to strengthen an anti-Judaistic polemic. On the whole, however, the N.T. authors employ Scripture as a source for doctrine that is peculiarly Christian. The Christian experience is set forth as the culmination of all that the O.T. has recorded and as therefore superior to anything that has preceded it. Jesus has introduced an age that is greater than Jonah (Mt. 12:41) or John the Baptist (Mt. 11:11); and according to Mt. 13:17, Jesus stated: "Many prophets and righteous men longed to see what you see, and did not see it." The early Christians saw themselves as the New Israel in whom God's purposes have been realized. Paul describes Christianity as qualitatively a fresh start (2 Cor. 5:17): "If any one is in Christ, he is a new creation; the old has passed away, behold, the new has come." And yet even in this affirmation of newness Paul is not departing from Scripture but clearly is citing the prophecy of Is. 43:18–19: "Remember not the former things . . . . Behold, I am doing a new thing." Prophetic words of God are found also in Is. 49:8: "In a time of favor I have answered you, in a day of salvation I have helped you." They are quoted by Paul in 2 Cor. 6:2 and then applied directly to the Christian situation: "Now is the acceptable time; behold, now is the day of salvation."

Early Christians were convinced that they were the people of God in their climactic time just as the Jews had been God's people in the past. The words of God spoken to the Jews in the wilderness (Ex. 19:5–6) were believed to be addressed principally to the time of Jesus: "You shall be my own possession among all peoples; . . . you shall be to me a kingdom of priests and a holy nation." Thus, in Tit. 2:14 it is written that Jesus died "to purify for himself a people of his own." The author of 1 Peter is thinking of the fulfillment of the same passage of Exodus when he declares (1 Pet. 2:9): "You are a chosen race, a royal priesthood, a holy nation, God's own people." Similarly, Rev. 1:6 states that Jesus Christ "made us a kingdom, priests to his God and Father." There is continuity in this development, and God has not acted capriciously. As the heirs of God's promises Christians are the spiritual descendants of Abraham. Paul argues (Gal. 3:16) that "the promises were made to Abraham and to his offspring" and is recalling the statement of Gen. 12:7: "The Lord appeared to Abram, and said, 'To your descendants I will give this land.'" It is Paul's contention that the true offspring of Abraham are Christ and his followers. The purely physical descendants of Abraham have cut themselves off from the possibility of salvation by adhering to the principle of obedience to the Law rather than to that of faith, which was first manifested in Abraham's trust in God.

Paul refers elsewhere (2 Cor. 3:12–16) to the fact that Moses had veiled his face when speaking to the Jewish people after he had been in God's presence (Ex. 34:29–35), and Paul adds that the same veil lies over the Jews whenever they read the Law. This is not true for Christians, however, for "when a man turns to the Lord the veil is removed." There are many other ways in which the followers of Jesus are to be distinguished from the Jews. It is recorded in Ex. 33:7 that "Moses used to take the tent and pitch it outside the camp," but in Heb. 8:2 Jesus is "a minister in the . . . true tent which is set up not by man but by the Lord." Paul states (Rom. 2:28): "He is not a real Jew who is one outwardly, nor is true circumcision something external and physical." The O.T. itself had recognized that the requirements of the Law were a matter of the heart (Deut. 30:6; Jer. 9:26). The physical fulfillment could mean nothing. Faith surpasses law.

As the N.T. writers saw it, the Jews had not been faithful to their missionary call to proclaim God's salvation to all the nations. But as the Lordship of Christ is universal, so is the area of Christian concern. In Acts 13:46–47 Paul explains his apostleship to the Gentiles by applying to himself the words of God in Is. 49:6: "I will give you as a light to the nations, that my salvation may reach to the end of the earth." Jeremiah writes of his call to be a prophet by citing God's words to him (Jer. 1:5): "Before you were born I consecrated you: I appointed you a prophet to the nations." Paul utilizes the same words to picture his commissioning to be an apostle for Christ (Gal. 1:15–16): "He who had set me apart before I was born . . . called me . . . , that I might preach him among the Gentiles." The mission of the followers of Christ is essentially the same as that which had been entrusted to the Jews but which the Jews had failed to accomplish.

GOD'S GIFT OF THE HOLY SPIRIT

The fourth assertion of apostolic preaching was that the power of God that is in Christ is available to all Christians through God's gift of the Holy Spirit. The amazing events of Pentecost are viewed (Acts 2:16–21) as the fulfillment of the pouring out of God's spirit prophesied in Joel 2:28–32. Paul reminds the Christians at Thessalonica (1 Thess. 4:8) that "God . . . gives his Holy Spirit to you." Ezekiel 36:27 contains God's promise: "I will put my spirit within you." These words and the prophecy of Joel lie behind the reference of Tit. 3:5–6 to "the Holy Spirit, which he poured out upon us richly." The reception of the Spirit is one more indication that the Christian experience is not contrary to the O.T. but rather its climax and completion.

The Future Coming of Christ

The fifth statement of the kerygma was that Jesus Christ, who once lived on earth and now reigns as Lord, will return in judgment and triumph. The new age that the O.T. awaited has indeed arrived, and Christians live in a critical present. Yet there are some things that are still to come, and the future has its own place in Christian theology. Peter, in a Jerusalem sermon (Acts 3:21), speaks of Jesus, "whom heaven must receive until the time for establishing all that God spoke by the mouth of his holy prophets from of old." Those sections of the N.T. which contain the most references to the future work of God, eschatology, are also sections which are heavily dependent upon the O.T. Thus, the "little apocalypse" of Mk., ch. 13, has 19 Scriptural citations, with a significantly larger number in the parallel but expanded accounts of Mt., ch. 24, and Lk., ch. 21. 1 Corinthians, ch. 15; 2 Cor., ch. 5; 1 Thess., ch. 4; and 2 Thess., ch. 2, are all markedly eschatological chapters and all refer constantly to the O.T. Revelation, the one completely apocalyptic writing in the N.T., is little more than a skillfully arranged patchwork of O.T. citations and references that are given a Christian interpretation. Moreover, N.T. eschatological statements are directly influenced by a relatively small number of O.T. passages, which are themselves pointedly eschatological. Heavily used in this manner are Ezekiel, Daniel, Joel, Zechariah, chs. 9 to 14, and Malachi.

In many instances the O.T. eschatological statement is faithfully cited in the N.T. without change in meaning, but often it is adapted to fit the new Christian situation. Jewish eschatology has provided much of the language and many of the concepts for the N.T. exposition of the things that it was believed were still to take place. The "little apocalypse" ascribes to Jesus (Mk. 13:26 = Mt. 24:30; Lk. 21:27) the prediction: "Then they will see the Son of man coming in clouds with great power and glory." The words are drawn from Dan. 7: 13–14, where the certainty of the future event has caused it to be presented as if it were past. The same prophecy is found in Mk. 14:62 (= Mt. 26:64; Lk. 22:69). The idea that on the Day of the Lord, the coming of the Son of man, God's chosen ones will be gathered together is found in both Testaments. It is predicted in Mk. 13:27 (= Mt. 24:31) that "then he will send out the angels, and gather his elect from the four winds, from the ends of the earth to the ends of heaven." We read in Deut. 30:4: "If your outcasts are in the uttermost parts of heaven, from there the Lord your God will gather you." There are references to "the four winds" in Jeremiah, Ezekiel, Daniel, and Zechariah.

Paul, in his defense before Felix (Acts 24:15), declares that "there will be a resurrection of both the just and the unjust." The reference is to Dan. 12:2: "Many of those who sleep in the dust of the earth shall awake, some to everlasting life, and some to shame and everlasting contempt." Both late Judaism and Christianity looked for a resurrection in the final times. But there was also to be a final judgment. Before that day arrives, however, there will be unmistakable indications of its approach. According to Mk. 13:4 (= Mt. 24:3; Lk. 21:7), four of the disciples asked Jesus: "Tell us, when will this be, and what will be the sign when these things are all to be accomplished?" The question is also asked in Dan. 12:6: "How long shall it be till the end of these wonders?" Matthew 24:3 speaks of "the close of the age," while Dan. 9:27 mentions "the decreed end" and Dan. 12:4 refers to "the time of the end." We are told (Mk. 13:24–25 = Mt. 24:29; Lk. 21:26) that in those days the sun and the moon will be darkened, the stars will fall, and heaven will be shaken. The composite picture is derived from verses of Joshua, Ecclesiastes, Isaiah, Ezekiel, Daniel, Joel, and Haggai. In Mk. 13:19 (= Mt. 24:21) it is stated that the tribulation at that time will be worse than anything yet experienced since the beginning of the world. The idea is drawn from Dan. 12:1: "There shall be a time of trouble, such as never has been since there was a nation till that time." Paul writes (1 Cor. 15:24) explicitly of the final days: "Then comes the end, when he delivers the kingdom to God the Father after destroying every rule and every authority and power." Daniel 7:14 speaks of the future role of the Son of man: "To him was given dominion and glory and kingdom." Paul declares (1 Cor. 15:52) that at the last day "the trumpet will sound"; he is citing Is. 27:13, "In that day a great trumpet will be blown," and Zech. 9:14. The sound of God's trumpet at the final time is mentioned also in 1 Thess. 4:16. In 1 Thess. 5:3 the tumult of the end is compared to the pangs of childbirth, a metaphor that is cited from Is. 13:8; 21:3; 26:17; and Mic. 4:9. In Zech. 14:5 it is prophesied that on the last day "the Lord your God will come, and all the holy ones with him." The prophecy is applied to Jesus and quoted in 2 Thess. 1:7, as the end is described as the time "when the Lord Jesus is revealed from heaven with his mighty angels." Before the final day, we are informed (2 Thess. 2:3–4), "the man of lawlessness . . . , who opposes and exalts himself against every so-called god," will take "his seat in the temple of God, proclaiming himself to be God." We find in these two verses a double indebtedness, first, to Dan. 11:36, where it is predicted: "The king . . . shall exalt himself and magnify himself above every god, and shall speak astonishing things against the God of gods. He shall prosper till the indignation is accomplished." There is also dependence on Ezek. 28:2: "You have said, 'I am a god, I sit in the seat of the gods.'" The instances of the O.T. basis for the apocalyptic pictures of Revelation are too numerous even to illustrate, and it must be concluded that N.T. eschatology is, at nearly every point, directly related to Jewish Scripture.

CALL TO REPENTANCE

The sixth and final proposition of the apostolic preaching is the call to repentance, to the abandonment of evil and the following of the good. Here, too, the O.T. provides the principal foundation and support. In Acts 3:19 Peter charges his hearers: "Repent therefore, and turn again, that your sins may be blotted out." The same thought is expressed in Jer. 36:3: "that every one may turn from his evil way, and that I may forgive their iniquity." The prophetic injunction to repentance is found in the words of God reported in Ezek. 33:11: "I have no pleasure in the death of the wicked, but that the wicked turn from his way and live." The words are reflected in 2 Pet. 3:9, where God is characterized as "not wishing that any should perish, but that all should reach repentance."

ETHICAL TEACHING AND THE OLD TESTAMENT

To repent is to turn from wrongdoing and toward the right. It is to stop one type of conduct and to substitute another for it. Very closely connected with the primitive Christian proclamation is the early teaching regarding the code of living to be followed by those who have accepted God's salvation in Christ, sometimes called the *didache* to distinguish it from doctrinal preaching. In this area also dependence on the teaching of the O.T. is striking. (Table 7 lists a number of examples of N.T. ethical and institutional principles with a direct relationship to the O.T.) Some of the instruction is of such fundamental religious importance that it might be regarded as part of the total kerygmatic tradition, but other illustrations are of secondary application and may represent a general moral and philosophical outlook that is not peculiar to Judaism and Christianity, although the immediate source of its Christian expression appears to be Jewish Scripture. In several instances rules for the life of the church are derived from O.T. teaching, but for the most part the *didache* consists of a standard of conduct for the individual follower of Christ. The majority of the N.T. books exhibit indebtedness to the O.T. for this form of instruction. The parts of the O.T. that are most influential are the Pentateuch, the writing prophets, and the Wisdom literature (Job, Proverbs, Ecclesiastes).

The primitive church was concerned to establish against many attacks the principle of a professional ministry. Even though Paul chose to support himself financially by manual labor, he defends the right of the church's ministers to be paid for their ministry by asking (1 Cor. 9:7): "Who plants a vineyard without eating any of its fruit?" The question is a direct quotation of Deut. 20:6. Paul also quotes, with an introductory formula (1 Cor. 9:9), Deut. 25:4, "You shall not muzzle an ox when it treads out the grain," and interprets this command as given not for the sake of the animals but for the sake of the Christian community. Finally, Paul reminds his readers (1 Cor. 9:13) that the servants of the Temple in Jerusalem were given a share of the food that was offered there, as is made clear in Leviticus, Numbers, and Deuteronomy. Another problem facing the church at Corinth was an extreme emphasis on the phenomenon of "speaking with tongues," which tended to crowd out the exercise of prophecy. To restore the role of the latter, Paul states (1 Cor. 14:5) that "he who prophesies is greater," and he probably is referring to the wish of Moses in Num. 11:29: "Would that all the Lord's people were prophets . . . !" Paul maintains that prophecy is necessary for the edification of believers (1 Cor. 14:21–22) and draws this conclusion from his own interpretation of Is. 28:11–12, which he quotes with a formula, "By men of strange lips and with an alien tongue the Lord will speak to this people . . . , yet they would not hear." The early church was required to reach some kind of working relationship with the Roman state, and Paul declares (Rom. 13:1) that "there is no authority except from God." He may have been thinking of Dan. 4:17: "The Most High rules the kingdom of men, and gives it to whom he will." The author of 1 Timothy writes (1 Tim. 2:1–2): "I urge that

. . . prayers . . . be made . . . for kings," and the advice is
in line with Ezra 6:10: "Pray for the life of the king." In dealing with the necessity for disciplining a member of the Corin-
thian church whose immoral conduct was threatening the integrity of the Christian community, Paul commands sternly
(1 Cor. 5:13): "Drive out the wicked person from among you";
but Paul is applying the order of Num. 15:30: "That person
shall be cut off from among his people." The virtually identical
command is given in Deut. 13:5 and repeated 7 times: "You
shall purge the evil from the midst of you." The primitive
church found in the O.T. detailed guidance for facing its own
problems.

The Ten Commandments, listed in Ex. 20:1–17 and Deut.
5:6–21, retain in the N.T. their primary position as a standard
for ethical conduct. Five of the commandments are quoted in
Mk. 10:19 (= Mt. 19:17–19; Lk. 18:20), and four are cited in
Rom. 13:9. Two of the commandments are listed in Rom. 2:21–
22 and Jas. 2:11, while one of them is quoted in each of the
following places: Mk. 7:10 (= Mt. 15:4); Mt. 5:21 and 27; Lk.
23:56; and Eph. 6:2–3. It should be added, of course, that Jesus
sums up the whole law, including the Decalogue, under two
other commandments, the love of God (Deut. 6:5), and the
love of neighbor (Lev. 19:18), and that these commandments
also appear many times in the N.T.

Hatred of one's Christian brother is condemned in 1 Jn. 2:9,
11; 3:15; and the foundation for the teaching is clearly Lev.
19:17: "You shall not hate your brother in your heart, but you
shall reason with your neighbor." This passage in Leviticus
concludes (19:18) with the positive command: "You shall love
your neighbor as yourself." The equation of "brother" and
"neighbor" in the poetic parallelism of Lev. 19:17 provides the
basis for applying the command to love one's neighbor to the
relationship among Christians that we find in 1 Jn. 4:21: "This
commandment we have from him, that he who loves God
should love his brother also." In 1 Pet. 4:8 the readers are ordered: "Above all hold unfailing your love for one another,

since love covers a multitude of sins"; and there is a reference to Prov. 10:12: "Love covers all offenses."

The wisdom of man is misleading and treacherous and always stands over against the wisdom of God. Paul warns the Christians in Rome (Rom. 11:25): "Lest you be wise in your own conceits." Prov. 3:7 (= 26:12) seems to be his source: "Be not wise in your own eyes"; and the same words occur in Is. 5:21. In 1 Cor. 1:19 Paul quotes with a formula Is. 29:14: "The wisdom of their wise men shall perish," and he asks (1 Cor. 1:20): "Has not God made foolish the wisdom of the world?" citing another verse of Isaiah (Is. 44:25): "I am the Lord . . . who turns wise men back, and makes their knowledge foolish." Jeremiah 8:9 predicts: "The wise men shall be put to shame," and Paul echoes (1 Cor. 1:27): "God chose . . . to shame the wise." In fact, Paul points out that the way of this world is futile. He declares (1 Cor. 15:32) that without Christ we would do well to accept the suggestion, "Let us eat and drink, for tomorrow we die," an exact quotation of Is. 22:13. Isaiah 49:4 (= Is. 65:23) says, "I have labored in vain," and Paul affirms (1 Cor. 15:58) that only "in the Lord your labor is not in vain."

Christians are admonished in 1 Pet. 3:3: "Let not yours be the outward adorning with braiding of hair, decoration of gold, and wearing of robes." It is a summary quotation of Is. 3:18–24, where the prophet pours scorn on "the headbands, and the crescents, the pendants, the bracelets, and the scarfs; the head-dresses, . . . the festal robes, . . . well-set hair, . . . a rich robe." Ezekiel 33:31–32 speaks of the contrast between hearing and doing: "They hear what you say, but they will not do it." This antithesis lies behind the injunction of Jas. 1:22: "Be doers of the word, and not hearers only." The command of Deut. 15:7, "If there is among you a poor man, . . . you shall not harden your heart or shut your hand," forms the basis of the observation of 1 Jn. 3:17 that God's love is not allowed to function "if any one has the world's goods and sees his brother in need, yet closes his heart against him."

CHRISTIAN DISTINCTIVENESS

We have now established the fact that the O.T. lies close to the surface in all the major emphases of apostolic proclamation, and we are brought face to face with the question of the nature of the uniqueness of the Christian message. The entire N.T. is dominated by the person and the work of Jesus. He is believed to be the Messiah sent to earth by God by whose power he did mighty deeds and was raised from the dead. Christian preaching begins with the experience and the conviction of Jesus' resurrection, and his relation to God is believed to be unique. Furthermore, N.T. writers make it clear that what Jesus has accomplished is efficacious for all time and all people and need not be repeated in any manner. Representative of the general early Christian interpretation of the sufficiency and finality of the work of Christ is Heb. 9:12: "He entered once for all into the Holy Place." It is true that in one sense "Christianity is Christ," but at the same time much of the very uniqueness of Christianity is arrived at through the utilization of O.T. material to support the convictions of Jesus' followers. Jesus and his work are explained in the N.T. by O.T. language and figures. He is the realization of all that the O.T. predicted would occur in God's time. The teaching of the N.T. seldom departs very far from O.T. doctrine, and the similarities are far more striking than the differences.

It is instructive to look negatively at the matter of N.T. dependence on the O.T. There are 260 chapters in the whole N.T., and only 12 of these contain no instance of a direct relationship of some form with the O.T. Another 19 chapters have only a single such instance in each. Thus, it can be quickly seen that 229 of the 260 chapters have in each at least 2 citations of or specific references to the O.T.; and, of course, most chapters contain far more than two such references. For example, Revelation has approximately 550 different references to the O.T. in its 22 chapters, an average of nearly 25 in each. The seventh chapter of Acts contains about 100 instances of direct dependence. Although the degree of use of the O.T. does vary somewhat from chapter to chapter and from author to author, direct employment of the O.T. is to be found almost everywhere. The principle of such use is at the heart of Christianity.

LIGHT FROM THE OLD TESTAMENT BACKGROUND

One final connection between the two Testaments remains to be considered briefly. The framework of the life and teaching of Jesus and of the first years of the existence of the church is the Judaism that is openly set forth in the O.T. The more clearly that background is understood the more accurate will be the picture of the rise of Christianity. At innumerable points the O.T. can throw valuable light on N.T. statements, and a few examples will suffice to prove the case. (Some of the many classifications are noted in Table 8.)

Jesus' command to the healed leper to go and show himself to the priest (Mk. 1:44 = Mt. 8:4; Lk. 5:14; and cf. Lk. 17:14) is founded upon the detailed law of Lev., chs. 13 and 14. The rebuke of Herod the tetrarch by John the Baptist that it was not lawful for him to marry the wife of his brother (Mk. 6:18 = Mt. 14:4) is an application of the regulation of Lev. 18:16 and 20:21. The fringe on the garment of Jesus (Mk. 6:56 = Mt. 9:20; 14:36; Lk. 8:44) and those on the garments of the scribes and Pharisees (Mt. 23:5) are commanded by God in Num. 15:37-39. According to Mt. 12:5, the priests of the Temple commit a technical violation of the Sabbath by offering sacrifice; but such a Sabbath offering is ordered in Num. 28:10. Matthew 17:24 refers to those who collect the half-shekel tax. This tax is described in Ex. 30:13 and 38:26. In Jesus' parable of the laborers in the vineyard (Mt. 20:1-16) we are told, "When evening came, the owner of the vineyard said to his steward, 'Call the laborers and pay them their wages.'" This procedure agrees with Lev. 19:13: "The wages of a hired servant shall not remain with you all night until the morning."

Deuteronomy 24:15 says of a hired servant: "You shall give him his hire on the day he earns it, before the sun goes down." Matthew 27:51 (= Lk. 23:45) tells us that during the crucifixion "the curtain of the temple was torn in two." The veil is first commanded in Ex. 26:31–33. In Lev. 24:16 it is ordered: "He who blasphemes the name of the Lord shall be put to death; all the congregation shall stone him." This law explains the comment of the Fourth Evangelist about Jesus (Jn. 5:18): "This was why the Jews sought all the more to kill him, because he . . . called God his Father." In Jn. 10:33 the Jews say to Jesus: "We stone you for . . . blasphemy." There is a further reference to Lev. 24:16 in the declaration of the Jews in Jn. 19:7: "We have a law, and by that law he ought to die, because he has made himself the Son of God." In connection with the stoning of Stephen we are told (Acts 7:58) that the witnesses laid their coats at Saul's feet before participating in the execution. The law of Deut. 17:7 requires that "the hand of the witnesses shall be first against him to put him to death."

When Paul is seized by the Jews in the Jerusalem Temple (Acts 21:28), it is charged that "he also brought Greeks into the temple, and he has defiled this holy place." In Ezek. 44:7 the admission of foreigners into God's sanctuary is seen as an act of profanation. According to Acts 21:30–31, it was after the Jews had dragged Paul out of the Temple that they tried to kill him. Clarification is provided by the story (2 Kings 11:15–16) of how Athaliah was seized and taken out of the Temple and then killed after the priest had said: "Let her not be slain in the house of the Lord." Acts 18:18 informs us that Paul cut his hair when he was at Cenchreae because he had taken a vow. In Acts 21:23–24 there is further mention of a vow, and purification and the shaving of heads; and in Acts 21:26–27 we read of the seven days of purification. These verses are clarified by the instructions laid down in Num. 6:5, 9: "All the days of his vow of separation no razor shall come upon his head; until the time is completed for which he separates himself to the Lord, he shall be holy; he shall let the locks of his hair grow long. . . . He shall shave his head on the day of his cleansing; on the seventh day he shall shave it."

The basic rule, "No person shall be put to death on the testimony of one witness," is stated in Num. 35:30, and the rule is made more specific in Deut. 17:6: "On the evidence of two witnesses or of three witnesses he that is to die shall be put to death." An even broader application is made in Deut. 19:15: "Only on the evidence of two witnesses, or of three witnesses, shall a charge be sustained." This principle of Jewish justice is reflected at many points in the N.T. The law is quoted by Jesus in Jn. 8:17, and it is included in a code for church discipline in Mt. 18:16. The principle is restated by Paul in 2 Cor. 13:1, and it appears also in 1 Tim. 5:19 and Heb. 10:28. The account of the trial of Jesus before Caiaphas presented in Mt. 26:60 has a new meaning when it is read in the light of the Pentateuchal law. "Many false witnesses came forward. At last two came forward" and gave the same testimony. On the evidence of these two witnesses the high priest could proceed with the condemnation.

The N.T. cannot be fully or properly understood without a knowledge of the Jewish Scripture, which was at every turn the raw material out of which most Christian teaching arose.

Chapter 6

The Book of Psalms in the New Testament

The N.T. has been influenced by Psalms more than by any other book of the O.T. In 70 cases N.T. quotations of Psalms are introduced by formulas. There are 60 more quotations that have no introductory formula, and in an additional 220 instances we can discover identifiable citations and references. More than 50 phrases are shared by the N.T. and Psalms. Early Christian writers are more dependent upon Psalms than they are upon Deuteronomy and Isaiah, which are the most frequently cited books of the Law and the Prophets. Before A.D. 90, Psalms was not included in the official Jewish canon of Scripture; but already in 1 Macc. 7:17, which is to be dated early in the first century B.C., the Psalter is quoted (Psalm 79:2–3), apparently as authoritative Scripture. The pseudepigraphic Psalms of Solomon, the Psalms of the Qumran Community, and the psalms (canticles) of the church all testify to the continuance of psalm composition among the Jews; but they also point to the established place held by the Psalter in common Jewish life. Early Christian preference for Psalms and Isaiah is found also at Qumran. The great majority of the psalms seem to have been composed before the exile, but the psalms as a whole exhibit numerous alterations and revisions that were made to take account of changing conditions. Yet the compilation of the Psalter, as we know it, must have been completed by 200 B.C. As it was increasingly used from that time, its acceptance as an authoritative writing became ever more certain. The primitive church not only received as an inheritance from Judaism a high view of Psalms but also carried it even farther. A large part of what has already been said about the relation of the N.T. to the rest of the O.T. applies with even greater intensity to Psalms. The latter is not regarded as less the word of God than the Law and the Prophets. Rather, its influence is even more pervasive, and it is used in the same ways as any other part of Scripture. It is an inseparable part of the O.T.

There is a reference to "the Book of Psalms" in Lk. 20:42 and Acts 1:20, while in Lk. 24:44 we find only "the psalms." In the N.T. as a whole the Davidic authorship of Psalms is unquestioned, and frequently the single word "David" is a synonym for the Psalter. In Mk. 12:36 Jesus' quotation of Ps. 110:1 is introduced by the words "David himself, inspired by the Holy Spirit, declared . . . ." This formula is itself reminiscent of the tradition of the last words of David preserved in 2 Sam. 23:2: "The Spirit of the Lord speaks by me." A similar reference occurs in Acts 1:16: "The scripture had to be fulfilled, which the Holy Spirit spoke beforehand by the mouth of David." In Peter's Pentecostal sermon a quotation of Ps. 16:8–11 is treated (Acts 2:25) as the words of David. The same is true of Acts 2:34; and in Acts 4:25 a citation of Ps. 2:1–2 is referred to as the speech of God by the Holy Spirit by the mouth of David. In Rom. 11:9 a citation of Ps. 69:22–23 is treated as the utterance of David, while in Heb. 4:7 the words of Ps. 95:7–8 are viewed as those of God spoken through David. Psalm 32:1–2 is introduced in Rom. 4:6 as the pronouncement of David. On the other hand, Ps. 8:4–6 is quoted in Heb. 2:6 after the vague formula: "It has been testified somewhere." Psalm 95:7–11 is cited in Heb. 3:7 as the direct words of the Holy Spirit. It is thus abundantly clear that for the N.T. authors the Psalter is accepted as the work of God through the agency of the Holy Spirit, which has been transmitted by the hand and mouth of David. It is thus of divine origin.

In its present form Psalms contains much evidence of the fact that it has been widely used in Jewish worship, both in the Jerusalem Temple and also in the synagogues. In its own worship Christianity continued the Jewish practice, and as the church was separated from the synagogue, the Psalter remained as a symbol of continuity. Exactly how psalms were utilized in worship is very difficult to determine, but it has been suggested that the singing of psalms in the synagogues is the source of the singing of hymns in the primitive church. In Mk. 14:26 (= Mt. 26:30) it is stated that Jesus and his disciples went to the Mount of Olives after they had sung a hymn, and it is supposed that this is a reference to the singing of Ps. 113 to 118 in connection with the Passover observance. According to Acts 16:25, Paul and Silas, imprisoned in Philippi, "were praying and singing hymns to God." Paul writes (1 Cor. 14:15): "I will sing with the spirit and I will sing with the mind also." In 1 Cor. 14:26 Paul describes the worship of the church at Corinth: "When you come together, each one has a hymn, a lesson, a revelation, a tongue, or an interpretation." Both Eph. 5:19 and Col. 3:16 describe the singing by Christians of "psalms and hymns and spiritual songs." The author of James instructs the members of the church (Jas. 5:13): "Is any cheerful? Let him sing praise." In all these N.T. references there is no proof that the Psalter is involved, and it is known that Christians often composed new hymns for their own use. On the other hand, it is very probable that Psalms provided the great bulk of Christian hymns. Wherever Christian worship has been offered down through the ages the Psalter has been present, and the roots of this practice are found in the primitive church.

Necessary Choices

It is significant that the whole Psalter is by no means reflected in the N.T. As many as 29 of the psalms may have no direct relationship with the N.T. at any point, and these are well scattered throughout the Psalter. Some of the psalms seem to have been judged unsuitable by early Christian authors and so rejected or ignored. Included in this group are Ps. 25; 43; 54; 58; 59; 60; 70; 85; 87; 100; 101; 108; 114; 120; 123; 127; 131; 133; and 142. Occasionally, psalms contain statements that appear to fall far below the high level of Christian thought. Sometimes there are expressions of vindictiveness, fanaticism, and hatred that cannot be reconciled with the love that is associated with Jesus. Those who are described in Psalms as "the righteous" often appear to be self-satisfied and arrogant. When psalms are clearly conditioned by the limitations of their time of composition, they are not worthy vehicles for the expression of Christian truth. A standard of judgment has to be applied and choices made. One of the verses most disturbing to Christian thinking is the expression of hatred and vengeance against the Babylonian oppressor in Ps. 137:9: "Happy shall he be who takes your little ones and dashes them against the rock!" The verse is reflected in the prediction of Jesus regarding the inhabitants of Jerusalem as set forth in Lk. 19:43–44: "Your enemies will . . . dash you to the ground, you and your children within you." Such behavior is of course not approved but only predicted of unredeemed human nature. In very few cases do passages from psalms which are religiously and morally suspect have any influence on early Christian writings. Use of Psalms in the N.T. is highly selective and thoroughly in accord with the example of Jesus.

As among the various N.T. books there are some differences as to the degree and manner of usage of Psalms. The Evangelists employ them freely in order to explain and interpret the life of Jesus. There are 10 Psalms quotations in Acts; and in Revelation the Psalter is often utilized in hymns and incidental allusions. Paul quotes psalms 20 or more times and employs them as practical exhortation and also authoritative doctrine. There are 14 quotations in Hebrews and many more direct references. In fact, of the twenty-seven N.T. books only five— Galatians, Philemon, 2 and 3 John, Jude—show no direct dependence on the Psalter. All the rest draw upon Psalms for their own purposes and in their own way.

The psalms are a product of a community at worship, and they convey a strong communal emphasis. The Mosaic religion of the covenant brought into being a sharp distinction between the righteous and the wicked and demanded that the latter have no part in the community. Psalms presupposes this separation at almost every turn, and the concept of the church in the N.T. is built upon it. Yet the psalms speak with equal force to personal religious experience, and in their balance between the group and the individual they are relevant to virtually every human situation in all periods of history. For this reason Christianity regarded Psalms as more meaningful to support and explain its own beliefs and practices than any other O.T. book. Thus, Artur Weiser has written of the Christian utilization of the Psalter: "Apart from its use in public worship it also serves as a means of individual edification, as the foundation of family worship, as a book of comfort, as a book of prayers, and as a guide to God in times of joy and affliction." (*The Psalms, A Commentary*, p. 19.)

Even though the N.T. writers are careful and restrained in their use of the Psalter, ignoring all passages that they view as unsuitable or unhelpful, they do draw upon the vast majority of the psalms. Nearly 500 verses out of a total of 2,450 are directly reflected in the N.T., approximately 20 percent; and these verses are drawn from approximately 120 of the 150 psalms. For the most part the N.T. allusions and citations do not overlap, and the selection of material to be used appears to be arrived at independently by the N.T. writers in most instances. A few verses of the Psalter, however, are part of a common Christian heritage. For example, Ps. 110:1,

"The Lord says to my lord, 'Sit at my right hand, till I make your enemies your footstool,'" appears more frequently in the N.T. than any other verse of the Psalter. It is quoted with an introductory formula in all three Synoptic Gospels, Acts, and Hebrews. It is cited without any introduction in Romans, 1 Corinthians, Ephesians, Colossians, and 1 Peter as well as additional times in Hebrews. The words of God in Ps. 2:7, "You are my son, today I have begotten you," are quoted in all three Synoptic Gospels and in 2 Peter. They are cited with formula in Acts and Hebrews, and they are reflected in John. The part of Ps. 8:4–6 that begins with the question, "What is man that thou art mindful of him . . . ?" is directly reflected in one way or another in Matthew, Mark, 1 Corinthians, Ephesians, and Hebrews. Likewise, Ps. 118:22, "The stone which the builders rejected has become the head of the corner," is quoted with formula in the three Synoptic Gospels and without introduction in Acts, Ephesians, and 1 Peter.

THE PSALMS MOST OFTEN USED

If there are about thirty psalms that have no direct influence upon the N.T., there are an equal number that the N.T. cites at least four or five times in each case. Often the use of the verses indicates that the Christian authors had in mind not simply the particular verses utilized but also their setting and even the entire psalm. Those psalms which are most frequently employed in the N.T. are Ps. 2; 22; 33; 34; 35; 39; 50; 69; 78; 89; 102; 105; 106; 107; 110; 116; 118; 119; 135; 145; 147.

Psalm 2 is in Jewish cultic use an "enthronement psalm" or a "royal psalm," and the king is pictured as anointed by God, who is the Lord of universal history. A Messianic interpretation seems to have been given to it in the Psalms of Solomon (Ps. of Sol. 17:26) as well as in some early rabbinical texts. Of its 11 verses, 7 are directly employed in the N.T. According to C. H. Dodd: "It appears then that the whole psalm was regarded as a description of messiahship, fulfilled in the mission and destiny of Jesus. Of all the scriptures . . . in the primary body of testimonies this is the only one except Is. 9:1–7 which is in the proper sense 'messianic.' " (*According to the Scriptures*, p. 105.)

Psalm 22 has been described as an "individual lament"; its theme is the seeking and the finding of God. Of its 31 verses, 11 are cited in the N.T.; and according to Mk. 15:34 (= Mt. 27:46), its opening words, "My God, my God, why hast thou forsaken me?" were spoken by Jesus as an expression of his faith in God. Following this lead, early Christianity looked upon Ps. 22 as having a special relation to Jesus. Other verses of the psalm were used to describe the passion of Jesus or as instances of the many ways in which Jesus had fulfilled O.T. prophecies.

Psalm 34 is in literary form an acrostic, an artificial composition in which successive verses begin with the advancing letters of the alphabet. In cultic usage it is an individual thanksgiving, and it consists largely of moral maxims that take into account the fear of the Lord. The N.T. employs 12 of its 22 verses, and F. F. Bruce has stated: "There is good reason to believe that from early days Ps. 34 was regularly used in the church's liturgy." (*New Testament Development of Old Testament Themes*, p. 63.) He notes especially the rather lengthy quotation of Ps. 34:12–16 made with an introduction in 1 Pet. 3:10–12.

Psalm 69 is an individual lament whose final 7 verses are in the form of a thanksgiving. It is quoted with an introductory formula 2 times each in John and Romans and once in Acts. It is also cited without formula or otherwise directly employed in Matthew, Mark, Luke, Philippians, Hebrews, Revelation. In the extent of its influence on the N.T. it is probably second only to Ps. 22. Its treatment of human suffering in general led at a very early time to its application to the sufferings of Jesus, and Christians quickly gave to it a Messianic interpretation. In fact, it has made more fundamental contributions to the passion narrative than has any other psalm.

Psalm 78 is of a different sort. It is basically a recital of the saving acts of God in the face of the continuing rebellion of his chosen people. It is quoted with an introductory formula by Matthew and John and is otherwise cited in Acts, Romans, 1 Corinthians, Hebrews, James, and Revelation. The sacred history of the Jews is recognized as an important part of the Christian heritage, and it is the object of further reflections.

Psalm 89 is another of the royal psalms, and the references to the throne of David are viewed by Christian writers as relating to Jesus as the Messiah. There is one formula-quotation of it in 1 Corinthians, but it is cited also in Luke, Acts, Romans, Colossians, Hebrews, and Revelation.

Psalm 110 is also a royal psalm, which, along with Ps. 2, was one of the "Messianic psalms" of late Judaism. The unique influence of its first verse on the N.T. has already been noted. It should also be pointed out that the words of God set forth in v. 4, "You are a priest for ever after the order of Melchizedek," are cited at least 6 times in Hebrews. Verse 5 is directly reflected in Romans. This short psalm of only seven verses is obviously treated in the N.T. as a testimony to Jesus as the Christ. This interpretation seems to spring from his own use of the psalm.

Psalm 118 is a liturgy of thanksgiving that was well known to the primitive church. It is probable that Jewish interpretation had already seen in it references to David and the Messiah, but in any case it was easily applied to the suffering and apparent defeat of Jesus, which were followed by his resurrection and glorification. Two of its verses are quoted with an introduction in Matthew (= Luke) and Hebrews. Other verses are cited in all four Gospels, Acts, Romans, 1 Corinthians, Ephesians, 1 Peter, and Revelation.

These eight psalms are those most frequently used in the N.T., but there are at least twelve others that exert a significantly wide influence through identifiable citations of all sorts. It must be added, however, that the way in which the Psalter was brought together from earlier smaller collections over

hundreds of years and the role of the community and its corporate worship in shaping it have resulted in the presence of
numerous duplications and repetitions. For example, Ps. 14
and Ps. 53 are identical. Many verses occur in more than one
place. It was the Psalter in this somewhat repetitive and final
form that the Christians knew and used. Where verses cited
by N.T. authors are to be found in more than one place among
the psalms, it is impossible to decide the precise source of the
Christian borrowing. For example, the ritual command "Praise
the Lord!" (or, "Hallelujah" in Hebrew), which is found 4
times in Rev., ch. 19, occurs 22 times in the last 50 psalms.
Similarly, the command "O sing to the Lord a new song,"
which is stated 2 times in Revelation to be fulfilled in heaven
(Rev. 5:9; 14:3), is a part of five different psalms, as well as
forming a verse in Isaiah. In such circumstances Christians
who utilized Psalms material were probably unaware of any
one specific source because of its general familiarity. A large
number of ideas and situations in Psalms are likewise so widely
diffused throughout that their influence on the N.T. proceeds
as much from the Psalter as a whole as from any individual
verses or passages of it.

Psalms are, of course, written as poetry; and in the vast majority of cases N.T. dependence is faithful to their poetic form.
This is always true when as much as a whole verse is cited. On
the other hand, the poetic form of the original is often forgotten
when only part of a verse is utilized or when the dominant
factor is the idea conveyed in the verse rather than the precise
words. One of the basic principles of Hebrew poetry is a
thought parallelism between the two lines of a single verse. A
clear illustration of this principle is provided by Ps. 69:25:
"May their camp be a desolation, let no one dwell in their
tents," which is cited with a formula introduction in Acts 1:20.
The two parts are parallel in that they are two ways of saying
the same thing. Hebrew poetry also contains antithetic parallelism, in which the second line contradicts the first, and
synthetic parallelism, in which the second line simply carries

farther the thought introduced in the first. Often Christian usage is impatient with the redundancies and artificialities required by the literary form, and the parallelism is abandoned. Some parts of the two lines of poetry may be combined in a single N.T. statement, or more often only one of the two poetic members is chosen for incorporation into the Christian writing. Occasionally, two or three successive verses will be summarized in a few words that remain unmistakably dependent on their source in Psalms.

CHRISTIAN ADAPTATION

The manner in which psalms are employed by the early Christian writers leaves no doubt that the furthering of the Gospel is their primary consideration. Passages from Psalms are very often interpreted arbitrarily without any regard to their context or original meaning. Occasionally, quotations are massed just for the sake of heightening their effect on the reader. We have already noted the bringing together of five different passages from the Psalter in Rom. 3:10–18, and we might also point to the mixing of quotations of two psalms with those of Deuteronomy and Isaiah in Rom. 15:9–12. Quotations of five psalms are joined with quotations from Deuteronomy, 2 Samuel, and Isaiah in Heb. 1:5–13. Such multiplications are not convincing to the modern reader, but they do agree with the practice of the rabbis at the time of Christian origins. Writers of the N.T. seem to have been very much influenced by what was already a traditional Jewish Messianic interpretation of Psalms. When they selected a passage from the Psalter for use as illustration or for dogmatic support, they did so because of its words as they understood them and not because of what it may have meant in past time. This was also the way of the rabbis. Thus, W. O. E. Oesterley has concluded: "Speaking generally, and apart from the Synoptic Gospels, the use of the Psalms in the N.T. follows Jewish methods." (*The Psalms,* p. 98.) Although the methods were for the most part Jewish, the goals were clearly Christian.

THE GREEK VERSION OF PSALMS

In the vast majority of instances the text of the Psalter that is used in the N.T. is Hebrew, or else the text of those verses which are cited is almost the same in the Greek as it is in the Hebrew. Thus it happens that there are relatively few instances in which the N.T. citation is obviously and significantly dependent upon the LXX rather than upon the Hebrew. However, in at least 11 cases a portion of the Psalter is quoted with an introductory formula, and some vital part of that quotation is found in the LXX and is either lacking or entirely different in the Hebrew. One each of these is found in Matthew, Romans, 2 Corinthians, and Ephesians, and there are 3 in Acts. The remaining 4 instances are in Hebrews. Furthermore, the 11 situations are to be compared with the 39 major instances in the rest of the O.T., which we have already described or listed.

Psalm 2:1-2 is quoted in Acts 4:25-26 as part of a speech attributed jointly to Peter and John. It is used to give a Scriptural background for the judgment and crucifixion of Jesus. The present tense is used in the Hebrew: "The kings of the earth set themselves, and the rulers take counsel together, against the Lord and his anointed." The past tense of the LXX is more readily applicable to the death of Jesus as a prediction which has come to pass: "The kings of the earth stood up and the rulers were gathered together." Herod and Pontius Pilate and the rulers of the Jews seem prefigured. It is the Greek form that is in fact cited.

Psalm 8:2 is quoted in Mt. 21:16 as the answer of Jesus to the complaints of the chief priests and the scribes that the children were crying out in the Temple. In the original we read: "Thou whose glory above the heavens is chanted by the mouth of babes and infants," while Matthew cites the more immediately applicable LXX: "By the mouth of babes and infants hast thou perfected praise." There is a strong implication that the passage has received fulfillment in the children's reception of Jesus.

Except for the omission of v. 6a, the whole of the three verses of Ps. 8:4–6 is quoted in Heb. 2:6–8. The LXX departs sharply from the Hebrew at v. 5, where the Hebrew says of God's relationship to man: "Thou hast made him little less than God," while the LXX reads: "Thou hast made him a little less than angels." Since the point being made by the author of the epistle is that God's promise to man of dominion over all creation is fulfilled only in Jesus and since the Hebrew reference to man as "little less than God" might seem to be theologically presumptuous, the LXX description of man as "little less than angels" is preferred. Furthermore, the Christology of the epistle, which sets forth Jesus as God's Son and as the unique and perfect victim and high priest, is more easily maintained.

In Peter's sermon at Pentecost (Acts 2:25–28) there is a rather lengthy quotation of Ps. 16:8–11, and here again it is the LXX which is employed. What in the Hebrew is expressed as the present confident faith of the worshiper is put in the past tense by the LXX. Thus, in the former it is said (v. 9): "My heart is glad, and my soul rejoices; my body also dwells secure," while the LXX tells of a past experience that gives rise to a future hope: "My heart rejoiced and my tongue exulted; moreover also my flesh shall rest in hope." The same situation is found in v. 11. The Hebrew describes a present relationship with God, but the LXX centers on a past encounter as the basis for future expectation: "Thou hast made known to me the ways of life; thou wilt fill me with joy with thy countenance." This characteristic of the LXX translation makes possible Peter's interpretation of the psalm as an account of David's meeting with Christ. David saw the Lord, and he rejoiced; he also had a ground for hope in what God would still do in Christ. Furthermore, the writer makes use of the LXX of v. 10 to find in it a prediction of the resurrection of Jesus. In the Hebrew the Psalmist gives further expression to his faith: "Thou dost not give me up to Sheol, or let thy godly one see the Pit," but in the LXX there is a possible distinction between the speaker and God's agent: "Thou wilt not leave my soul in hell; neither wilt thou suffer thy holy one to see corruption." In Acts 2:31 Peter declares, in reference to Ps. 16:10, that David "foresaw and spoke of the resurrection of the Christ, that he was not abandoned to Hades, nor did his flesh see corruption." The way in which Ps. 16 has been utilized would not have been possible on the basis of the Hebrew text.

Psalm 40:6 is quoted in Heb. 10:5 as the words of Christ himself. The wording of the Hebrew is confusing: "Sacrifice and offering thou dost not desire; but thou hast given me an open ear." In the LXX the second part is clearer: "but a body hast thou prepared for me." (There is some textual disagreement at this point.) According to the author of Hebrews, the Jewish system of sacrifices and offerings must always be ineffective and has in fact been done away with by the perfect offering of Jesus Christ. The LXX of Ps. 40 can be used to support the writer's thesis. The body prepared is that of Christ offered upon the cross.

Psalm 68:18 pictures the mighty triumph of God over the forces that opposed him and mentions the captives that he took and the tribute that he received. In the LXX version the triumph is seen as an exaltation and glorification from which man will receive divine gifts: "Thou art gone up on high, thou hast led captivity captive, thou hast received gifts for man." It is the LXX form of the verse that is quoted in Eph. 4:8 in reference to the ascension of Christ and his subsequent boundless gifts to his followers.

In Rom. 11:10 Paul quotes the words of Ps. 69:23 to bolster his suggestion that God had predestined Israel not to believe in Christ. The Hebrew wording says: "Let their eyes be darkened, so that they cannot see; and make their loins tremble continually." The second half of the verse in the LXX, which is used here by Paul, is stronger and suggests more of God's power: ". . . and bow down their back continually."

Psalm 95:7–11, which speaks of God's displeasure at the

rebellion of the Jews in the wilderness, is quoted in Heb. 3:7–11. Verse 8 of the psalm contains in the Hebrew the proper names of Meribah and Massah. They are omitted in the LXX, which chooses to translate their meaning rather than to transliterate them. The author of Hebrews uses the LXX, which he undoubtedly believes to be more edifying for the reader not skilled in the details of O.T. history: "Harden not your hearts as in the provocation, according to the day of irritation in the wilderness."

Psalm 109:8 is part of a prayer for the destruction of a wicked man, and the second half of the verse asks in the original Hebrew: ". . . may another seize his goods!" The verse is used by Peter in Acts 1:20 as the Scriptural justification for the selection of a successor to the traitor Judas in the body of the twelve apostles. It is the LXX rather than the Hebrew that is utilized, however, as the former states: "Let another take his office of overseer." Obviously the LXX translation is far more relevant to the critical situation in the infant church.

Psalm 116:10 declares in the original: "I kept my faith, even when I said . . . ," but a somewhat different sense is given in the LXX: "I believed, wherefore I have spoken." In 2 Cor. 4:13 Paul makes the point that his belief is the very ground of his speech, and he bases his position on the LXX wording of Ps. 116:10. The Hebrew wording would have led to a quite different conclusion.

Finally, Ps. 135:14 is quoted in Heb. 10:30, where the author is concerned to emphasize the constant danger of the inevitable judgment of God. The Hebrew of the psalm verse would not have agreed with the thought of the Christian writer because it states that "the Lord will vindicate his people"; but the LXX translation is most useful in its reading, "The Lord will judge his people."

These 11 examples of N.T. use of the LXX version of Psalms are adequate proof that although the Psalter was regarded as authoritative by both Christians and Jews long before it became a part of the official canon of Jewish Scripture, for Chris-

tians its authority was by no means tied to the Hebrew text.
The LXX version could be employed when it seemed advan-
tageous to do so, with no apology or awareness of abandoning
the original word. Moreover, it should not be overlooked that
in large numbers of N.T. quotations from Psalms use of the
LXX is not immediately apparent because the Greek is not
significantly different from the Hebrew; but it is significant
that in some cases the Hebrew should have been used rather
than the LXX. In the 11 instances studied, 6 N.T. books are
represented and 4 or 5 different Christian writers. Utilization
of the LXX version of Psalms for apologetic purposes was apparently widespread, and it was not believed to be inconsistent
with the admitted fact that they were written in the Hebrew
language. Circumstances of their composition were not ulti-
mately important to the Christian author; but their message
did matter a great deal, and their significance for Christianity
was often found in their precise wording, either in Hebrew or
in Greek.

FORMULA-QUOTATIONS

The importance of Psalms for the N.T. writers is indicated
by the number of class-one quotations that they draw from
them. There are 239 such quotations in the N.T., of which 70
are taken from the Psalter, almost 30 percent of the total. The
239 quotations represent 185 different O.T. passages. The 70
such quotations from Psalms are derived from 55 different
verses or sections of the Psalter, which is again nearly 30 percent of the whole. However, only 11 of the 27 N.T. books contain formula-quotations of Psalms. There are 18 in Hebrews
and 15 in Romans. The remaining 37 are rather evenly distributed among the four Gospels, Acts, 1 and 2 Corinthians,
Ephesians, and 1 Peter.

There is a great variety in the wording of the formulas used
to introduce Psalms quotations, but they are not substantially
different from those which the N.T. employs to present cita-

tions of older parts of Scripture. In 20 of the 70 instances the quotation is set forth with the words, or their equivalent, "It is written"; and in 2 more cases the passage is simply referred to as Scripture. There are 9 references to what is to follow as the words of David, and in 3 cases the source is described as a psalm. In 6 uses the words are called the utterance of God, and in 1 they are ascribed to Christ. In 6 instances the single word "for" suggests a forensic setting for the quotation; 7 times the introduction is simply "and," almost always as the next in a series of O.T. quotations. Once a Psalm quotation is described as a part of the Jewish law (Jn. 15:25). Once the quotation is curiously referred to as that which was "spoken by the prophet" (Mt. 13:35). In 4 cases the similarity of a Christian event to words of the Psalter is said to constitute the fulfilling of Scripture. Use of the psalms for recitation by the Christian community is suggested by the prefacing (Heb. 13:6) of a quotation of Ps. 118:6 with the words, "Hence we can confidently say . . . ." Writers of the N.T. are using the Psalter as an integral part of Scripture, and they therefore feel free to make unlimited use of it to suit their own needs and purposes. It is more helpful to them than any other O.T. book.

In some cases a psalm verse that is apparently quoted in the N.T. is paralleled almost exactly elsewhere in the O.T., making it impossible to identify the precise source utilized by the N.T. writer. He may in fact be drawing upon a tradition that is permanently preserved in two or more literary expressions, and he may not therefore be citing Psalms consciously. There is no question that in Heb. 2:6–8 there is a quotation of Ps. 8:4–6, but the opening line of that passage appears also in Job 7:17: "What is man, that thou dost make so much of him." The class-one quotation that Paul makes in Rom. 11:26–27 is probably drawn primarily from Is. 59:20–21 (LXX), but the same tradition is also found in Ps. 14:7 (= 53:6). The source of Paul's quotation in Rom. 15:9 is either Ps. 18:49 or 2 Sam. 22:50. The two verses are almost identical. John 19:36 declares: "For these things took place that the scripture might be fulfilled, 'Not a bone of him shall be broken.'" The source is apparently Ps. 34:20: "He keeps all his bones; not one of them is broken"; but Ex. 12:46 says of the Passover sacrifice: "You shall not break a bone of it," and the order is repeated in Num. 9:12. Again, the command of Jesus in Mt. 5:33 to "perform to the Lord what you have sworn" may be a citation of Ps. 50:14, "Pay your vows to the Most High"; or it may be drawn from Num. 30:2: "When a man vows a vow to the Lord, . . . he shall do according to all that proceeds out of his mouth." On the other hand, Jesus may be citing Deut. 23:21: "When you make a vow to the Lord your God, you shall not be slack to pay it."

A few of the class-one quotations of Psalms are found in more than one place in the Psalter, and again the precise source cannot be concluded. Psalm 8:4, quoted in Heb. 2:6, is paralleled in Ps. 144:3. In 1 Cor. 10:26 Paul writes: "For 'the earth is the Lord's, and everything in it'"; he may have been quoting Ps. 24:1; 50:12; or 89:11. Such a saying would obviously be very familiar to anyone who had a knowledge of the whole Psalter, as Paul surely did. The words quoted in Jn. 15:25, "They hated me without a cause," are found in Ps. 35:19 and also in Ps. 69:4. The quotation in Jn. 6:31, "He gave them bread from heaven to eat," may be taken from Ps. 78:24 in a combination of elements from each of the two poetically parallel lines or it may be derived from Ps. 105:40.

A single verse of a psalm may be quoted, with differing introductory formulas, by two or more writers; or a verse may be quoted 2 or 3 times by the same writer though with varying introductions. Thus, Ps. 2:7 is quoted in Acts 13:33 and in Heb. 1:5 and 5:5. Psalm 95:7–11 is quoted in Heb. 3:7–11, while vs. 7–8 are quoted in Heb. 3:15 and 4:7. There are class-one quotations of Ps. 110:1 in Matthew, Mark, Luke, Acts, and Hebrews. The first part of Ps. 69:9 is quoted in Jn. 2:17; the second part is quoted completely independently by Paul in Rom. 15:3.

OTHER CITATIONS

Quotations with introductions can be examined with relative accuracy and objectivity. Unacknowledged quotations are not so easily recognized or so surely classified. The dividing line between a quotation and a reference is sometimes hard to determine, but there are about 45 different passages of the Psalter that are quoted without introductory formulas a total of 65 times in the N.T. In this category also Psalms accounts for approximately 30 percent of the entire N.T. usage. These class-two quotations are found in 14 of the 27 N.T. books, and nearly one half of them occur in the four Gospels. Of these, 11 are in Revelation and 7 in Acts. The remainder are scattered. There is a marked tendency to quote without formula psalm verses that occur in more than one place in the Psalter. This is true in more than one half of the 45 passages that are so cited. Perhaps it was true that material which was so commonly known needed no identification or acknowledgment. In no instance is more than one verse quoted without an introductory formula, and often only a half verse or even a few words is reproduced. In every case the quoted material is presented casually and with no indication at all of its source. However, even though so many of the verses have exact parallels elsewhere in the Psalter, in only 7 of the 45 sections that are cited is the tradition found also in other O.T. books. In only one case is a quoted psalm verse that is duplicated in another O.T. writing without parallel expression in the Psalter. In other words, where duplication is not just a phenomenon of Psalms, it is a question of a tradition with many different attestations, both within the Psalter and beyond it. The freedom with which N.T. writers incorporate these class-two quotations of Psalms into their own writings indicates that the authority rests with the borrowed material and does not in any way require the inclusion of an introductory formula.

PHRASES FROM THE PSALTER

As previously noted, the use in the N.T. of phrases that occur in the O.T. constitutes an extended and specialized form
of the class-two quotation. There are at least 21 such phrases
that belong to the N.T. and the Psalter but to no other part of
the O.T. (See Table 9.) In many cases the borrowing by the
N.T. writer must have been quite unconscious, but the indebtedness is undeniable. Thus, the words "the kings of the
earth" can be found 6 times in Psalms and also 1 time in Acts
and 5 times in Revelation. The combination "fear and trem-
bling" occurs in 2 psalms and in 4 Pauline epistles. Two psalms
contain the phrase "hairs of the head," and it recurs in Matthew
and Luke. Other phrases may be found in only 1 psalm and
1 N.T. book. Altogether, 14 N.T. writings make use of phrases
that belong only to the Psalter.

In addition, there are at least 35 more phrases used in the
N.T. that may be borrowed from Psalms but are to be found
also in other books of the O.T. (See Table 10.) Several metaphors are included in this list. It is impossible, of course, to
conclude that in each case the N.T. borrowing has been from
Psalms because there are parallels elsewhere in the O.T.; but
the wide use of Psalms by Christian writers, which we have
already established, would seem to indicate that here, too, the
dependence is more likely to be on Psalms than on other writings. It should also be pointed out that 25 of the 35 phrases of
this type are found more than once in the Psalter, many of them
5 or more times. Here we are dealing with phrases that are
obviously in rather common use and that have been given
literary expression in numerous places. Nevertheless, it is the
Psalter to which we must look as the probable influence upon
the N.T. author. In this category we discover such familiar
phrases as "the name of the Lord," "the birds of the air," "the
glory of God," "the fear of the Lord," "God's holy name," and
"the people of Israel." Furthermore, these phrases occur in the
majority of the N.T. writings.

REFLECTIONS IN JESUS' TEACHINGS

Jesus knew Psalms well, and according to the Gospel tradition he used the Psalter more than any other part of the O.T. He applied Psalms to a wide variety of circumstances and at various times in his life. His use of them is careful and constructive and springs from a deep understanding of their nature and meaning. Apparently Jesus often prayed in their words. He found psalms a proper vehicle for expressing his own feelings and for explaining his deeds or those of others. At times he employs the Psalter as a source for authoritative teaching, as, for example, in argument with the scribes and Pharisees. He may quote literally or he may cite freely, but in either case he views Psalms as the word of God for him and for all men. His own attitude and his own dependence on Psalms are the principal foundation upon which the practice of the N.T. authors is constructed.

The words that are ascribed to Jesus in the Gospels are filled with references to Psalms, direct and indirect, quotations and allusions. In at least 31 separate instances, many of which have double or triple attestations because of Gospel interdependence, the teaching or personal speech of Jesus manifests a very close relationship to the Psalter; and in many cases deliberate borrowing may be assumed even where there is no acknowledgment of the source. (See Table 11.) It may also be assumed that among the hearers of Jesus there was a rather wide knowledge and a strong appreciation of Psalms and that by utilizing material from the Psalter in his teaching Jesus could proceed from at least a partial common basis of understanding.

The Sermon on the Mount provides many examples of Jesus' use of Psalms. The third beatitude in Mt. 5:5, "Blessed are the meek, for they shall inherit the earth," is closely related to Ps. 37:11, "The meek shall possess the land." We have already examined in another light Jesus' class-one quotation of Ps.

50:14 in Mt. 5:33. In Mt. 5:34 Jesus refers to heaven as the throne of God, and both Ps. 11:4 and 103:19 state that God's throne is in heaven. In Mt. 6:26 (= Lk. 12:24), Jesus states that God feeds the birds of the air; it is said in Ps. 147:9 that God "gives . . . food . . . to the young ravens . . . ." In Mt. 6:27 (= Lk. 12:25), Jesus asks: "Which of you by being anxious can add one cubit to his span of life?" The thought of life as measured in terms of distance seems strange until we note the background statement in Ps. 39:5, "Thou hast made my days a few handbreadths." In Mt. 6:30 (= Lk. 12:28) Jesus speaks of "the grass of the field, which today is alive and tomorrow is thrown into the oven." The basic idea is set forth in Ps. 90:5–6: "Grass . . . in the morning . . . flourishes and . . . in the evening it fades and withers." In Mt. 7:23 (= Lk. 13:27), Jesus pictures his future role as a judge in determining who is to be admitted into God's Kingdom and states that he will say to those who have rendered him only lip service: "Depart from me, you evildoers." The words are an exact quotation of Ps. 119:115 and also almost identical with Ps. 6:8. It should also be noted that in the Lukan version of the sermon Jesus says (Lk. 6:28): "Bless those who curse you." There may well be some influence extended from Ps. 109:28: "Let them curse, but do thou bless!"

In the teaching of Jesus that is preserved by Mark and included in Matthew and/or Luke we find further borrowing. In the parable of the mustard seed Jesus tells (Mk. 4:32 = Mt. 13:32 and Lk. 13:19) how the shrub "puts forth large branches, so that the birds of the air can make nests in its shade." The same picture is drawn in Ps. 104:12: "The birds of the air have their habitation; they sing among the branches." In Mk. 8:37 (= Mt. 16:26), Jesus asks: "What can a man give in return for his life?" Similarly, Ps. 49:8 says of a man: "The ransom of his life is costly, and can never suffice." In Jesus' parable of the vineyard (Mk. 12:1 = Mt. 21:33 and Lk. 20:9) "a man planted a vineyard . . . and dug a pit . . . and built a tower." As the parable develops, it seems clear that the vineyard is Israel. The fundamental idea is presented in Ps. 80:8: "Thou didst bring a vine out of Egypt; thou didst drive out the nations and plant it."

Dependence on Psalms is indicated, too, in the teaching material presented by both Matthew and Luke but not by Mark, the hypothetical Gospel source Q. In Mt. 8:11 Jesus speaks of the coming time when "many will come from east and west," while Lk. 13:29 says: "Men will come from east and west, and from north and south." The concept is present in Ps. 107:3: "[The Lord has] gathered in from the lands, from the east and from the west, from the north and from the south." In Mt. 23:37 (= Lk. 13:34), Jesus expresses his lament over Jerusalem: "How often would I have gathered your children together as a hen gathers her brood under her wings . . . ." Again the germ of the idea is found in the Psalter (Ps. 91:4): "Under his wings you will find refuge." Jesus begins his parable of the lost sheep (Mt. 18:12 = Lk. 15:4; 19:10) with the words: "If a man has a hundred sheep, and one of them goes astray . . ."; and Ps. 119:176 states succinctly: "I have gone astray like a lost sheep; seek thy servant." According to Mt. 24:45 (= Lk. 12:42), it is the function of the faithful and wise servant "to give them their food at the proper time," and in Ps. 104:27 (= Ps. 145:15) it is the work of God "to give them their food in due season."

In teaching, other than the Sermon on the Mount, that is found only in Matthew there are further examples of the pervasive influence of Psalms. According to Mt. 16:27, Jesus warns that in the final days the Son of man "will repay every man for what he has done." The thought is found also in Proverbs and Jeremiah, but it is prominent in Psalms. Regarding the wicked, Ps. 28:4 asks God to "requite them according to their work," and in Ps. 62:12 the statement is made that God does do precisely that. At the end of the parable of the vineyard it is stated in Mt. 21:41 that the new tenants "will give him the fruits in their seasons," and the righteous man is likened in Ps. 1:3 to "a tree . . . that yields its fruit in its season."

The material that is peculiar to Luke is especially rich in illustrations of Jesus' use of Psalms. Thus, in Lk. 7:46 Jesus charges his host, Simon the Pharisee: "You did not anoint my head with oil," whereas it is said of God in Ps. 23:5: "Thou anointest my head with oil," and in Ps. 92:10 it is added: "Thou hast poured over me fresh oil." In Lk. 10:19 Jesus tells the seventy apostles that he has given to them "authority to tread upon serpents," and in Ps. 91:13 it is promised: "The young lion and the serpent you will trample under foot." In the parable of the rich fool (Lk. 12:20) God warns: "This night your soul is required of you; and the things you have prepared, whose will they be?" In Ps. 39:6 it is observed: "Man heaps up, and knows not who will gather!" while Psalm 49:10 contains the similar thought: "The fool and the stupid alike must perish and leave their wealth to others." The influence of Genesis, Deuteronomy, and Proverbs on the parable of the prodigal son has already been studied; but we note further that the confession in Lk. 15:18 and 21, "Father, I have sinned against heaven and before you," is related to the penitence of Ps. 41:4, "I have sinned against thee," and the similar admission of Ps. 51:4, "Against thee, thee only, have I sinned." Jesus asks in Lk. 18:7: "Will not God vindicate his elect, who cry to him day and night?" The situation has been presented in Ps. 88:1: "O Lord, my God, I call for help by day; I cry out in the night before thee." The prediction of Jesus in Lk. 21:24 that "Jerusalem will be trodden down by the Gentiles" has some remarkable parallels with the image presented in Ps. 79:1: "O God, the heathen . . . have defiled thy holy temple; they have laid Jerusalem in ruins." The following prediction in Lk. 21:25 that there will be "distress of nations in perplexity at the roaring of the sea and the waves" is obviously connected with the description of God in Ps. 65:7 as one "who dost still the roaring of the seas, the roaring of their waves."

Even in the Gospel of John, which contains little teaching of Jesus of the type found in the Synoptic Gospels, there are several instances of dependence on Psalms. In Jn. 4:24 Jesus states: "God is spirit, and those who worship him must worship in spirit and truth." The idea is at least partly presented in Ps. 145:18: "The Lord is near . . . to all who call upon him in truth." Jesus' formula-quotation of Ps. 78:24 (= Ps. 105:40) in Jn. 6:31 has been examined earlier. Another such quotation is ascribed to Jesus in Jn. 10:34, where he cites Ps. 82:6. In Jn. 13:18 he apparently cites Ps. 41:9 in predicting his betrayal by Judas; and in Jn. 15:25 he sees in his own experience a fulfillment of Ps. 35:19 (= Ps. 69:4).

Not all the parallels suggested represent certain borrowing from Psalms. In some cases the agreement may be accidental, or the link may be custom or tradition rather than any direct dependence. In some cases the parallel may not be attributable to Jesus but may be the shaping of the form of the teaching by the Evangelists to conform, consciously or unconsciously, to the wording of Psalms. Yet it remains evident that Jesus was so immersed in the psalms that in his teaching he frequently availed himself of their ideas and their wording as a means of setting forth his own thoughts.

There are three occasions during the final hours of his life when Jesus is reported to have turned to the Psalter in order to phrase his views and at the same time to receive strength to meet the extreme demands laid upon him. Thus, in Gethsemane he is said, in Mk. 14:34 (= Mt. 26:38; cf. Jn. 12:27), to have revealed to Peter, James, and John: "My soul is very sorrowful, even to death." The garden experience clearly involved an initial shrinking from the prospect of immediate death, and he thought at once of psalms. Psalm 6:3–5 was relevant: "My soul also is sorely troubled. . . . O Lord, save my life; . . . for in death there is no remembrance of thee." The question of Ps. 42:5, 11; 43:5: "Why are you cast down, O my soul?" is also involved, as is the statement of Ps. 42:6: "My soul is cast down within me." According to Mk. 15:34 and Mt. 27:46 the only statement of Jesus while he was hanging on the cross was an exact quotation of Ps. 22:1, preserved by Mark in Aramaic as well as in Greek and by Matthew in Hebrew and in Greek, "My God, my God, why hast thou forsaken me?" According to Luke, 1 of the 3 times that Jesus spoke from the cross he cried (Lk. 23:46): "Father, into thy hands I commit my spirit!" Except for the personal address, "Father," which was characteristic of Jesus, the words agree exactly with Ps. 31:5. According to John, Jesus spoke 3 times while on the cross, and the content of his words is different from those of Luke (or of Mark). In Jn. 19:28 Jesus says, in order to fulfill the Scripture, "I thirst." Exactly what verse of the O.T. the Evangelist has in mind it is impossible to say, but only three verses from Psalms have been proposed. The situation of Jesus seems to be described in Ps. 22:15: "My strength is dried up like a potsherd, and my tongue cleaves to my jaws." Perhaps, however, Jesus is citing Ps. 63:1: "O God, . . . my soul thirsts for thee." Since, according to Jn. 19:29, vinegar was immediately applied to Jesus' lips, it is possible that Jesus had in mind Ps. 69:21: "For my thirst they gave me vinegar to drink."

The centrality of Psalms for Jesus in the climactic experience of his life stands forth strongly from the Gospel accounts. It is of one piece with what must have been true throughout his whole ministry. The Psalter was first in his heart and first upon his lips. He found it highly useful for public instruction and for private prayer and meditation. His constant utilization of it argues powerfully that for him it was the most faithful expression of the religious inheritance of the Jewish people.

PSALMS AND THE GOSPEL NARRATIVES

The usage of Jesus was, of course, well known to the Evangelists and provides one of the most persuasive reasons why they also used Psalms so often in their accounts of Jesus' words and deeds or why the Psalter played such an important part in the formation of the early traditions about Jesus with which the Evangelists worked in composing their finished narratives. Whether it was done very early in the formation of the stories about Jesus or whether it was done later in the process of transmission, at some point portions of Psalms have been introduced as explanations or comments on the story or as words addressed to Jesus by others. Often the employment of material from Psalms to round out the narrative marks the beginning of theological interpretation.

We are told in Mt. 2:11 that when the Wise Men arrived at the place of Jesus' birth in Jerusalem, "they fell down and worshiped him. Then, opening their treasures, they offered him gifts, gold . . . ." The account is sharply reminiscent of Ps. 72:10–11, 15: "May the kings . . . render him tribute, may the kings . . . bring gifts! May all kings fall down before him . . . ! May gold . . . be given to him!" Moreover, the relationship between the Matthean narrative and Psalms accounts for the birth of the Christian tradition that the Wise Men were actually kings.

The account of the visit of the boy Jesus to the Temple at Jerusalem is, at Lk. 2:46, 49, closely related to the Psalter. Jesus was found "among the teachers, . . . asking them questions; and all . . . were amazed at his understanding . . . . And he said . . . , 'Did you not know that I must be in my Father's house?'" The first point of contact is with Ps. 27:4: "One thing have I asked of the Lord . . . that I may dwell in the house of the Lord . . . to inquire in his temple." The second point of contact is with Ps. 119:99: "I have more understanding than all my teachers."

According to Mk. 1:11 (= Mt. 3:17 and Lk. 3:22), the heavenly voice at the baptism of Jesus proclaimed, "Thou art my beloved Son; with thee I am well pleased." This proclamation can be analyzed as a composite of three different verses of the O.T. In Gen. 22:2 God in addressing Abraham refers to Isaac as "your only son . . . , whom you love." In Is. 42:1 God's servant is called "my chosen, in whom my soul delights." In Ps. 2:7, which as we have seen is more widely quoted than any other verse in the Psalter, we find the heart of the proclamation: "I will tell of the decree of the Lord: He said to me, 'You are my son, today I have begotten you.'" Jesus' baptismal ad-

dress, with which he begins his ministry and in which it is
rooted, is based on Psalms, with some elaboration from Genesis
and Isaiah.

The baptism is followed at once by the temptation in the
wilderness, where Jesus clarifies his vocation. One of the three
temptations of Jesus, according to Mt. 4:6 (= Lk. 4:10–11),
arose from the protection that was apparently promised by Ps.
91:11–12: "For he will give his angels charge of you to guard
you . . . . On their hands they will bear you up, lest you dash
your foot against a stone."

At many different points the Evangelists relate the ministry
of Jesus to the Psalter. After some of Jesus' parables Matthew
states (Mt. 13:35) that Jesus employed this mode of teaching
to fulfill Scripture and then quotes Ps. 78:2; "I will open my
mouth in a parable; I will utter dark sayings from of old." In
the episode of the healing of the centurion's servant, the centurion answers Jesus (Mt. 8:8 = Lk. 7:7): "Say the word, and
my servant will be healed." The same words are used of God
in Ps. 107:20: "He sent forth his word, and healed them." In
Mk. 4:39 it is written that when Jesus was with his disciples
in a boat on the lake of Galilee and a storm arose, "He . . .
rebuked the wind. . . . And the wind ceased, and there was
a great calm." The incident suggests Ps. 107:29: "He made the
storm be still, and the waves of the sea were hushed"; but the
telling of the story in Mt. 8:26 (= Lk. 8:24) is brought even
more closely into line with the Psalms passage by preserving
the thought of each of the poetically parallel lines of the
original with reference to both the storm of wind and the
raging waves: "He rebuked the winds and the sea; and there
was a great calm." In Mk. 6:48 (= Mt. 14:26 and Jn. 6:19) it
is stated that Jesus saw that his disciples were in trouble in a
boat on the lake and that "he came to them, walking on the
sea." Psalm 77 opens as a cry to God for help in a time of
trouble, and in v. 19 it is claimed: "Thy way was through the
sea, . . . yet thy footprints were unseen."

In the narrative of the transfiguration we are told in Mk. 9:7

(= Mt. 17:5 and Lk. 9:35) that there was a message from the cloud similar to that at Jesus' baptism: "This is my beloved Son; listen to him." Once more we have a composite of Gen. 22:2, "your only son . . . whom you love," and Deut. 18:15: ". . . a prophet like me from among you, . . . —him you shall heed," and Ps. 2:7: "You are my son."

There are two narratives of Jesus' ministry in John that closely reflect the Psalter. At the end of the story of the cleansing of the Temple as told in Jn. 2:17 there is an explanation that involves a direct quotation of Ps. 69:9: "His disciples remembered that it was written, 'Zeal for thy house will consume me.' " In the episode, uniquely recorded in John, of Jesus' healing of the man born blind, dependence on Psalms is suggested at several points. In Ps. 66:18 it is said: "If I had cherished iniquity in my heart, the Lord would not have listened," while in Jn. 9:31 the Jews declare: "We know that God does not listen to sinners." The Jews then add: "If any one is a worshiper of God and does his will, God listens to him." Possible sources for their words are Ps. 34:17: "When the righteous cry for help, the Lord hears," and Ps. 145:19: "He fulfils the desire of all who fear him." The healed man is then charged (Jn. 9:34): "You were born in utter sin," and we may well have a reference to Ps. 51:5: "I was brought forth in iniquity, and in sin did my mother conceive me."

THE PASSION STORY

It is within the passion narrative that we find the largest concentration of direct and indirect citations of the Psalter. Since the psalms have so much to say regarding man's experience of suffering and its relationship to God, it is not surprising that they are so much used to present and interpret the final sufferings of Jesus. No other portions of Scripture are as productive for this purpose.

In the episode of Jesus' triumphal entry into Jerusalem, with which his final week begins, it is reported in Mk. 11:8 (= Mt.

154   FINDING THE OLD TESTAMENT IN THE NEW

21:8 and Jn. 12:13) that "others spread leafy branches." The action seems to be taken in obedience to the command of Ps. 118:27: "Bind the festal procession with branches." The cry of the multitude who welcomed Jesus is preserved in Mk. 11:9 (= Matt. 21:9; Lk. 19:38; Jn. 12:13): "Hosanna! Blessed is he who comes in the name of the Lord!" The quotation is from Ps. 118:25–26: "Save us [Hebrew: "Hosannah"] . . . ! Blessed be he who enters in the name of the Lord!" It is significant that Ps. 118 marks the conclusion of the Hallel, the grouping of Ps. 113 to 118, which were sung at the Passover celebration. Jesus' entry into Jerusalem, the Jewish Passover, and the impending death of Jesus are all closely interwoven.

At the last supper of Jesus with his disciples his betrayal by Judas is predicted, and Jesus says in Mk. 14:18: "One of you will betray me, one who is eating with me." The words are different, but the substance is the same in Lk. 22:21: "The hand of him who betrays me is with me on the table." In Jn. 13:18 the betrayal is pictured as a fulfillment of Scripture: "He who ate my bread has lifted his heel against me." The source of the words in Mark, Luke, and John is to be found in Ps. 41:9: "Even my bosom friend in whom I trusted, who ate of my bread, has lifted his heel against me." In John we have a class-one quotation and in Mark and Luke variant allusions to the same Scriptural verse.

In Ps. 31:13 the psalmist admits that he is fearful of his adversaries "as they scheme together against me, as they plot to take my life." These words appear to have worked their influence upon the Evangelists. In Mk. 14:1 (= Mt. 26:4 and Lk. 22:2) it is stated that "the chief priests and the scribes were seeking how to arrest him by stealth, and kill him." The scheming and plotting against the life of Jesus were regarded as in some sense foreshadowed in the experience of the author of Ps. 31.

At the trial of Jesus before the high priest it is emphasized (Mk. 14:56–57 = Mt. 26:60) that there were many false witnesses against him. The account may have been influenced by two verses in the Psalter. In Ps. 27:12 the writer admits: "False witnesses have risen against me," and in Ps. 35:11 it is added: "Malicious witnesses rise up."

According to Mt. 27:24, Pilate "washed his hands before the crowd, saying, 'I am innocent of this man's blood' "; and we are reminded of Deut. 21:7: "Our hands did not shed this blood." However, it seems more likely that there is direct dependence on Ps. 26:6: "I wash my hands in innocence," and on Ps. 73:13: "I . . . washed my hands in innocence."

We are informed by Mk. 15:24 (= Mt. 27:35 and Lk. 23:34) that after they had crucified Jesus the soldiers "divided his garments among them, casting lots for them." In Jn. 19:23–24 the situation is elaborated with the addition of a reference to Jesus' tunic, woven without seam. It is for the tunic that the lots are cast according to John, and the equal division of the garments and the casting of lots for the tunic are said to fulfill Ps. 22:18: "They divide my garments among them, and for my raiment they cast lots." In the simpler accounts of Matthew, Mark, and Luke there is a clear reference to Ps. 22:18, and there is an application of the meaning of the whole verse without regard to its poetic parallelism. In John there is a formula-quotation, and the narrative is made to conform to a literal understanding of the two lines of the verse.

We are informed by Mk. 15:29 (= Mt. 27:39; cf. Lk. 23:35–36) that while Jesus was hanging on the cross, "those who passed by derided him, wagging their heads." The account appears to be indebted to Ps. 109:25 for a description of the situation: "I am an object of scorn to my accusers; when they see me, they wag their heads." Psalm 22:7 may also be influential: "All who see me mock at me, . . . they wag their heads," and Ps. 79:4 cannot be overlooked: "We have become a taunt to our neighbors, mocked and derided by those round about us."

At the conclusion of the narrative of the crucifixion, Mk. 15:40 (= Mt. 27:55 and Lk. 23:49) adds that "there were also women looking on from afar." Perhaps the wording has been suggested by Ps. 38:11: "My friends and companions stand aloof from my plague."

Among the taunts hurled at the dying Jesus was the mockery of the chief priests, the scribes, and the elders reported by Mt. 27:43: "He trusts in God; let God deliver him now, if he desires him." The words seem to be a slightly altered version of Ps. 22:8, which is presented as the speech of those who scorn the psalmist: "He committed his cause to the Lord; let him deliver him, . . . for he delights in him!" Thus, the words that are used to mock the psalmist are also used to mock Jesus.

Only in Jn. 20:25 do we learn that in the act of crucifixion the hands of Jesus were pierced by nails. Thomas, who had been absent when Jesus first appeared to the gathered disciples, declared that he would not believe that Jesus had risen from the dead "unless I see in his hands the print of the nails." Indirectly, at least, we have here another of the many correspondences between the N.T. and Ps. 22 because Ps. 22:16 relates: "They have pierced my hands and feet."

Mark 15:36 (= Mt. 27:48 and Lk. 23:36) tells the reader that at a moment when Jesus was suffering acutely, "one ran and, filling a sponge full of vinegar, put it on a reed and gave it to him to drink." According to Jn. 19:29, this was done right after Jesus had admitted his thirst. Behind the reference in all four Gospels stands Ps. 69:21: "For my thirst they gave me vinegar to drink."

According to Jn. 19:33, because the soldiers saw that Jesus was already dead they did not break his legs in order to hasten the end. In Jn. 19:36 it is stated that "these things took place that the scripture might be fulfilled, 'Not a bone of him shall be broken.'" The commandment not to break a bone of the Passover sacrifice occurs in Ex. 12:46 and Num. 9:12, but the Johannine narrative is probably directly related to Ps. 34:20, which speaks of the righteous man under affliction: "He keeps all his bones; not one of them is broken."

Other Narratives

The influence of the Psalter is not confined entirely to narratives about Jesus, although it is of course evident there to an overwhelming degree. For example, in the story of Zechariah, father of John the Baptist, Gabriel, messenger of God, informs Zechariah (Lk. 1:20) that because of his failure to believe that he was to have a son, "you will be silent and unable to speak." Perhaps there is a relationship to Ps. 39:9: "I am dumb, I do not open my mouth; for it is thou who hast done it." In Acts 12:7 the freeing of Peter from prison by an angel is described as consisting of two developments: "A light shone in the cell . . . . And the chains fell off his hands." The two events correspond strikingly with the parallel lines of Ps. 107:14: "He brought them out of darkness and gloom, and broke their bonds asunder."

Psalms and Prophetic Fulfillment

Wherever among the numerous possibilities that we have surveyed there is actual dependence upon Psalms by the Evangelists or their sources, whether they were aware of it or not, there is at least a strong implication that in the events connected with Jesus' life there has been a fulfillment of prophecy. Christian writers and readers alike would have been aware that in these instances what had been written long before in Scripture had come true in Jesus. In some cases the fact of such fulfillment is openly stated; in others it is set forth by significant changes in language.

Matthew, who makes many references in his Gospel to the specific fulfillment of words of the prophets in events of Jesus' life, in Mt. 13:35 quotes Ps. 78:2: "I will open my mouth in a parable; I will utter dark sayings from of old"; and he points out the reason that Jesus used parabolic teaching was "to fulfil what was spoken by the prophet." The Psalms and the Prophets are used by Matthew with equal authority as sources of predictions of Jesus' life. There is one similar instance in Acts 13:32–33, where the sermon of Paul is reported: "What God promised to the fathers, this he has fulfilled to us their children by raising Jesus; as also it is written in the second psalm"; and a quotation of Ps. 2:7 follows.

There are four examples of specific fulfillment of Psalms presented in John. In Jn. 13:18 Jesus states that the betrayal by Judas "is that the scripture may be fulfilled," and he then quotes Ps. 41:9. In Jn. 15:25 Jesus indicates that the hatred of his opponents for him "is to fulfil the word that is written in their law," and then he quotes Ps. 35:19 (= Ps. 69:4). The reference to Psalms here as "law" is also of interest. In Jn. 19:24 the casting of lots by the soldiers for Jesus' tunic is said by the Evangelist to have been "to fulfil the scripture," and then Ps. 22:18 is quoted. Finally, the failure of the soldiers to break the legs of Jesus is declared in Jn. 19:36 to have been "that the scripture might be fulfilled," and then Ps. 34:20 is quoted.

Less direct but no less definite cases of recognized fulfillment of Psalms may be discovered in the N.T. adaptation of quotations. In Ps. 39:12 the psalmist appeals to God: "Hear my prayer, O Lord, and give ear to my cry." The realization of this supplication may be seen in the reference to Jesus in Heb. 5:7: "Jesus offered up prayers and supplications with loud cries . . . , and he was heard."

Another appeal to God may be noted in Ps. 22:21–22: "Save me from the mouth of the lion . . . ! I will tell of thy name to my brethren." In 2 Tim. 4:17 the imperative and the future tense of the psalm have become past events although their order is reversed: "The Lord gave me strength to proclaim the message fully, that all the Gentiles might hear it. So I was rescued from the lion's mouth."

In Ps. 33:3 we find the command: "Sing to him a new song." It is repeated in Ps. 96:1; 98:1; and 149:1. It is found also in Is. 42:10. The command becomes a simple future statement in

Ps. 144:9: "I will sing a new song to thee." In Revelation the fulfillment of the command is stressed 2 times. In Rev. 5:9 it has taken place: "And they sang a new song"; and in Rev. 14:3 it is a present reality: "And they sing a new song."

There is a promise given in Ps. 37:28 (= 94:14): "The Lord . . . will not forsake his saints." As Paul wrestles with the problem of the almost total rejection by the Jews of belief in Jesus as the Christ, he is sure that the promise has been carried out (Rom. 11:2): "God has not rejected his people."

Abraham admits in Gen. 23:4: "I am a stranger and a sojourner." In Lev. 25:23 it is stated: "You are strangers and sojourners with me"; and again in 1 Chron. 29:15 it is written: "We are strangers before thee, and sojourners." So, too, in Ps. 39:12 the same thought is expressed: "I am . . . a sojourner"; and we find it again in Ps. 119:19: "I am a sojourner on earth." This well-attested tradition does not apply to Christians, however; and in Eph. 2:19 they are reminded: "You are no longer strangers and sojourners."

The same contrast between promise and fulfillment is apparent in Ps. 50:23 (= 91:16): "To him who orders his way aright I will show the salvation of God!" The experience of every Christian is to be seen in the corresponding words of Simeon in Lk. 2:30: "Mine eyes have seen thy salvation."

Psalm 79:10 contains a heartfelt cry to God: "Let the avenging of the outpoured blood of thy servants be known"; and the completed action of God is stated in Rev. 19:2: "He has avenged on her the blood of his servants."

Another statement of faith in God's future deeds occurs in Ps. 130:8: "He will redeem Israel from all his iniquities." The direct answer to this firm expectation is provided 2 times in the N.T. At Lk. 1:68 Zechariah, aware of the direct intervention of God in the birth of John the Baptist, proclaims: "The Lord God of Israel . . . has redeemed his people"; and in Tit. 2:14 the statement corresponds even more closely: "Christ . . . gave himself for us to redeem us from all iniquity."

CHRISTIAN DOCTRINE AND PSALMS

The Gospels are written in the context of a belief in the unique relationship between God and Jesus which had been developing in the forty or fifty years of the church's existence. The early expressions of that theology take place in the N.T. epistles, which antedate the writing of the Gospels, and its growth is indicated in all later Christian literature. In their concern for adequate theological statement Christian writers looked to the Psalter, as they did for so many other purposes. One reason why the psalms were so useful for this end was that they represent no unified theological viewpoint but reflect the many varieties of religious faith that existed within Judaism and that were evident also within early Christianity. However, Psalms has much to say about God; and there is a common understanding that he is the exalted Lord, who has made the world and all mankind. He is the ruler of men and of nations, and the starting point of distinctively Jewish theology is the proclamation of the mighty deeds whereby he has formed a people for himself. In many places the Psalter recites, and everywhere it assumes, a somewhat standardized list of the divine acts in history whereby God has chosen to further his aims. In general the pattern followed by Psalms is that of the books of the Law, but in a few details there are variants from the received tradition. Thus, in Ps. 105:39 it is said that God "spread a cloud for a covering" for the Jews in the wilderness, whereas the Pentateuch says nothing of the cloud as a shelter. In 1 Cor. 10:1 the Psalter is followed as Paul writes: "Our fathers were all under the cloud." In Psalms we are given a picture of the absolute goodness and holiness of God, whose demands for moral conduct will be supported by his inescapable judgments. He is the champion of the oppressed and the helpless. He is also seen as One who makes himself available to all who have faith in him. He brings salvation by meeting man's deepest and most vital needs.

THE NATURE OF GOD

For the early Christians the truth of God revealed in Jesus was not unrelated to the O.T. or in any way contrary to it. God's decisive acts were viewed as the realization of his promises that were made long before. Even the newness that Christianity recognized as belonging to it had been foretold in the O.T., which speaks of the coming of "a new covenant" (Jer. 31:31), "a new spirit" (Ezek. 11:19), and "new heavens and a new earth" (Is. 65:17). In Is. 43:18-19 God says: "Remember not the former things . . . . Behold, I am doing a new thing." These predictions were believed to have been fulfilled in Jesus. It is true that the new experience brought forth some fresh interpretations of Scripture that had not hitherto been conceived, but with these new understandings the O.T. became the primary resource by which N.T. authors could express, explain, and support their statements of Christian doctrine. To this end Psalms made its unique contribution as theological references were repeated, expanded, interpreted, and applied in Christian writings.

The personal attributes and characteristics of God are not argued in Psalms or in the N.T.; but they are stated constantly. Thus, in Ps. 86:10, as also in Deuteronomy and Isaiah, it is stated: "Thou alone art God." This strict monotheism is repeated in Mk. 12:32: "He is one, and there is no other but he," and again in 1 Cor. 8:4: "There is no God but one." The declaration of Ps. 90:4, "A thousand years in thy sight are but as yesterday when it is past," is only slightly varied in 2 Pet. 3:8: "With the Lord one day is as a thousand years, and a thousand years as one day." God is seen as exalted and majestic, and Ps. 10:16 (= Ps. 29:10; 93:1; 96:10; 99:1) declares: "The Lord is king for ever and ever." The same thought is set forth in Rev. 11:15: "He shall reign for ever and ever." The psalmist says of God in Ps. 36:6: "Thy judgments are like the great deep." Paul reflects this verse when he writes in Rom.

11:33: "How unsearchable are his judgments." That God brings his judgments to bear on the life of the individual is the thought of Ps. 94:12 (cf. Ps. 118:18): "Blessed is the man whom thou dost chasten, O Lord." Paul clarifies the concept in 1 Cor. 11:32: "When we are judged by the Lord, we are chastened." God's holiness is far removed from man's imperfections, and Ps. 104:2 describes God as one "who coverest thyself with light." Similarly, in 1 Tim. 6:16 God is he "who . . . dwells in unapproachable light." Psalm 34:8 urges: "O taste and see that the Lord is good!" This verse is directly reflected twice in the N.T. In Heb. 6:5 it is written that Christians "have tasted the goodness of the word of God," and in 1 Pet. 2:3 the reader is told: "You have tasted the kindness of the Lord." God is not fooled by external appearance, but in Ps. 7:9 (= Ps. 26:2; 139:23) he is addressed as "thou who triest the minds and hearts," and he speaks in Rev. 2:23: "I am he who searches mind and heart."

The omnipotent and holy God, who is far above man, at the same time is concerned about him. He has special thought for the disadvantaged and the oppressed. According to Ps. 145:14 (= Ps. 146:8; 147:6), "the Lord . . . raises up all who are bowed down." In Lk. 1:52 this divine attribute is the basis of his action: "[The Lord] has exalted those of low degree." In Ps. 68:5 (= Ps. 146:9; cf. also Ex. 22:22; Is. 1:17, 23; and Mal. 3:5), God is portrayed as "Father of the fatherless and protector of widows," and Jas. 1:27 characterizes pure religion as "to visit orphans and widows in their affliction," in obvious imitation of God. God cares what happens to men and observes what they are doing. We are told in Ps. 11:4 (= Ps. 14:2; 33:13) that the "eyes [of the Lord] behold . . . the children of men"; and for Heb. 4:13 this fact creates our solemn responsibility: "Before him no creature is hidden, but all are open and laid bare to the eyes of him with whom we have to do." In fact, God's observation has personal meaning. Psalm 40:17 (= Ps. 56:9; 118:6) affirms: "The Lord takes thought for me"; and 1 Pet. 5:7 tells the reader: "He cares about you." It is simply stated in Ps. 34:18 (= Ps. 119:151; 145:18) that "the Lord is near"; and in Acts 17:27 the statement is repeated, though in the literary form of litotes: "[God] is not far from each one of us." The experience of the believer is stated in Ps. 18:28 (= Ps. 118:27): "The Lord lightens my darkness"; and in 1 Pet. 2:9 God is presented as he "who called you out of darkness into his marvelous light."

God, who created man and knows every human action, is also Lord of nature. He is the author of all creation. Five times in the Psalter (Ps. 115:15; 121:2; 124:8; 134:3; and 146:6) he is represented as "the Lord, who made heaven and earth." Exactly the same words are used of him in Acts 4:24; 14:15; Rev. 10:6; 14:7. In Ps. 74:16 it is declared: "Thou hast established the luminaries and the sun"; and in Jas. 1:17 God is pictured as "the Father of lights." Moreover, God's work of creation in the past results in his present dominion. The assertion of Ps. 24:1 (= Ps. 50:12; 89:11) that "the earth is the Lord's and the fulness thereof" is quoted by Paul in 1 Cor. 10:26. God cares for nature even as he cares for men. Psalm 147:8 (= Job 5:10) states: "He prepares rain for the earth"; and in Acts 14:17 it is said again: "He gave you from heaven rains and fruitful seasons." Psalm 147:9 (= Job 38:41) adds that "he gives . . . food . . . to the young ravens"; and Jesus agrees in Lk. 12:24: "Consider the ravens: . . . God feeds them."

The Nature of Man

When man is looked upon objectively and freely, he is seen to be of little value in himself. It is written in Ps. 39:11 that "every man is a mere breath," and the identical view is set forth also in Ps. 78:39; 102:3; and 144:4 and also Job 7:7. The same assessment is present in Jas. 4:14: "You are a mist that appears for a little time and then vanishes." Further, it is said in Ps. 94:11 that "the Lord, knows the thoughts of man, that they are but a breath"; and a class-one quotation of the verse appears in 1 Cor. 3:20. The same appraisal is given in Ps. 90:5–6 (= Ps. 102:11; 103:15). "[Men] are like grass . . . : in the morning it flourishes . . . ; in the evening it fades and withers." James 1:10 says of man: "Like the flower of the grass he will pass away." Not only is man weak; he is also thoroughly sinful. The five passages from the Psalter that Paul quotes, along with Is. 59:7–8, in Rom. 3:10–18 are intended to support his claim (Rom. 3:9) that "all men, both Jews and Greeks, are under the power of sin." Typical of these verses is Ps. 14:1, 3 (= Ps. 53:1, 3): "There is none that does good. . . . They have all gone astray, they are all alike corrupt." This realistic approach underlies the psalmist's question in Ps. 8:4 (= Ps. 144:3 and Job 7:17): "What is man that thou are mindful of him, and the son of man that thou dost care for him?" The question is quoted in Heb. 2:6.

God's Salvation

Although man does not deserve any consideration, God offers him the chance to be freed from his disabilities. According to Ps. 3:8, "Deliverance belongs to the Lord"; and the words are only slightly changed in Rev. 7:10: "Salvation belongs to our God." In Ps. 35:9 it is said in faith: "My soul shall rejoice in the Lord, exulting in his deliverance," whereas in Lk. 1:47 salvation is a present experience: "My spirit rejoices in God my Savior." In Ps. 130:7 it is affirmed of God: "With him is plenteous redemption," and in Eph. 1:7 the words are transferred to Christ, "in him we have redemption."

Moreover, God's salvation is intended for all people and thus requires a mission of the Jews to the Gentiles. Psalm 18:49, "For this I will extol thee, O Lord, among the nations," is quoted in Rom. 15:9. Psalm 19:4, "Their voice goes out through all the earth," is cited in Rom. 10:18. The prediction of Ps. 86:9, "All the nations thou hast made shall come and bow down before thee, O Lord," is reproduced in Rev. 15:4: "All nations shall come and worship thee." The substance of

Ps. 98:2, "He has revealed his vindication in the sight of the nations," is found in Lk. 2:30–31: "Mine eyes have seen thy salvation which thou hast prepared in the presence of all peoples." The command of Ps. 117:1, "Praise the Lord, all nations!" is given in a formula-quotation in Rom. 15:11.

God accomplishes his salvation through the people whom he has selected. Psalm 135:4 (= Ex. 19:5 and Deut. 7:6) states: "The Lord has chosen Jacob for himself, Israel as his own possession." But the tragedy of the Jews' rejection of Jesus is stated in Jn. 1:11: "His own people received him not." Thus, the early Christians saw themselves, rather than the Jews, as constituting henceforth God's chosen people. According to Tit. 2:14, it was the work of Jesus Christ "to purify for himself a people of his own," and 1 Pet. 2:9 says to the Christian readers: "You are a chosen race, . . . God's own people."

The N.T. agrees with Psalms that God was active in the events of Jewish history. Thus, it is asserted in Ps. 44:2 (= Ps. 78:55; 80:8; Josh. 23:9; 24:18), "Thou with thy own hand didst drive out the nations"; and in Acts 7:45 Stephen relates that the Jews "dispossessed the nations which God thrust out before our fathers." The crossing of the Red Sea, which is recorded in Ex. 14:22, 29, is reviewed in Ps. 66:6, where it is said: "[God] turned the sea into dry land; men passed through the river on foot." The statement is echoed in 1 Cor. 10:1 and Heb. 11:29. God's continuing activity is chronicled in Ps. 78: 15–16: "He cleft rocks in the wilderness, and gave them drink abundantly as from the deep. He made streams come out of the rock." Paul recognizes the hand of God in these events as he writes of the Jews in 1 Cor. 10:4: "They drank from the supernatural Rock which followed them." The account continues in Ps. 78:24–25: "He rained down . . . manna to eat, and gave them the grain of heaven. Man ate of the bread of the angels." God's role is stressed in Jn. 6:31: "He gave them bread from heaven to eat," and it is echoed in 1 Cor. 10:3: "All ate the same supernatural food." The rebellion in the wilderness is recounted in Ps. 78:31: "The anger of God rose against them and he slew the strongest of them, and laid low the picked men of Israel"; and a summary is given in 1 Cor. 10:5: "With most of them God was not pleased; for they were overthrown in the wilderness." God speaks of his involvement in Jewish history in Ps. 89:20: "I have found David, my servant; with my holy oil I have anointed him." The story is told in the same way in Acts 13:22, though with the order of the two parts reversed: "He raised up David to be their king; . . . and said, 'I have found in David . . . a man . . . who will do all my will.'"

THE PERSON OF JESUS

Writers of the N.T. are anxious to further the understanding of their readers as to the person and nature of Jesus, and psalms are utilized to assist in this goal, just as they had furnished material for contemporary Jewish Messianic speculation. It is of interest that in Hebrews all the many quotations from the Psalter are used for Christological purposes. Correspondences include quotations, references, and allusions.

The declaration of Ps. 8:6, "Thou hast put all things under his feet," is made regarding God's gracious treatment of man; but in 1 Cor. 15:27 the verse is quoted with an introductory formula and applied to Jesus. It is a statement of God's action in Christ in Eph. 1:22. The righteous man affirms in Ps. 16:10: "Thou dost not give me up to Sheol, or let thy godly one see the Pit." The words are quoted in Acts 2:27 and 13:35, and referred to in Acts 2:31, as the prediction of David regarding Jesus. The beatitude of Ps. 32:2, "Blessed is the man to whom the Lord imputes no iniquity, and in whose spirit there is no deceit," has become a description of Jesus in 1 Pet. 2:22: "He committed no sin; no guile was found on his lips." In Rom. 15:3 Paul quotes Ps. 69:9: "The insults of those who insult thee have fallen on me"; and he concludes that since this happened to Jesus he did not please himself but God. God speaks of an idealized David in Ps. 89:27 and promises: "I will make him the first-born, the highest of the kings of the earth." Correspondingly, Christ is spoken of in Rom. 8:29 as "the first-born among many brethren," in Col. 1:15 as "the first-born of all creation," and in Col. 1:18 as "the first-born from the dead." In Rev. 1:5 both the original statement and its Christian development are applied, in reverse order, to Jesus Christ who is "the first-born of the dead, and the ruler of kings on earth." The solemn pronouncement of Ps. 110:4, "You are a priest for ever after the order of Melchizedek," is interpreted by the author of Hebrews as addressed to Jesus and so used as the basis for the special Christology of that epistle. Psalm 118:22, "The stone which the builders rejected has become the head of the corner," has been very influential on the N.T. It appears as a class-one quotation in Mk. 12:10 (= Mt. 21:42 and Lk. 20:17). It is cited and applied to Jesus by Peter in Acts 4:11. It is referred to in connection with Jesus in Eph. 2:20, and it is quoted again in 1 Pet. 2:7. It was obviously believed to be a prediction of the rejection of Jesus by the Jews and his exaltation as head of the church. Finally, in Ps. 132:11 it is reported: "The Lord swore to David a sure oath . . . : 'One of the sons of your body I will set on your throne'"; and in Peter's sermon at Pentecost the verse is cited (Acts 2:30): "God had sworn with an oath to him that he would set one of his descendants upon his throne." Jesus is identified as that son of David.

In spite of the manifestations of God's grace, reaching a climax in the redemptive work of Christ, man dare not presume upon the goodness of God because he is also just and will judge all men. It is declared 3 times in the Psalter (Ps. 9:8; 96:13; and 98:9) that "he judges the world with righteousness," and the N.T. agrees. In Acts 17:31 Paul declares in his Athens sermon that God "will judge the world in righteousness" by the agency of Jesus Christ, and in Rev. 19:11 it is declared of God: "In righteousness he judges." The nature of God's judgment is stated in Ps. 62:12 (= Ps. 28:4; Prov. 24:12; Jer. 17:10; 25:14; and 32:19): "Thou dost requite a man according to his work." The N.T. sees that the principle is true

whether God judges by himself or whether Christ acts on his
behalf. Jesus asserts in Mt. 16:27: "The Son of man . . . will
repay every man for what he has done," and Paul writes in
Rom. 2:6 (= 1 Cor. 3:8) that God "will render to every man
according to his works." He speaks of the judging of Christ in
2 Cor. 5:10: "We must all appear before the judgment seat of
Christ, so that each one may receive good or evil, according to
what he has done in the body." This rule of just compensation
appears also in 1 Pet. 1:17; Rev. 2:23; 20:12–13; and 22:12.
Psalm 76:7 (= Nahum 1:6 and Mal. 3:2) asks: "Who can
stand before thee when once thy anger is roused?" The thought
is retained in Rev. 6:17: "The great day of their wrath has
come, and who can stand before it?" Psalm 110:5 (= Zeph.
1:18; 2:3) speaks of "the day of his wrath," and Paul uses the
same phrase in Rom. 2:5. God's forgiveness and God's justice
are equally emphasized in the Psalms; and the N.T., using the
Psalter, also finds place for both even though they may seem
logically incompatible.

Christian Ethical Teaching

The early church proclaimed the *kerygma,* the core of theological truth that was formulated as a series of propositions
regarding God, Jesus, and man. The Psalter provided much of
the Scriptural material used in this proclamation. Psalms were
drawn upon heavily, too, for the church's instruction in moral
and ethical behavior, the *didache.*

The command of Ps. 4:4, "Be angry, but sin not," is quoted
exactly in Eph. 4:26. The righteous man is defined in Ps. 24:4
as "he who has clean hands and a pure heart," and in Jas. 4:8
the definition has become two commands: "Cleanse your
hands, . . . and purify your hearts." A statement of the action
of faith in Ps. 26:1, "I have trusted in the Lord without wavering," has been transformed into an exhortation in Heb. 10:23:
"Let us hold fast the confession of our hope without wavering."
The injunction of Ps. 31:24 (= Josh. 1:6, 7, 9, 18; 1 Chron.

22:13; and 28:20), "Be strong, and let your heart take courage," reappears in reverse order in 1 Cor. 16:13: "Be courageous, be strong." In Ps. 34:2 it is asserted: "My soul makes its boast in the Lord"; and in 2 Cor. 10:17 Paul changes the form of the verse to make it into a command: "Let him who boasts, boast of the Lord." The imperative of Ps. 34:13, "Keep your tongue from evil, and your lips from speaking deceit," has become a very brief reference in Jas. 3:8: "The tongue—a restless evil." The double injunction of Ps. 34:14, "Seek peace, and pursue it," is slightly altered by Paul in Rom. 14:19: "Let us then pursue what makes for peace," and is abbreviated in Heb. 12:14: "Strive for peace." Psalm 49:17 (= Job 1:21) makes a comment on the man who has become rich: "When he dies he will carry nothing away"; and the observation is made again in 1 Tim. 6:7: "We brought nothing into the world, and we cannot take anything out of the world." The injunction of Ps. 55:22, "Cast your burden on the Lord," is cited in 1 Pet. 5:7: "Cast all your anxieties on him." The command of Ps. 62:10, "If riches increase, set not your heart on them," is reiterated in 1 Tim. 6:17: "As for the rich in this world, charge them not to . . . set their hopes on uncertain riches." The simple assertion of Ps. 97:10 (cf. Amos 5:15), "The Lord loves those who hate evil," stands behind Paul's double command in Rom. 12:9: "Hate what is evil, hold fast to what is good."

SOME PROVERBS

The Psalter is basically a hymnbook, but it contains a wide variety of literary forms and at times it closely resembles the Wisdom literature of the Jews. It includes a number of proverbs and practical observations on the workings of the world. Even in this area the N.T. manifests dependence on Psalms.

In Ps. 1:3 there is reference to "a tree . . . that yields its fruit in its season," and in Mt. 21:41 we find mention of "the fruits in their seasons." In Ps. 12:3 there is an allusion to "the tongue that makes great boasts," while Jas. 3:5 observes: "The tongue . . . boasts of great things." Psalm 32:9 tells of a horse "which must be curbed with bit," and Jas. 3:3 argues: "If we put bits into the mouths of horses . . . ." The course of nature is discussed in Ps. 90:5–6: "Grass . . . in the morning . . . flourishes . . . ; in the evening it fades and withers." Jesus cites this section in Mt. 6:30, when he says: "The grass of the field . . . today is alive and tomorrow is thrown into the oven." The words of Ps. 83:14, "As fire consumes the forest," are reflected in Jas. 3:5: "How great a forest is set ablaze by a small fire!"

The Psalter contributed to the early Christians' theological formulations and ethical principles and even practical observations. In addition, it furnished hymns of penitence, praise, and thanksgiving for the worship of the church, brief phrases and sentences that could be quickly learned and meaningfully repeated by Christian worshipers, and probably some suggestions as to how worship might be conducted.

PSALMS AND CHRISTIAN WORSHIP

One of the dominant moods of the Psalter is exultation, and the injunction of Ps. 33:1 is thoroughly representative: "Rejoice in the Lord." Precisely the same words are used by Paul in Phil. 3:1 and 4:4; and the claim of Lk. 1:47, "My spirit rejoices in God," is similar. In Ps. 118:24 the suggestion is made: "Let us rejoice and be glad"; and it is repeated in Rev. 19:7: "Let us rejoice and exult." Psalm 33:2 (= Ps. 27:6; 147:7) orders the worshiper to "make melody to [the Lord]," and the identical action is described in Eph. 5:19. An exclamation of praise, which was undoubtedly employed often in Jewish services, appears 3 times in the Psalter (Ps. 41:13; 72:18; 106:48): "Blessed be the Lord, the God of Israel"; and it forms the opening of the hymn of Zechariah in Lk. 1:68: "Blessed be the Lord God of Israel." The worshipers are exhorted in Ps. 134:1: "Come, bless the Lord, all you servants of the Lord"; and there are variant expressions in Ps. 135:1: "Praise the Lord, . . . O servants of the Lord," and Ps. 135:20: "You that fear the Lord, bless the Lord!" The command is renewed in Rev. 19:5 as a message from the heavenly throne, but the form is a combination of elements from all three verses in the Psalms: "Praise our God, all you his servants, you who fear him." In its corporate praise of God, as well as in the private devotional life of its members, the Psalter is a treasured part of the heritage of the church.

New Testament Passages Illuminated

Because the Psalter is an expression of diverse types of Jewish experience under varied circumstances and over a period of centuries, it affords insights into the life of the people that illuminate some N.T. passages by means of casual references to common customs. Thus, in Acts 3:1 "the hour of prayer, the ninth hour" is spoken of; and in Acts 10:9 it is said that "Peter went up on the housetop to pray, about the sixth hour." There is further reference to the ninth hour of prayer in Acts 10:30. That the hours of prayer were a regular part of Jewish religious life is evident from many verses in the Psalter. The psalmist reveals in Ps. 119:147: "I rise before dawn and cry for help"; and he cries in Ps. 5:3 (= Ps. 88:13): "In the morning thou dost hear my voice." He adds in Ps. 92:2 that it is good "to declare thy steadfast love in the morning, and thy faithfulness by night." In Ps. 141:2 he asks that the lifting up of his hands may be accepted as an evening sacrifice. The comprehensive statement of Ps. 55:17 may suggest the course of the Jewish day, which began at sunset: "Evening and morning and at noon I utter my complaint." We are told in 1 Tim. 2:8 that "men should pray, lifting holy hands"; and that posture is described in Ps. 28:2: "As I cry to thee for help, as I lift up my hands," and also in Ps. 63:4: "I will lift up my hands and call on thy name." 1 Corinthians 14:16 indicates that "Amen" was said at the close of corporate prayer by all the worshipers in the church at Corinth. In the book of Revelation (Rev. 19:4) it is stated that the symbolic twenty-four elders and the four living creatures say "Amen" in the course of their heavenly worship. In Ps. 106:48, just after the liturgical cry, "Blessed be the Lord, the God of Israel," and just before the liturgical command, "Praise the Lord"—in other words, in the context of worship—we find the order, "And let all the people say, 'Amen!' " The "Amen" of the Christian church is the "Amen" of Jewish liturgy, and psalms provide the line of continuity.

The extent of the dependence of the N.T. on Psalms is to be observed not only in major categories of fulfillment, doctrine, ethics, and worship but also in the relatively secondary areas of imagery and imitation. Psalms have become so much a part of the thinking of the N.T. authors that their language is employed in Christian composition even when the borrowing is entirely unconscious. At other times the Psalter contributes word pictures or statements of generally accepted religious or theological truth. It is significant that psalms are invoked not just for primary and recognizable purposes but also for reasons that often cannot be defined. The material of Psalms is a familiar and available starting point for much Christian thought and writing.

According to Ps. 1:2 (= Ps. 119:14, 16, 24, 47, 70, 92, 143, 174), the righteous man is blessed and "his delight is in the law of the Lord." Paul applies the assertion to himself in Rom. 7:22, when he says that in his inmost self "I delight in the law of God." Many of Paul's declarations are directly related to verses in Psalms. In 1 Cor. 3:17 he writes that "God's temple is holy," and he may have in mind Ps. 11:4, "The Lord is in his holy temple," or Ps. 138:2, "I bow down toward thy holy temple." In Rom. 6:14 Paul states that when God's salvation provided in Christ is accepted in faith, "sin will have no dominion over you." The language, at least, is derived from Ps. 19:13: "Keep back thy servant also from presumptuous sins; let them not have dominion over me!" The same prayer is found in Ps. 119:133: "Let no iniquity get dominion over me." Paul believes that the answer to the anguished prayer of the psalmist is found in Christ. In Rom. 11:33 Paul writes regarding God: "How unsearchable are his judgments"; and the source of the statement may be Ps. 36:6: "Thy judgments are like the great deep." In 2 Cor. 4:9 Paul, with special reference to himself, characterizes the sufferings of all those who are faithful to Christ and states that they are "struck down, but not destroyed." The thought is also that of Ps. 37:24, where it is said of the man who trusts in God: "though he fall, he shall not be cast headlong." In Rom. 2:21 Paul criticizes the typical prideful Jew by asking: "While you preach against stealing, do you steal? You who say that one must not commit adultery, do you commit adultery?" Although Paul mentions two of the Ten Commandments of Ex., ch. 20, and Deut., ch. 5, the reversing of their order suggests that he has been influenced primarily by Ps. 50:18: "If you see a thief, you are a friend of his; and you keep company with adulterers." In Rom. 3:19 Paul, who is convinced that under the law all men are guilty, asserts that the goal of the law is "that every mouth may be stopped." Probably, he is recalling the prediction of Ps. 63:11 that "the mouths of liars will be stopped." In his condemnation of the pagan world Paul charges (Rom. 1:23) that men "exchanged the glory of the immortal God for images," and he is citing Ps. 106:20: "They exchanged the glory of God for the image." In 1 Cor. 10:20 Paul remarks that "what pagans sacrifice they offer to demons," and he may be remembering the words of Ps. 106:37 (cf. also Deut. 32:17): "They sacrificed . . . to the demons." In 1 Thess. 3:9 Paul asks: "What thanksgiving can we render to God . . . ?" This is the same question raised in Ps. 116:12: "What shall I render to the Lord for all his bounty to me?" Paul's indebtedness to the Psalter is apparent everywhere and in all degrees from formula-quotation to casual allusion.

Two further instances of this type of borrowing from the Psalter are found in words attributed to Paul in Acts. In Acts 13:11 Paul declares to Elymas the magician: "The hand of the Lord is upon you, and you shall be blind." The idea of Ps. 32:4 is very closely related: "Thy hand was heavy upon me." Moreover, the connection between God's hand and man's adversity is made again in Ps. 38:2; and 39:10 (cf. Ex. 9:3; 1 Sam. 5:6–7; and Job 19:21). In Acts 22:16 Paul reports Ananias' order to him: "Wash away your sins"; it may be a recollection of Ps. 51:2: "Wash me thoroughly from my iniquity, and cleanse me from my sin!" but this borrowing has forgotten the poetic parallelism and has retained only the beginning and the end.

The author of Hebrews believes that material sacrifices no longer have any place because of the completely efficacious self-offering of Christ, and he therefore proposes in Heb. 13:15: "Let us continually offer up a sacrifice of praise to God." The concept of gratitude as a proper offering to God is expressed at least 5 times in the Psalter. The command is given in Ps. 50:14: "Offer to God a sacrifice of thanksgiving"; the identical thought is found also in Ps. 50:23; 107:22; 116:17; and 119:108.

In Jas. 3:8 the human tongue is characterized as "full of deadly poison," and there seems to be a clear reference to Ps. 140:3, where it is said that evil men "make their tongue sharp as a serpent's, and under their lips is the poison of vipers." Again the poetic form is dropped, and the "tongue" of the first line is joined directly to the "poison" of the second.

1 Peter 1:17, with obvious recollection of the address of the Lord's Prayer (Mt. 6:9 = Lk. 11:2), declares, "If you invoke as Father him who . . . ," while it is written of God's servant in Ps. 89:26 (cf. Jer. 3:19) that "he shall cry to me, 'Thou art my Father.'" In 2 Pet. 2:9 it is stated that "the Lord knows how to rescue the godly from trial," and the thought is not far removed from that of Ps. 37:33, where it is stated of the righteous man: "The Lord will not . . . let him be condemned when he is brought to trial."

THE DEBT OF THE BOOK OF REVELATION

Revelation is more in debt to the O.T. than any other N.T. writing even though it contains no class-one quotations. As an apocalyptic composition it has naturally borrowed heavily from eschatological sections of Isaiah and Ezekiel and from Daniel and Zechariah. More surprising, however, is the intensity of its use of Psalms, which is reflected throughout and in almost limitless ways.

Some of the assertions made in Revelation have their origin in the Psalter. God's decrees are the subject in Rev. 16:7: "True and just are thy judgments!" and in Rev. 19:2: "His judgments are true and just." The borrowing is from Ps. 19:9: "The ordinances of the Lord are true, and righteous"; and there are parallels in Ps. 119:75, 137, 142. Similar in nature is the chant of praise in Rev. 15:3: "Great . . . are thy deeds, O Lord"; and the basis of the song is seen in Ps. 92:5 (= Ps. 111:2): "How great are thy works, O Lord!" In Rev. 11:18 (= Rev. 19:5) there is a reference to "those who fear thy name, both small and great," and the author is citing Ps. 115:13: "Those who fear the Lord, both small and great."

Even more influential on Revelation are the word pictures that are presented in the Psalter, for the most part in an incidental manner. The author of Revelation desires to employ as many images as possible in order to express his own vivid imagination and to stimulate that of his readers, and he finds suitable for his purpose a large number of passages from Psalms.

A representative instance of this type of borrowing is the declaration of Rev. 14:1 that "on Mount Zion stood the Lamb." It is a reenactment of Ps. 2:6: "I have set my king on Zion." So, too, in Rev. 22:4 we are told that the faithful "shall see his face," and the picture is drawn from Ps. 11:7 (cf. Ps. 17:15; 42:2): "The upright shall behold his face." In Rev. 14:14 we are given the vision of a heavenly being "with a golden crown on his head," while in Ps. 21:3 the king approved by God is wearing "a crown of fine gold upon his head." The description of the glorious future awaiting all who have been faithful to Christ includes the statement in Rev. 7:17 that "the Lamb . . . will be their shepherd, and he will guide them to springs of living water." There is here a clear reflection of the familiar words of Ps. 23:1–2: "The Lord is my shepherd . . . . He leads me beside still waters." In the extended and moving account of the heavenly Jerusalem that is given in Rev., chs. 21 and 22, we are told about "the river of the water of life . . . , flowing from the throne of God . . . through the middle of the street of the city." This graphic description seems to be an elaboration of Ps. 46:4: "There is a river whose streams make glad the city of God." Another heavenly vision reveals in Rev. 4:2 that "a throne stood in heaven, with one seated on the throne!" The declaration is repeated in Rev. 4:9, 10; 5:1, 7, 13; 6:16; 7:10, 15; 19:4; and 21:5. The essence of the scene is presented in Ps. 47:8 (= Is. 6:1): "God sits on his holy throne."

In Rev. 16:1 the seven angels are instructed, as if they were dealing with some form of liquid: "Pour out on the earth . . . the wrath of God." The idea is present in the prayer of Ps. 69:24 that God should act against evil men: "Pour out thy indignation upon them." It is found again in Ps. 79:6 (cf. Jer. 10:25; Ezek. 22:31; and Zeph. 3:8). In Rev. 3:5 the promise of the exalted Christ is given to him who remains constant in his allegiance: "I will not blot his name out of the book of life." The picture of names written in a heavenly book is drawn also in Rev. 13:8; 17:8; 20:12, 15; and 21:27. Furthermore, Heb. 12:23 tells about "the first-born who are enrolled in heaven." Although Moses cries out to God in Ex. 32:32, "Blot me . . . out of thy book," the author of Revelation is drawing upon Ps. 69:28: "Let them be blotted out of the book of the living; let them not be enrolled among the righteous." While recounting disasters which must take place on earth before the Day of the Lord, Rev. 16:4 (cf. Rev. 8:9; 11:6) relates: "The rivers . . . became blood." The ultimate source is of course the narration of Ex. 7:17, 19, but the literary relationship is with Ps. 78:44: "He turned their rivers to blood." In Rev. 21:23 it is stated that in the heavenly Jerusalem there will be no need of any outside illumination because "the glory of God is its light," and in Ps. 84:11 we are informed that "the Lord God is a sun." In Rev. 11:5 we read that "fire . . . consumes their foes," while Ps. 97:3 says about God, that "fire . . . burns up his adversaries."

Revelation 9:20 speaks scornfully of those who still rely on "the works of their hands . . . idols of gold and silver and bronze and stone and wood, which cannot either see or hear or walk." Dependence on Ps. 115:4–7 (cf. also Ps. 135:15–17; Deut. 4:28; Is. 2:20; Dan. 5:4, 23) is evident: "Their idols are silver and gold, the work of men's hands. They have mouths but do not speak; eyes, but do not see. They have ears, but do not hear; . . . feet, but do not walk." In Rev. 5:8 incense is equated with the prayers of the saints, and in Rev. 8:3–4 incense and the prayers of the saints are mingled and rise together before God. The origin of the figure appears to be Ps. 141:2: "Let my prayer be counted as incense before thee." According to Rev. 7:16, the faithful Christians will be kept safe in God's presence and "the sun shall not strike them." It is promised in Ps. 121:6 to him who trusts only in God: "The sun shall not smite you."

PSALMS AS CHRISTIAN WRITING

In the numerous class-one quotations of Psalms in the N.T. the Psalter is invoked because the Christian authors believe that it is the authoritative word of God. This is true also in the case of many of the class-two quotations that have no introductory formula because their source is so well known by the readers that they need none to identify them. Other quotations in class two and all the quotations in class three, which includes references and allusions, may be utilized because of their recognized authority or simply because they were part of the religious furnishings of the minds of the N.T. writers. In any case the authority is not tied to the pronouncements of an official assembly (for Psalms was not yet technically a part of Scripture) or conceived of in a fixed, literal, or mechanical sense. No reluctance is felt to make alterations in the wording so as to conform more closely to the situations that have called for the quotations in the first place. Furthermore, some psalms had been in use for centuries before the time of Jesus, and

the Psalter was in form the product of a long evolution and
always changing in understanding and meaning. Most of the
Psalter is timeless in that it relates not to moments of past
history but to that human experience which seems essentially
the same in all generations. That is why the present tense is
much more characteristic of the Psalter than the past tense.
The psalms suggest that they speak to every time and place.
The authority of Psalms is in the end conferred not by eccle-
siastical decision but by the testimony of successive ages of
man that they do in fact convey the word of God to human
need.

The N.T. use of Psalms is a part of this process. Christian authors are certain that the true meaning of the Psalter is understandable for the first time now that Christ has come, and they
therefore utilize the psalms with complete freedom and creativity and apply them to the new situation brought about by
the coming of Jesus. The psalmist offers the general truth in
Ps. 18:28: "The Lord my God lightens my darkness"; but 1
Pet. 2:9 speaks specifically to Christians and says that God
"called *you* out of darkness into his marvelous light." The command is universal in Ps. 34:8: "O taste and see that the Lord is
good!" but it is altered in form and applied to the followers of
Jesus in Heb. 6:5, those who have "tasted the goodness of the
word of God," and also in 1 Pet. 2:3: "*You* have tasted the
kindness of the Lord." Those who are faithful to God are
described in Ps. 44:22: "For thy sake we are slain all the day
long, and accounted as sheep for the slaughter"; but as Paul
makes a class-one quotation of the verse in Rom. 8:36, it is
held to pertain to Christians. The psalmist affirms in Ps. 56:9
(= Ps. 118:6): "God is for me"; but Paul uses the verse to relate to his fellow believers, in Rom. 8:31, when he says: "If
God is for us." The prayer of Ps. 79:10 (cf. Deut. 32:43 and 2
Kings 9:7), "Let the avenging of the outpoured blood of thy
servants be known among the nations," becomes a statement
of specifically Christian confidence in Rev. 6:10: "Thou wilt
judge and avenge our blood on those who dwell upon the

earth." Finally, we must consider Ps. 95:7: "O that today you would hearken to his voice!" The reader is exhorted not to harden his heart against God as was done in the rebellion of the Jews in the wilderness but to receive God openly and humbly. Although the events of the wandering reviewed in Ps. 95:8–11 are tied to a particular period of the past, the "today" of the exhortation is timeless. The author of Hebrews makes much of this fact but applies it exclusively to the new age of Christ. After a class-one quotation of Ps. 95:7 in Heb. 3:7, he discusses it further in Heb. 3:13 and cites it again in Heb. 3:15 and 4:7. His Christian readers are strenuously urged to accept once and for all the revelation of God in Jesus Christ, and he adds significantly in Heb. 4:12: "The word of God is living and active." For Christians the Psalter is the instrument of the God who has brought salvation to all in Jesus Christ.

Epilogue

The preceding study of relationships between the two Testaments has been necessarily complicated in order that we might deal with factual evidence rather than with generalizations. No attempt has been made to be exhaustive in the survey, and many examples remain untreated. However, there has been the intent to be comprehensive and to determine the main principles of N.T. usage of Scripture. It is hoped that these procedures have been thoroughly illustrated by proposed instances. Some of the suggested correspondences will undoubtedly seem questionable, and the possibility that others may be only coincidental must be admitted. Nevertheless, the vast majority of the cases considered demonstrate forcibly the many ways in which the N.T. is dependent upon the O.T. From the review now completed four conclusions emerge.

The Meaning of the Whole Bible

In the first place, early Christian authors believed that the O.T. possessed a unique authority as God's written word. Although they reveal in their writings an awareness of other literature, both Jewish and Greek, they very rarely make any use of it. At the most there are in the N.T. only four quotations from Greek authors, and virtually all the N.T. parallels with extracanonical Jewish writings can be explained as arising from a common dependence on an O.T. source. On the other hand, the high degree to which the O.T. is invoked and the variety of ends to which it is put are most impressive. As the N.T. writers were proclaiming the gospel in their writings, they were sure that only the O.T. was a fit literary tool for their own high calling because both were from God.

Secondly, we are forced to admit that the manner in which the O.T. is used grows out of the conviction that it is in itself incomplete just because it is preparatory to something higher and is predictive of its own fulfillment in Christ. Wherever the O.T. is utilized, it is made to fit into the Christian perspective. Thus, entirely fresh meanings are given to Scriptural texts that Jewish tradition had understood in other ways. In a very real sense it can be said that the O.T. has become a Christian book and that its Jewish origins and nature are often forgotten. It sometimes appears that it has become subservient to Christian goals.

Thirdly, by such an examination of the parallels between the Testaments as has been presented we are enabled to discover the true nature of the Bible as the vehicle of God's truth for all ages. That the N.T. writers often find new meanings in O.T. verses is a reminder of the fact that even within the O.T. later portions sometimes provide a reassessment of earlier sections. It is of the essence of Scripture to put forward God's truth so that its meaning will be understood with increasing clarity and with relevance for all human situations even though they may be forever changing. The historicocritical study of Biblical literature, which is concerned with all the circumstances of the original composition, is only a beginning. The task of interpretation and application is never finished. Thus, the manner in which the N.T. draws upon the O.T. is true to the nature of Scripture. The interrelationship of the two Testaments is an expression of the continuity of God's revelation and the strongest testimony to the true unity of the Bible.

The Uniqueness of Christianity

Finally, we are brought to a consideration of the uniqueness of Christianity. The multitudinous instances in which N.T. writers have appropriated O.T. verses, most of the time without any formal acknowledgment of their indebtedness, point to the fact that Christian origins lie deeply embedded in Judaism. It is unthinkable that the Christian Bible should not contain the O.T. Yet Christianity is distinct from Judaism, and the Testaments are distinguished in Christian terminology by the judgmental adjectives "Old" and "New." Part of the distinctiveness of Christianity is centered in the principles by which N.T. authors chose not to cite some parts of the O.T. while deciding to make use of others. Most of all, however, the N.T. emphasizes, both openly and implicitly, the fact that in Jesus Christ all parts of the O.T. have been fulfilled. The uniqueness of Christianity is found not in the proclamation of completely new truth but in the full revelation of that truth which is imperfectly perceived in the O.T.

Tables

TABLE 1

N.T. FULFILLMENT OF THE O.T.

Reference	Quotation
1. Deut: 15:4	There will be no poor among you.
Acts 4:34	*There was not a needy person among them.*
2. Is. 11:2	And the Spirit of the Lord shall rest upon him.
Mt. 3:16	*He saw the Spirit of God descending . . . and alighting on him.*
3. Is. 42:16	I will turn the darkness before them into light.
Eph. 5:8	*Once you were darkness, but now you are light.*
4. Is. 52:3	You shall be redeemed without money.
1 Pet. 1:18	*You were ransomed . . . , not with perishable things such as silver or gold.*
5. Is. 61:6	You shall be called the priests of the Lord.
Rev. 1:6	*. . . who . . . made us . . . priests to his God.*
Rev. 5:10	*Thou . . . hast made them . . . priests to our God.*
6. Ezek. 36:26–27	A new spirit I will put within you.
Joel 2:28	It shall come to pass afterward, that I will pour out my spirit on all flesh.
Tit. 3:5–6	*. . . by the . . . renewal in the Holy Spirit, which he poured out upon us richly.*
7. Hos. 2:23	I will say to Not my people, "You are my people."
1 Pet. 2:10	*Once you were no people, but now you are God's people.*
8. Zech. 2:11	I will dwell in the midst of you.
Jn. 1:14	*The Word . . . dwelt among us.*
Rev. 21:3	*The dwelling of God is with men.*

TABLE 2

APPARENT N.T. CONTRADICTIONS OF THE O.T.

Reference	Quotation
1. Ex. 23:7	I will not acquit the wicked.
Prov. 17:15	He who justifies the wicked [is] . . . an abomination to the Lord.

TABLE 2—*Continued*

Reference	*Quotation*
Rom. 4:5	. . . *trusts him who justifies the ungodly.*

2. 2 Sam. 5:8 (LXX) — The lame and the blind shall not enter into the house of the Lord.

    Mt. 21:14 — *The blind and the lame came to him in the temple.*

3. Is. 49:4 — But I said, "I have labored in vain."

    1 Cor. 15:58 — *In the Lord your labor is not in vain.*

TABLE 3

SOME PHRASES THAT OCCUR IN BOTH TESTAMENTS

I. GENERAL PHRASES	*O.T.*	*N.T.*
1. in the beginning	Gen. 1:1	Jn. 1:1
2. the tree of life	Gen. 2:9; 3:22, 24; Prov. 3:18; 11:30; 13:12; 15:4	Rev. 2:7; 22:2, 14, 19
3. thorns and thistles	Gen. 3:18	Heb. 6:8
4. forty days and forty nights	Gen. 7:4; Ex. 24:18; 34: 28; Deut. 9:9, 11; 1 Kings 19:8	Mt. 4:2
5. everlasting covenant	Gen. 17:7, 19; Is. 55:3; Jer. 32:40; 50:5; Ezek. 16:60; 37:26	Heb. 13:20
6. three measures of meal	Gen. 18:6	Mt. 13:33
7. his only son	Gen. 22:2, 16	Jn. 3:16; 1 Jn. 4:9; Heb. 11:17
8. a stranger and a sojourner	Gen. 23:4; Lev. 25:23, 35; 1 Chron, 29:15	Eph. 2:19
9. hail and fire	Ex. 9:23, 24, 28 (LXX)	Rev. 8:7
10. the glory of the Lord	Ex. 16:7, 10; 24:16, 17; Is. 58:8; 60:1	2 Cor. 3:18; Rev. 21:11, 23
11. thirty shekels of silver	Ex. 21:32; Zech. 11:12	Mt. 26:15; 27:3
12. blood of the covenant	Ex. 24:8; Zech. 9:11	Heb. 10:29; 13:20
13. tables of stone	Ex. 24:12; 31:18; 34:1, 4; Deut. 4:13; 9:10– 11; 10:1, 3	2 Cor. 3:3

I. GENERAL PHRASES	*O.T.*	*N.T.*
14. the finger of God	Ex. 8:19; 31:18	Lk. 11:20
15. stiff-necked people	Ex. 32:9; 33:3, 5	Acts 7:51
16. outside the camp	Ex. 29:14; 33:7; Lev. 4: 12, 21; 8:17; 9:11; 16:27; Num. 12:14–15; 19:3, 9	Heb. 13:11, 13
17. branches of palm trees	Lev. 23:40	Jn. 12:13; Rev. 7:9
18. uncircumcised heart	Lev. 26:41; Jer. 9:26	Acts 7:51
19. golden altar	Num. 4:11	Rev. 8:3
20. the God of the spirits	Num. 27:16	Rev. 22:6
21. fire, darkness, and gloom	Deut. 4:11	Heb. 12:18
22. devouring fire	Deut. 4:24; 9:3; 2 Sam. 22:9; Is. 33:14	Heb. 12:29
23. the tables of the covenant	Deut. 9:9, 11, 15	Heb. 9:4
24. the early rain and the later rain	Deut. 11:14; Joel 2:23	Jas. 5:7
25. forty lashes	Deut. 25:3	2 Cor. 11:24
26. beloved of the Lord	Deut. 33:12	2 Thess. 2:13
27. from his mother's womb	Judg. 15:17	Lk. 1:15
28. a full reward	Ruth 2:12	2 Jn. 8
29. vain things	1 Sam. 12:21	Acts 14:15
30. burnt offerings and sacrifices	1 Sam. 15:22	Mk. 12:33
31. horn of salvation	2 Sam. 22:3	Lk. 1:69
32. blameless before God	2 Sam. 22:24	Eph. 1:4
33. God's servants the prophets	2 Kings 9:7; Dan. 9:6, 10; Amos 3:7; Zech. 1:6	Rev. 10:7; 11:18
34. on the third day	2 Kings 20:5, 8; Hos. 6:2	Mt. 16:21; Lk. 9:22; 24: 46; 1 Cor. 15:4
35. sabbaths, new moons, and feast days	1 Chron. 23:31; 2 Chron. 31:3	Col. 2:16
36. nation against nation	2 Chron. 15:6	Mt. 24:7; Mk. 13:8; Lk. 21:10
37. the Sheep Gate	Neh. 3:1, 32; 12:39	Jn. 5:2
38. the holy city	Neh. 11:1, 18; Is. 52:1; Dan. 9:24	Mt. 4:5; Rev. 11:2; 21:2, 10; 22:19

TABLE 3—*Continued*

I. GENERAL PHRASES	O.T.	N.T.
39. sackcloth and ashes	Esther 4:1; Is. 58:5; Jer. 6:26; Dan. 9:3; Jon. 3:6	Mt. 11:21; Lk. 10:13
40. a moth-eaten garment	Job 13:28	Jas. 5:2
41. faithful witness	Prov. 14:5; Jer. 42:5	Rev. 1:5; 3:14
42. slow to anger	Prov. 16:32	Jas. 1:19
43. wine and oil	Prov. 21:17	Lk. 10:34; Rev. 6:6
44. kingdom against kingdom	Is. 19:2	Mt. 24:7; Mk. 13:8; Lk. 21:10
45. things to come	Is. 44:7	Jn. 16:13
46. everlasting salvation	Is. 45:17	Heb. 5:9; 9:12
47. to the end of the earth	Is. 48:20; 49:6; 62:11	Acts 1:8
48. sharp sword	Is. 49:2	Rev. 1:16; 2:12; 19:15
49. the cup of wrath	Is. 51:17; Jer. 25:15	Rev. 14:10; 16:19
50. the righteous one	Is. 53:11	Acts 3:14; 7:52
51. seed to the sower and bread	Is. 55:10	2 Cor. 9:10
52. the bonds of wickedness	Is. 58:6	Acts 8:23
53. gold and frankincense	Is. 60:6	Mt. 2:11
54. the oil of gladness	Is. 61:3	Heb. 1:9
55. a new name	Is. 62:2	Rev. 2:17; 3:12
56. new heavens and a new earth	Is. 65:17; 66:22	2 Pet. 3:13; Rev. 21:1
57. a voice from the temple	Is. 66:6	Rev. 16:1, 17
58. the voice of the bridegroom and the voice of the bride	Jer. 7:34; 16:9; 25:10	Rev. 18:23
59. day of slaughter	Jer. 12:3	Jas. 5:5
60. by the sword, by famine, and by pestilence	Jer. 14:12; 15:2; 21:7; 24:10; 29:17–18; 34:17; Ezek. 5:12, 17; 14:21	Rev. 6:8
61. beasts of the earth	Jer. 34:20; Ezek. 29:5; 34:28	Rev. 6:8
62. the four winds	Jer. 49:36; Ezek. 37:9; Dan. 11:4; 7:2; 8:8; Zech. 2:6; 6:5	Mt. 24:31; Mk. 13:27; Rev. 7:1

I. General Phrases	*O.T.*	*N.T.*
63. lost sheep	Jer. 50:6	Mt. 10:6
64. a golden cup	Jer. 51:7	Rev. 17:4
65. offscouring and refuse	Lam. 3:45	1 Cor. 4:13
66. four living creatures	Ezek. 1:5	Rev. 4:6
67. full of eyes	Ezek. 1:18; 10:12	Rev. 4:6, 8
68. the four corners of the land	Ezek. 7:2	Rev. 7:1
69. the house of Israel	Ezek. 36:22, 32, 37; 45:6	Acts 2:36
70. the God of heaven	Dan. 2:19, 44	Rev. 11:13; 16:11
71. peoples, nations, and languages	Dan. 3:4; 5:19; 6:25; 7:14	Rev. 5:9; 7:9; 10:11; 11:9; 13:7; 17:15
72. furnace of fire	Dan. 3:6, 23	Mt. 13:42, 50
73. he who lives for ever	Dan. 4:34; 12:7	Rev. 4:9; 10:6
74. gods of gold and silver, bronze, iron, wood, and stone	Dan. 5:4, 23	Rev. 9:20
75. the abomination that makes desolate	Dan. 11:31; 12:11	Mt. 24:15; Mk. 13:14
76. the fruit of lips	Hos. 14:2	Heb. 13:15
77. dumb idols	Hab. 2:18	1 Cor. 12:2
78. two olive trees	Zech. 4:3, 11	Rev. 11:4

II. Idioms		
1. to find favor in the eyes of the Lord	Gen. 6:8; Ex. 33:13	Lk. 1:30
2. to take away reproach	Gen. 30:23; Is. 4:1	Lk. 1:25
3. to see face to face	Gen. 32:30	1 Cor. 13:12
4. this shall be the sign for you	Ex. 3:12; 1 Sam. 2:34; 2 Kings 19:29; 20:9; Is. 37:30; 38:7	Lk. 2:12
5. to gird up one's loins	Ex. 12:11; 1 Kings 18:46; 2 Kings 4:29; 9:1; Job 38:3; 40:7; Prov. 31:17; Jer. 1:17	Lk. 12:35; Eph. 6:14
6. to put a stumbling block before	Lev. 19:14	Rom. 14:13
7. to worship the host of heaven	Deut. 17:3; 2 Chron. 33:3; Jer. 7:18 (LXX); 19:13; Zeph. 1:5	Acts 7:42
8. to put dust upon one's head	Josh. 7:6; Job 2:12; Lam. 2:10; Ezek. 27:30	Rev. 18:19

TABLE 3—Continued

II. IDIOMS	O.T.	N.T.
9. the Lord is with you	Judg. 6:12; Ruth 2:4	Lk. 1:28; 2 Thess. 3:16
10. the woman bore a son and called his name	Judg. 13:24	Mt. 1:25
11. to go in peace	1 Sam. 1:17; 20:42; 2 Sam. 15:9; 2 Kings 5:19	Mk. 5:34
12. peace be to your house	1 Sam. 25:6	Lk. 10:5
13. to go and wash	2 Kings 5:10	Jn. 9:7, 11
14. to profane the sabbath	Neh. 13:18	Mt. 12:5
15. to fall on one's face	Ezek. 1:28; Dan. 10:9	Mt. 17:6

III. METAPHORS AND SIMILES		
1. like the sand of the sea	Gen. 22:17; 32:12; Josh. 11:4	Heb. 11:12; Rev. 20:8
2. as many as the stars of heaven	Gen. 22:17; Ex. 32:13; Deut. 1:10; 10:22	Heb. 11:12
3. like the sound of many waters	Ezek. 1:24; 43:2	Rev. 1:15; 14:2; 19:6
4. like lions' teeth	Joel 1:6	Rev. 9:8

IV. PHRASES WITH PROPER NAMES		
1. the great river Euphrates	Gen. 15:18; Deut. 1:7; Josh. 1:4	Rev. 9:14; 16:12
2. Moses the servant of the Lord	Ex. 14:31; Josh. 14:7; 22:5	Rev. 15:3
3. Balaam the son of Beor	Num. 22:5; Deut. 23:4; Mic. 6:5	2 Pet. 2:15
4. Rahab the harlot	Josh. 2:1; 6:17, 25	Heb. 11:31; Jas. 2:25
5. the hill country of Judah	Josh. 20:7; 21:11	Lk. 1:39
6. the days of Noah	Is. 54:9	Mt. 24:37
7. Babylon the great	Dan. 4:30	Rev. 14:8; 16:19; 17:5

TABLE 4

SOME N.T. USES OF LXX PASSAGES THAT DIFFER SIGNIFICANTLY FROM THE HEBREW

Classes of Citations:

(1) Acknowledged quotations preceded by a formula
(2) Unacknowledged quotations, without a formula
(3) Identifiable citations or allusions, but with some rewording

O.T.	N.T.	Class
1. Gen. 12:7	Gal. 3:16	(1)
2. Gen. 46:27	Acts 7:14	(3)
3. Gen. 47:31	Heb. 11:21	(3)
4. Ex. 2:14	Acts 7:27	(2)
5. Ex. 9:28	Rev. 8:7	(3)
6. Num. 12:7	Heb. 3:2	(2)
7. Deut. 18:19	Acts 3:23	(1)
8. Deut. 29:18	Heb. 12:15	(3)
9. Deut. 32:43	Heb. 1:6	(1)
10. 2 Sam. 22:3	Heb. 2:13	(2)
11. Job 13:16	Phil. 1:19	(3)
12. Prov. 3:12	Heb. 12:6	(1)
13. Prov. 3:34	1 Pet. 5:5	(1)
14. Prov. 4:26	Heb. 12:13	(2)
15. Prov. 11:31	1 Pet. 4:18	(1)
16. Prov. 22:8	2 Cor. 9:7	(1)
17. Prov. 23:31	Eph. 5:18	(2)
18. Is. 9:2	Mt. 4:15–16	(1)
19. Is. 11:10	Rom. 15:12	(1)
20. Is. 28:16	Rom. 10:11	(1)
21. Is. 29:13	Mt. 15:8–9; Mk. 7:6–7	(1)
22. Is. 29:14	1 Cor. 1:19	(1)
23. Is. 40:3–5	Mt. 3:3; Mk. 1:3; Lk. 3:4–6; Jn. 1:23	(1)
24. Is. 42:4	Mt. 12:21	(2)
25. Is. 52:5	Rom. 2:24	(1)
26. Is. 53:8	Acts 8:33	(1)
27. Is. 53:12	Rom. 4:25	(3)
28. Is. 59:20	Rom. 11:26–27	(1)
29. Is. 61:1	Mt. 11:5; Lk. 4:18–19; 7:22	(1)
30. Is. 65:2	Rom. 10:21	(1)
31. Is. 66:5	2 Thess. 1:12	(2)
32. Jer. 31:32	Heb. 8:9	(1)
33. Ezek. 9:11	Rev. 1:13	(3)

TABLE 4—*Continued*

O.T.	N.T.	Class
34. Hos. 6:6	Mt. 9:13; 12:7	(1)
35. Amos 9:12	Acts 15:17–18	(1)
36. Hab. 1:5	Acts 13:41	(1)
37. Hab. 2:4	Heb. 10:38	(1)
38. Zech. 8:6	Mk. 10:27	(3)
39. Zech. 11:12	Mt. 26:15; 27:3,9	(1)

TABLE 5

O.T. PARALLELS (OTHER THAN PSALMS) TO TEACHINGS OF JESUS

Classes of Citations:
    (1) Acknowledged quotations preceded by a formula
    (2) Unacknowledged quotations, without a formula
    (3) Identifiable citations or allusions, but with some rewording

I. MARK, WITH PARALLELS IN MATTHEW AND/OR LUKE

Class	Mark	N.T.	O.T.	Subject
(3)	Mk. 1:17	= Mt. 4:19; Lk. 5:10	2 Kings 6:19; Jer. 16:16	fishers of men
(3)	Mk. 1:44	= Mt. 8:4; Lk. 5:14; 17:14	Lev. 13:49; 14:2	show to priests
(3)	Mk. 2:26	= Mt. 12:4; Lk. 6:4	1 Sam. 21:6	David and holy bread
(3)	Mk. 3:27	= Mt. 12:29; Lk. 11:21	Is. 49:24	strong man's goods
(2)	Mk. 4:12	= Mt. 13:13; Lk. 18:10 (and Jn. 12:40)	Is. 6:9–10	seeing and hearing
(1)	Mk. 7:6–7	= Mt. 15:8–9	Is. 29:13 (LXX)	lips and heart
(1)	Mk. 7:10	= Mt. 15:4; Lk. 18:20	Ex. 20:12; 21:17; Deut. 5:16; Lev. 20:9	honor parents
(2)	Mk. 8:17–18	= Mt. 13:13	Jer. 5:21; Ezek. 12:2	eyes and ears
(2)	Mk. 9:12	= Mt. 17:10–11	Mal. 4:5	coming of Elijah
(2)	Mk. 9:43, 48	= Mt. 3:12; Lk. 3:17	Is. 66:24	unquenchable fire
(2)	Mk. 10:6–7	= Mt. 19:4–5	Gen. 1:27; 2:24; 5:2	male and female

Class	Mark	N.T.	O.T.	Subject
(1)	Mk. 10:19	= Mt. 19:18–19; Lk. 18:20	Ex. 20:12–16; Deut. 5:16–20	commandments
(3)	Mk. 10:27	= Mt. 19:26; Lk. 18:27	Job 42:2	God's power
(3)	Mk. 10:38	= Mt. 20:22	Jer. 49:12	to drink the cup
(3)	Mk. 10:45	= Mt. 20:28	Is. 53:12	ransom for many
(1)	Mk. 11:17	= Mt. 21:13; Lk. 19:46	Is. 56:7; Jer. 7:11	house of prayer
(3)	Mk. 12:1	= Mt. 21:33; Lk. 20:9	Is. 5:1–2	parable of vineyard
(1)	Mk. 12:26	= Mt. 22:32; Lk. 20:37	Ex. 3:6	God of Abraham
(1)	Mk. 12:29–31	= Mt. 22:37–39; Lk. 10:27	Deut. 6:4–5; Lev. 19:18	summary of law
(3)	Mk. 13:8	= Mt. 24:7; Lk. 21:10	2 Chron. 15:6; Is. 19:2	nation vs. nation
(2)	Mk. 13:12	= Mt. 10:21, 35–36; Lk. 12:53; 21:16	Mic. 7:6	children vs. parents
(3)	Mk. 13:14	= Mt. 24:15	Dan. 11:31; 12:11	desolating sacrilege
(3)	Mk. 13:16	= Mt. 24:18; Lk. 17:31	Gen. 19:17	no turning back
(3)	Mk. 13:19	= Mt. 24:21	Dan. 12:1	future tribulation
(3)	Mk. 13:24–25	= Mt. 24:29; Lk. 21:26	Eccles. 12:2; Is. 13:10; 34:4; Ezek. 32:7; Joel 2:10; 3:15; Hag. 2:6, 21	heaven darkened
(2)	Mk. 13:26; 14:62	= Mt. 24:30; 26:64; Lk. 21:27; 22:69	Dan. 7:13–14	Son of man
(3)	Mk. 13:27	= Mt. 24:31	Ex. 19:16; Deut. 30:4	gathering of elect
(3)	Mk. 14:7	= Mt. 26:11 (and Jn. 12:8)	Deut. 15:11	poor always
(2)	Mk. 14:24	= Mt. 26:28	Ex. 24:8; Is. 53:12; Jer. 31:34; Zech. 9:11	blood of the covenant
(1)	Mk. 14:27	= Mt. 26:31	Zech. 13:7	scattered sheep

TABLE 5—*Continued*

II. MARK ONLY

Class	Mark	N.T.	O.T.	Subject
(3)	Mk. 1:15		Ezek. 7:7	the time fulfilled
(2)	Mk. 4:29		Joel 3:13	reaping the harvest
(3)	Mk. 13:36		Mal. 3:1	sudden coming

III. MATTHEW, WITH PARALLELS IN LUKE

Class	Mark	N.T.	O.T.	Subject
(1)	Mt. 4:4	= Lk. 4:4	Deut. 8:3	God's word
(1)	Mt. 4:7	= Lk. 4:12	Deut. 6:16	tempting God
(1)	Mt. 4:10	= Lk. 4:8	Deut. 6:13	worship of God
(3)	Mt. 5:12a	= Lk. 6:23a	Gen. 15:1	great reward
(3)	Mt. 5:12b	= Lk. 6:23b	2 Chron. 36:16	persecution of prophets
(3)	Mt. 5:25	= Lk. 12:58	Prov. 25:8–9	reconciliation
(3)	Mt. 5:39	= Lk. 6:29	Is. 50:6; Lam. 3:30	turn the cheek
(3)	Mt. 5:48	= Lk. 6:36	Lev. 11:44–45; 19:2; 20:26	to be like God
(3)	Mt. 6:9b	= Lk. 11:2	Ezek. 36:23	God's holy name
(3)	Mt. 6:11	= Lk. 11:3	Ex. 16:4; Prov. 30:8	daily bread
(3)	Mt. 6:23	= Lk. 11:35	Is. 5:20	light and darkness
(2)	Mt. 7:7	= Lk. 11:9	Deut. 4:29; Prov. 8:17	seek and find
(3)	Mt. 7:24–25	= Lk. 6:48	Prov. 12:7	foundation on rock
(3)	Mt. 8:21	= Lk. 9:59	Lev. 21:11; Num. 6:6–7	burying a father
(3)	Mt. 10:32–33	= Lk. 12:8–9	1 Sam. 2:30	acknowledging Christ
(2)	Mt. 11:5	= Lk. 4:18–19; 7:22	Is. 26:19; 29:18–19; 35:5–6; 61:1	signs of God's servant
(1)	Mt. 11:10	= Lk. 7:27 (cf. Mk. 1:2)	Mal. 3:1	John the Baptist

Class	Matthew	N.T.	O.T.	Subject
(2)	Mt. 11:19	= Lk. 7:34	Deut. 21:20; Prov. 23:20	glutton and winebibber
(3)	Mt. 11:23	= Lk. 10:15	Is. 14:13, 15	brought down to Hades
(3)	Mt. 12:41–42	= Lk. 11:31–32	1 Kings 10:1; 2 Chron. 9:2; Jon. 3:4–5	Queen of south and Nineveh
(3)	Mt. 17:17	= Lk. 9:41	Deut. 32:5, 20	faithless generation
(3)	Mt. 18:12	= Lk. 15:4; 19:10	Ezek. 34:4, 11–12, 16	lost sheep
(3)	Mt. 19:28	= Lk. 22:30	Dan. 7:9–10	thrones and judgment
(3)	Mt. 23:12	= Lk. 14:11; 18:14	Job 5:11; 22:29; Prov. 29:23; Ezek. 21:31(LXX)	self-exaltation
(3)	Mt. 23:23	= Lk. 11:42	Lev. 27:30	tithing of herbs
(3)	Mt. 23:34	= Lk. 11:49	Jer. 7:25	sending of prophets
(3)	Mt. 23:38	= Lk. 13:35	Jer. 12:7; 22:5	a forsaken house
(3)	Mt. 24:37–38	= Lk. 17:26–27	Gen. 6:10; 7:1, 7	days of Noah

IV. MATTHEW ONLY

Class	Matthew		O.T.	Subject
(3)	Mt. 5:3		Is. 57:15	poor in spirit
(3)	Mt. 5:8		Job 19:26	seeing God
(3)	Mt. 5:21b		Lev. 24:17	liable to judgment
(1)	Mt. 5:31		Deut. 24:2–3	divorce
(1)	Mt. 5:33		Lev. 19:12; Deut. 23:21; Num. 30:2	oath to God
(2)	Mt. 5:35		Is. 66:1	God's footstool
(1)	Mt. 5:38		Ex. 21:24; Lev. 24:20; Deut. 19:21	eye for eye
(3)	Mt. 6:6		2 Kings 4:33; Is. 26:20	prayer in secret
(3)	Mt. 6:7		1 Kings 18:29	many words to God

TABLE 5—*Continued*

Class	Matthew	N.T.	O.T.	Subject
(3)	Mt. 6:9a		Eccles. 5:2	God in heaven
(3)	Mt. 6:17		2 Sam. 12:20	fasting and washing
(3)	Mt. 7:22		Jer. 14:14; 27:15	prophecy in the Lord's name
(3)	Mt. 9:4		Zech. 8:17	evil in heart
(1)	Mt. 9:13; 12:7		Hos. 6:6	mercy
(2)	Mt. 10:5–6; 15:24		Jer. 50:6; Ezek. 3:4, 6	to house of Israel
(3)	Mt. 10:29		Amos 3:5	a bird's fall
(2)	Mt. 11:28		Ex. 33:14	to give rest
(2)	Mt. 12:40		Jon. 1:17	Jonah and the whale
(1)	Mt. 13:14–15 (and Jn. 12:40)		Is. 6:9–10	closed eyes
(3)	Mt. 13:44		Prov. 2:4	hidden treasure
(3)	Mt. 16:18		Job. 38:17; Is. 38:10	powers of death
(3)	Mt. 16:19 (and Jn. 20:23)		Is. 22:22	shutting and opening
(3)	Mt. 16:27; 25:31		Zech. 14:5	Son of man and angels
(3)	Mt. 18:16 (and Jn. 8:17)		Num. 35:30; Deut. 17:6; 19:15	two witnesses
(3)	Mt. 19:17		Lev. 18:5; Neh. 9:29; Ezek. 20:21	commands and life
(1)	Mt. 21:5 (and Jn. 12:15)		Zech. 9:9	the king comes
(3)	Mt. 23:19		Ex. 29:37	God's holy altar
(3)	Mt. 23:21		1 Kings 8:13	God's house
(3)	Mt. 25:32		Ezek. 34:17	sheep and goats
(3)	Mt. 25:35–36		Job 31:32; Is. 58:7; Ezek. 18:7, 16	last judgment

Class	Matthew	N.T.	O.T.	Subject
(3)	Mt. 25:46 (and Jn. 5:29)		Dan. 12:2	eternal punishment
(3)	Mt. 26:36		Gen. 22:5	stay and I go

V. LUKE ONLY

Class	Matthew	N.T.	O.T.	Subject
(3)	Lk. 4:25–27		1 Kings 17:1, 9; 18:2; 2 Kings 5:1, 14	Elijah and Elisha
(3)	Lk. 7:44, 45, 47		Gen. 18:4; 19:2; 43:24; Judg. 19:21; 2 Sam. 15:5; Prov. 10:12	Jesus' anointing
(2)	Lk. 11:20		Ex. 8:19; 31:18	the finger of God
(3)	Lk. 11:28		Prov. 8:32	hearing and doing
(3)	Lk. 12:47–48		Num. 15:29–30	the knowing servant
(3)	Lk. 13:6 (cf. Mt. 21:19; Mk. 11:13)		Jer. 8:13	parable of the fig tree
(3)	Lk. 13:14		Ex. 20:9–10; Deut. 5:13–14	six days to work
(3)	Lk. 14:8–10		Prov. 25:6–7	parable of the chief seats
(3)	Lk. 14:20		Deut. 24:5	married a wife
(3)	Lk. 15:12–13, 22, 30		Gen. 41:42; Deut. 21:16; Prov. 29:3	prodigal son
(3)	Lk. 16:15		1 Sam. 16:7; 1 Chron. 28:9; Prov. 21:2; 24:12	justification before men
(3)	Lk. 17:29		Gen. 19:15, 24; Jer. 50:40	Lot and Sodom
(3)	Lk. 18:13		Ezra 9:6	parable of Pharisee and tax collector
(2)	Lk. 19:40		Hab. 2:11	cry of stones
(3)	Lk. 19:43–44		Is. 29:3; Jer. 6:6	destruction of Jerusalem

TABLE 5—*Continued*

Class	Luke	N.T.	O.T.	Subject
(3)	Lk. 21:18		1 Sam. 14:45	hair of the head
(1)	Lk. 22:37		Is. 53:12	reckoned with transgressors

VI. JOHN ONLY

Class		N.T.	O.T.	Subject
(3)	Jn. 3:5		Ezek. 36:25–27	born of water and Spirit
(3)	Jn. 3:13–14		Num. 21:9; Deut. 30:12; Prov. 30:4; Is. 52:13	Jesus' ascent
(3)	Jn. 6:39; 17:12		Jer. 23:4	to lose nothing
(1)	Jn. 6:45		Is. 54:13	taught of God
(3)	Jn. 6:63		Ezek. 37:14	life-giving spirit
(2)	Jn. 7:24		Deut. 1:16–17; 16:18; Is. 11:3–4	right judgment
(3)	Jn. 8:12		Is. 49:6	light of the world
(3)	Jn. 8:35		Gen. 21:10; Ex. 21:2; Deut. 15:12	slave not forever
(3)	Jn. 11:10; 12:35		Prov. 4:19	walking in darkness
(3)	Jn. 12:48		Deut. 18:19	rejection of Christ
(3)	Jn. 16:21		Is. 13:8; 21:3; 26:17; Hos. 13:12; Mic. 4:9	woman in travail
(3)	Jn. 16:22		Is. 66:14	rejoicing hearts
(3)	Jn. 16:32 (cf. Mt. 26:31; Mk. 14:27)		Zech. 13:7	future scattering
(3)	Jn. 17:9		Jer. 7:16; 14:11	no prayer for world
(3)	Jn. 18:20		Is. 45:19	no secret speech
(3)	Jn. 21:15–17		Ezek. 34:2	feeding sheep

TABLE 6

THE O.T. AND NARRATIVES OF THE N.T.

I. STORIES ABOUT JESUS

A. *Birth*   *N.T.*   *O.T.*

1. return from Egypt	Mt. 2:20	Ex. 4:19
2. presentation in the Temple	Lk. 2:22–24	Ex. 13:2, 12; 34:19; **Lev.** 5:7; 12:6, 8; Num. 6: 10; 18:15
3. Jesus' growth	Lk. 2:52	1 Sam. 2:26

B. *Ministry*

1. baptism		
a. heaven opened	Mt. 3:16; Mk. 1:10; Lk. 3:21	Ezek. 1:1
b. God's Spirit	Mt. 3:16; Mk. 1:10; Lk. 3:22	Is. 11:2
2. temptation		Gen. 7:4, 12; Ex. 24:18; 34:28; Deut. 9:9, 11; 1 Kings 19:8
a. forty days and forty nights	Mt. 4:2	
b. the holy city	Mt. 4:5	Neh. 11:1, 18; Ezek. 40: 2; Dan. 9:24
c. a high mountain	Mt. 4:8	Ezek. 40:1–2
d. fall down and worship	Mt. 4:9	Dan. 3:5–6, 10, 15
e. wild beasts	Mk. 1:13	Is. 11:6–9; 65:25; Hos. 2:18
3. plucking grain		
a. by hand	Mk. 2:23 =Mt. 12:1; Lk. 6:1	Deut. 23:25
b. on Sabbath	Mk. 2:24 = Mt. 12:2; Lk. 6:2	Ex. 20:10; Deut. 5:14
c. holy bread	Mk. 2:26 = Mt. 12:4–6; Lk. 6:4	Lev. 24:9; 1 Sam. 21:6; Neh. 13:18
4. raising of widow's son	Lk. 7:15	1 Kings 17:23; 2 Kings 4:36
5. appointment of seventy	Lk. 10:1, 4–5, 7	Ex. 24:1; Num. 11:16; Deut. 24:15; 1 Sam. 25:6; 2 Kings 4:29
6. feeding of multitude		
a. sheep without a shepherd	Mt. 9:36; Mk. 6:34	Num. 27:17; 1 Kings 22: 17; 2 Chron. 18:16

TABLE 6—*Continued*

B. *Ministry*	N.T.	O.T.
b. enough to eat	Mt. 14:16, 20; 15:33, 37; Mk. 6:37, 42; 8:8; Lk. 9:13, 17; Jn. 6:5, 9, 12, 13	2 Kings 4:42–44
7. transfiguration	Mk. 9:5, 7 = Mt. 17:2, 4–6; Lk. 9:33, 35	Ex. 34:29–30; 40:34; Ezek. 1:28
8. Jesus in Jerusalem	Jn. 7:34, 37–42	Lev. 23:36; Deut. 18:15, 18; Prov. 1:28; Is. 44:3; 55:1; Ezek. 36:26–27; Joel 2:28; Mic. 5:2
9. man born blind	Jn. 9:2, 7, 11, 24	Ex. 20:5; Deut. 5:9; Josh. 7:19; 2 Kings 5:10; Is. 49:6

C. *The passion*		
1. triumphal entry	Mk. 11:7–9 = Mt. 21:8–9; Lk. 19:35–40; Jn. 12:13	2 Kings 9:13; Zech. 9:9; Hab. 2:11
2. cleansing of Temple	Mt. 21:12–13; Mk. 11:15–17; Lk. 19:45–46; Jn. 2:14–16	Ex. 30:13; Lev. 1:14; 5:7; 12:8; Is. 56:7; Jer. 7:11; Zech. 14:21; Mal. 3:1–3
3. barren fig tree	Mk. 11:13 = Mt. 21:19	Jer. 8:13
4. thirty pieces of silver	Mt. 26:15; 27:3	Ex. 21:32; Zech. 11:12
5. Jesus' silence	Mt. 26:63; 27:12, 14; Mk. 14:61; 15:5; Lk. 23:9; Jn. 19:9	Is. 53:7
6. rending of clothes	Mt. 26:65	Num. 14:6; 2 Sam. 13:19; Esther 4:1; Job 1:20
7. blasphemy and death	Mk. 14:64 = Mt. 26:65–66	Lev. 24:16
8. spitting	Mt. 26:67; Mk. 15:19	Is. 50:6
9. striking of Jesus	Jn. 18:22; 19:3	Mic. 5:1
10. carrying of the cross	Jn. 19:17	Gen. 22:6
11. Jesus' robe intact	Jn. 19:24	Ex. 28:32
12. crucified with robbers	Mt. 27:38; Mk. 15:27; Lk. 23:33; Jn. 19:18	Is. 53:12
13 darkness at noon	Mk. 15:33 = Mt. 27:45; Lk. 23:44	Ex. 10:21; Amos 8:9

C. *The passion*	*N.T.*	*O.T.*
14. curtain of the Temple	Mt. 27:51 = Lk. 23:45	Ex. 26:33
15. the dead raised	Mt. 27:52–53	Is. 26:19; Ezek. 37:12
16. the body removed	Lk. 23:52–53; Jn. 19:31	Ex. 34:25; Deut. 21:23; Josh. 10:27
17. Sabbath rest	Lk. 23:56	Ex. 20:10; Deut. 5:14
18. buried with the rich	Mt. 27:57, 60	Is. 53:9
19. the tomb sealed	Mt. 27:66	Dan. 6:17
20. raiment white as snow	Mt. 28:3	Dan. 7:9; 10:6

II. OTHER STORIES

1. John the Baptist		
a. clothing	Mk. 1:6 = Mt. 3:4	2 Kings 1:8
b. Herod's unlawful marriage	Mk. 6:18 = Mt. 14:3–4	Lev. 18:16; 20:21
2. Herod Antipas	Mk. 6:21, 23	Esther 1:3; 2:18; 5:3, 6; 7:2
3. Peter	Acts 3:7–8	Is. 35:6
4. Stephen	Acts 7:58	Lev. 24:16; Deut. 13:10; 17:7
5. Paul		
a. conversion	Acts 9:7	Deut. 4:12; Dan. 10:7
b. escape	Acts 9:25	Josh. 2:15
6. Herod Agrippa I	Acts 12:22–23	2 Sam. 24:17; 2 Kings 19:35; Ezek. 28:2
7. Eutychus	Acts 20:10	1 Kings 17:21; 2 Kings 4:34–35

TABLE 7

N.T. ETHICAL TEACHING AND THE O.T.

Subject	*N.T.*	*O.T.*
1. the evil present	Mt. 17:17; Acts 2:40; Phil. 2:15	Deut. 32:5, 20
2. the commandments	Mt. 19:17–19; Mk. 10:19; Lk. 18:20; Rom. 13:9; Gal. 5:14; Jas. 2:8, 11	Ex. 20:13–17; Lev. 19:18; Deut. 5:17–21
3. humility and pride	Mt. 23:12; Lk. 14:11; 18:14; Jas. 4:6, 10; 1 Pet. 5:5	Job 5:11; 22:29; Prov. 3:34; 29:23

TABLE 7—*Continued*

Subject	N.T.	O.T.
4. in sight of God and man	Lk. 16:15; 2 Cor. 8:21; Heb. 4:13	1 Sam. 16:7; 1 Chron. 28:9; Prov. 3:4; 21:2; 24:12
5. love	Jn. 13:34; 1 Pet. 4:8; 1 Jn. 2:9–11; 3:15; 4:21	Lev. 19:18; Prov. 10:12
6. man's wisdom	Rom. 11:25; 1 Cor. 1:19–20, 27; 3:18	Prov. 3:7; 26:12; Is. 5:21; 19:12; 29:14; 44:25; Jer. 8:9
7. authority from God	Rom. 13:1; 1 Tim. 2:1–2	Prov. 8:15; Dan. 4:17
8. living with step-mother	1 Cor. 5:1	Deut. 22:30; 27:20
9. the wicked expelled	1 Cor. 5:13	Num. 15:30; Deut. 13:5; 17:7, 12; 19:19; 21:21; 22:21, 24; 24:7
10. a professional ministry	1 Cor. 9:7, 9, 13; 1 Tim. 5:18	Lev. 6:16, 26; 7:6; Num. 5:10; 18:31; Deut. 18:3; 20:6; 25:4
11. prophecy and tongues	1 Cor. 14:5, 8, 21	Num. 11:29; Is. 28:11–12; Ezek. 33:4
12. worldly futility	1 Cor. 15:32, 58; Phil. 2:16	Is. 22:13; 49:4; 65:23
13. poverty and wealth	2 Cor. 6:10; Jas. 2:5	Prov. 13:7
14. the cost of truth	Gal. 4:16; Eph. 4:25	Amos 5:10; Zech. 8:16
15. retribution	Gal. 6:8	Job 4:8
16. drunkenness	Eph. 5:18	Prov. 23:31 (LXX)
17. head of the family	Eph. 5:22, 28; Col. 3:18	Gen. 1:26–27; 2:18, 22–24; 3:16; 5:1; 9:6
18. parents and children	Eph. 6:1, 4	Gen. 18:19; Ex. 20:12; Deut. 5:16; 6:7; 8:5; 11:19; Prov. 6:20; 13:24; 19:18
19. the armor of God	Eph. 6:14–17; 1 Thess. 5:8	Is. 11:5, 52:7; 59:17; Nahum 1:15
20. the peace of God	Phil. 4:7	Is. 26:3
21. hearty work	Col. 3:23	Eccles. 9:10
22. prayer for kings	1 Tim. 2:1–2	Ezra 6:10
23. firmness and strength	Heb. 12:12	Prov. 4:26; Is. 35:3; Ezek. 7:17
24. hospitality	Heb. 13:2	Gen. 19:1, 3
25. hearers and doers	Jas. 1:22–23	Ezek. 33:31–32

Subject	N.T.	O.T.
26. rich clothing	1 Pet. 3:3	Is. 3:18–24
27. help for the needy	1 Jn. 3:17	Deut. 15:7

TABLE 8

THE N.T. EXPLAINED BY THE O.T.

Subject	N.T.	O.T.
1. show to the priest	Mk. 1:44 = Mt. 8:4; Lk. 5:14; 17:14	Lev. 13:49; 14:2
2. brother's wife	Mk. 6:18 = Mt. 14:4	Lev. 18:16; 20:21
3. fringes on garments	Mk. 6:56 = Mt. 9:20; 14:36; 23:5; Lk. 8:44	Num. 15:38
4. days of unleavened bread	Mk. 14:12 = Mt. 26:17; Lk. 22:7	Ex. 12:15
5. Sabbath offering	Mt. 12:5	Num. 28:10
6. half-shekel tax	Mt. 17:24	Ex. 30:13; 38:26
7. two or three witnesses	Mt. 18:16; 26:60; Jn. 8:17; 2 Cor. 13:1; 1 Tim. 5:19; Heb. 10:28	Num. 35:30; Deut. 17:6; 19:15
8. daily wage	Mt. 20:8	Lev. 19:13; Deut. 24:15
9. veil of the Temple	Mt. 27:51 = Lk. 23:45	Ex. 26:33
10. Sabbath travel	Jn. 5:10	Ex. 16:29; Neh. 13:19; Jer. 17:21
11. death for blasphemy	Jn. 5:18; 10:33; 19:7; Acts 7:58	Lev. 24:16
12. cast lots	Acts 1:26	Lev. 16:8; Josh. 14:2; Neh. 10:34; 11:1; Prov. 16:33
13. laying on of hands	Acts 6:6	Deut. 34:9
14. witnesses as executors	Acts 7:58	Deut. 17:7
15. days of a vow	Acts 18:18; 21:23–24, 25–27	Num. 6:5, 9
16. profaning the sanctuary	Acts 21:28	Ezek. 44:7
17. no killing in the Temple	Acts 21:30–31	2 Kings 11:15
18. cursing and throwing dust	Acts 22:23	2 Sam. 16:13

TABLE 8—*Continued*

Subject	N.T.	O.T.
19. the guilty to be beaten	Acts 23:3	Deut. 25:2
20. homosexuality	Rom. 1:27	Lev. 18:22; 20:13
21. sexual deformity	Gal. 5:12	Deut. 23:1

TABLE 9

PHRASES FOUND IN PSALMS AND IN THE N.T.

Phrase	Psalms	N.T.
1. the kings of the earth	Ps. 2:2; 48:4 (LXX); 89:27; 102: 15; 138:4; 148:11	Acts 4:26; Rev. 6:15; 17:2, 18; 19:19; 21:24
2. rod of iron	Ps. 2:9	Rev. 2:27; 12:5; 19:15
3. fear and trembling	Ps. 2:11; 55:5	1 Cor. 2:3; 2 Cor. 7:15; Eph. 6:5; Phil. 2:12
4. fiery shafts	Ps. 7:13	Eph. 6:16
5. he who does what is right	Ps. 15:2	Acts 10:35
6. the end of the heavens	Ps. 19:6	Mt. 24:31
7. without wavering	Ps. 26:1	Heb. 10:23
8. the God of glory	Ps. 29:3	Acts 7:2
9. my God and my Lord	Ps. 35:23	Jn. 20:28
10. the fountain of life	Ps. 36:9	Rev. 21:6
11. hairs of the head	Ps. 40:12; 69:4	Mt. 10:30; Lk. 12:7
12. secrets of the heart	Ps. 44:21	1 Cor. 14:25
13. city of the great king	Ps. 48:2	Mt. 5:35
14. temple of God	Ps. 48:9	Mt. 21:12
15. the roaring of the seas and of the waves	Ps. 65:7	Lk. 21:25
16. blessed be God	Ps. 66:20; 68:35	Rom. 9:5; 2 Cor. 1:3; 11:31
17. pure in heart	Ps. 73:1	Mt. 5:8
18. the appointed time	Ps. 102:13	Gal. 4:2
19. the holy one of the Lord	Ps. 106:16	Mk. 1:24
20. double-minded men	Ps. 119:113	Jas. 1:8; 4:8
21. clashing cymbals	Ps. 150:5	1 Cor. 13:1

Table 10

PHRASES FOUND IN PSALMS AND OTHER O.T. BOOKS AND IN THE N.T.

Phrase	Psalms and Other O.T. Books	N.T.
1. the law of the Lord	Ps. 1:2; 19:7; 119:1; Is. 5:24 et al.	Lk. 2:39
2. how long, O Lord?	Ps. 6:3; 13:1; 79:5; 89: 46; 90:13; 119:84; Is. 6:11; Zech. 1:12	Rev. 6:10
3. the name of the Lord	Ps. 7:17; 20:7; 102:15, 21; 113:1, 2, 3; 116:4, 13, 17; 118:10, 11, 12, 26; 122:4; 124:8; 129: 8; 135:1; 148:5, 13; Ex. 20:7 et al.	Acts 8:16 et al.
4. the birds of the air	Ps. 8:8; 50:11; 79:2; 104: 12; Gen. 1:26 et al.	Mt. 6:26 et al.
5. fire and brimstone	Ps. 11:6; Gen. 19:24; Ezek. 38:22	Lk. 17:29; Rev. 14:10; 20:10; 21:8
6. the horn of my salvation	Ps. 18:2; 2 Sam. 22:3	Lk. 1:69
7. the glory of God	Ps. 19:1; Prov. 25:2 et al.	Jn. 11:4 et al.
8. the fear of the Lord	Ps. 19:9; 34:11; 111:10; Job 28:28 et al.	Acts 9:31
9. to wag the head	Ps. 22:7; 64:8; 109:25; 2 Kings 19:21; Lam. 2:15	Mt. 27:39; Mk. 15:29
10. like a roaring lion	Ps. 22:13; Prov. 28:15	1 Pet. 5:8
11. the voice of the Lord	Ps. 29:3, 4, 5, 7, 8, 9; 106:25; Is. 6:8 et al.	Acts 7:31
12. the hand of the Lord	Ps. 32:4; 38:2; 39:10; 75:8; Ex. 9:3 et al.	Lk. 1:66; Acts 11:21; 13:11
13. the word of the Lord	Ps. 33:4, 6; 105:19; 141: 6; Ex. 9:20 et al.	Lk. 22:61 et al.
14. God's holy name	Ps. 33:21; 103:1; 105:3; 106:47; 111:9; 145:21; 1 Chron. 16:10 et al.	Lk. 1:49
15. to gnash the teeth	Ps. 35:16; 37:12; 112:10; Job 16:9	Mt. 8:12; 13:42, 50; 22: 13; 24:51; 25:30; Lk. 13:28; Acts 7:54
16. the fear of God	Ps. 36:1; Gen. 20:11 et al.	2 Cor. 7:1

TABLE 10—*Continued*

Phrase	Psalms and Other O.T. Books	N.T.
17. the house of God	Ps. 42:4; 52:8; 55:14; 84:10; Gen. 28:17 *et al.*	Mt. 12:4; Mk. 2:26; Lk. 6:4; Heb. 10:21
18. myrrh and aloes	Ps. 45:8; Prov. 7:17; Song 4:14	Jn. 19:39
19. bulls and goats	Ps. 50:13; Lev. 16:6–7, 14, 16, 18	Heb. 9:13; 10:4
20. sharp swords	Ps. 57:4; Is. 49:2	Rev. 1:16; 2:12; 19:15
21. to fear God	Ps. 66:16; Gen. 42:18 *et al.*	Lk. 23:40; Acts 13:16; Rev. 14:7
22. grass of the field	Ps. 72:16; Dan. 4:15, 23	Mt. 6:30
23. beasts of the earth	Ps. 79:2; Deut. 28:26; Job 35:11; Jer. 7:33; 15:3; 16:4; 19:7; 34:20; Ezek. 29:5	Rev. 6:8
24. to come and bow down before	Ps. 86:9; Is. 45:14; 60:14	Rev. 3:9
25. edge of the sword	Ps. 89:43; Jer. 21:7	Lk. 21:24; Heb. 11:34
26. the house of Israel	Ps. 98:3; 115:12; 135:19; Lev. 10:6 *et al.*	Acts 2:36 *et al.*
27. the glory of the Lord	Ps. 104:31; 138:5; Ex. 16:7 *et al.*	Lk. 2:9; 2 Cor. 3:18
28. God's chosen ones	Ps. 105:6, 43; 106:5; Is. 65:9, 15, 22	Rom. 8:33
29. the house of David	Ps. 122:5; Is. 7:2 *et al.*	Lk. 1:27, 69; 2:4
30. signs and wonders	Ps. 135:9; Jer. 32:20 *et al.*	Mt. 24:24 *et al.*
31. the Lord of lords	Ps. 136:3; Deut. 10:17	1 Tim. 6:15; Rev. 17:14; 19:16
32. the people of Israel	Ps. 148:14; Josh. 8:33 *et al.*	Acts 4:27
33. praise the Lord (hallelujah)	Ps. 104:35; Judg. 5:2 *et al.*	Rev. 19:1, 3, 6
34. God the Savior	Ps. 106:21; Is. 43:3 *et al.*	Lk. 1:47; 1 Tim. 1:1; 2:3; Tit. 1:3; 2:10; 3:4; Jude 25
35. the pangs of death	Ps. 18:4–5; 116:3; 2 Sam. 22:6	Acts 2:24

TABLE 11

THE WORDS OF JESUS AND THE PSALMS

N.T.	Psalms	O.T. Background
1. Mt. 5:5	Ps. 37:11	
2. Mt. 5:33	Ps. 50:14	Lev. 19:12; Num. 30:2; Deut. 23:21
3. Mt. 5:34	Ps. 11:4; 103:19	Is. 66:1
4. Mt. 6:26 (= Lk. 12:24)	Ps. 147:9	Job 38:41
5. Mt. 6:27 (= Lk. 12:25)	Ps. 39:5	
6. Mt. 6:30 (= Lk. 12:28)	Ps. 90:5–6	
7. Mt. 7:23 (= Lk. 13:27)	Ps. 6:8; 119:115	
8. Mt. 8:11 (= Lk. 13:29)	Ps. 107:3	Is. 49:12
9. Mt. 16:27	Ps. 28:4; 62:12; 137:8	2 Sam. 3:39; Prov. 24:12; Jer. 25:14; 32:19; 50:29
10. Mt. 18:12 (=Lk. 15:4; 19:10)	Ps. 119:176	Ezek. 34:4, 11–12, 16
11. Mt. 21:41	Ps. 1:3	
12. Mt. 23:37 (= Lk. 13:34)	Ps. 91:4	
13. Mt. 24:45 (= Lk. 12:42)	Ps. 104:27; 145:15	
14. Mk. 4:32 (= Mt. 13:32; Lk. 13:19)	Ps. 104:12	Ezek. 17:23; 31:6; Dan. 4:12
15. Mk. 8:37 (= Mt. 16:26)	Ps. 49:8	
16. Mk. 12:1 (= Mt. 21:33; Lk. 20:9)	Ps. 80:8	Song 8:11; Is. 5:1–2
17. Mk. 14:34 (= Mt. 26:38)	Ps. 6:3–5; 42:5, 6, 11; 43:5	
18. Mk. 15:34 (= Mt. 27:46)	Ps. 22:1	
19. Lk. 6:28	Ps. 109:28	
20. Lk. 7:46	Ps. 23:5; 92:10	

TABLE 11—*Continued*

N.T.	Psalms	O.T. Background
21. Lk. 10:19	Ps. 91:13	
22. Lk. 12:20	Ps. 39:6; 49:10	Job 27:8
23. Lk. 15:18, 21	Ps. 41:4; 51:4	
24. Lk. 18:7	Ps. 22:2; 88:1	
25. Lk. 21:24	Ps. 79:1	
26. Lk. 21:25	Ps. 65:7	
27. Lk. 23:46	Ps. 31:5	
28. Jn. 4:24	Ps. 145:18	
29. Jn. 6:31	Ps. 78:24; 105:40	Ex. 16:4, 15; Neh. 9:15
30. Jn. 10:34	Ps. 82:6	Is. 41:23
31. Jn. 13:18	Ps. 41:9	
32. Jn. 15:25	Ps. 35:19; 69:4	
33. Jn. 19:28	Ps. 22:15; 63:1; 69:21	

Bibliography

Black, Matthew, "The Christological Use of the Old Testament in the New Testament," *New Testament Studies,* Vol. XVIII (1971).

Box, G. H., "The Value and Significance of the Old Testament in Relation to the New," *The People and the Book,* ed. by A. S. Peake. Oxford: Clarendon Press, 1925.

Bruce, F. F., *New Testament Development of Old Testament Themes.* Wm. B. Eerdmans Publishing Company, 1968.

Cerfaux, Lucien, "Citations scriptuaires et tradition textuelle dans le livre des Actes," *Aux Sources de la Tradition Chrétienne.* Neuchâtel: Delachaux & Niestlé, 1950.

Cunliffe-Jones, Hubert, *The Authority of the Biblical Revelation.* London: James Clarke & Co., Ltd., 1945.

Dodd, C. H., *According to the Scriptures.* Charles Scribner's Sons, 1953.

———, *The Apostolic Preaching.* Harper & Brothers, 1935.

———, *The Old Testament in the New.* Rev. ed. Fortress Press, 1965.

Doeve, J. W., *Jewish Hermeneutics in the Synoptic Gospels and Acts.* Assen, Netherlands: Royal Van Gorcum & Co., 1953.

Ellis, E. Earle, *Paul's Use of the Old Testament.* London: Oliver & Boyd, Ltd., 1961.

Fitzmyer, J. A., "The Use of Explicit Old Testament Quotations in the Qumran Literature and in the New Testament," *New Testament Studies,* Vol. VII (1961).

Freed, Edwin D., *Old Testament Quotations in the Gospel of John.* Leiden: E. J. Brill, 1965.

Goppelt, Leonhard, *Apostolic and Post-Apostolic Times,* tr. by R. A. Guelich. Harper & Row, Publishers, Inc., 1970.

Grant, Robert M., *The Bible in the Church.* The Macmillan Company, 1948.

Gundry, Robert H., *The Use of the Old Testament in St. Matthew's Gospel.* Leiden: E. J. Brill, 1967.

Hanson, A. T., *Jesus Christ in the Old Testament.* London: S.P.C.K., 1965.

Hebert, A. G., *The Authority of the Old Testament.* London: Faber & Faber, Ltd., 1947.

Jeremias, Joachim, *New Testament Theology: The Proclamation of Jesus.* Charles Scribner's Sons, 1971.

Lamb, J. A., *The Psalms in Christian Worship.* London: The Faith Press, 1962.

Lindars, Barnabas, *New Testament Apologetic: The Doctrinal Significance of the Old Testament Quotations.* The Westminster Press, 1962.

Manson, T. W., "The Argument from Prophecy," *Journal of Theological Studies,* Vol. XLVI (1945).

Metzger, Bruce M., "The Formulas Introducing Quotations of Scripture in the New Testament and the Mishnah," *Journal of Biblical Literature,* Vol. LXX (1951).

Moule, C. F. D., *The Birth of the New Testament.* London: Adam & Charles Black, Ltd., 1962.

Oesterley, W. O. E., *The Psalms.* London: S.P.C.K., 1962.

Rowley, H. H., *The Unity of the Bible.* The Westminster Press, 1955.

Scott, R. B. Y., *The Psalms as Christian Praise.* London: Lutterworth Press, 1958.

Stendahl, Krister, *The School of St. Matthew.* 2d ed. Lund: C. W. K. Gleerup Publishers, 1961.

Sundberg, A. C., Jr., *The Old Testament of the Early Church.*
Harvard University Press, 1964.

Swete, H. B., *Introduction to the Old Testament in Greek.*
2d ed. London: Cambridge University Press, 1914.

Tasker, R. V. G., *The Old Testament in the New Testament.*
2d ed. London: SCM Press, Ltd., 1954.

Venard, L., "Citations de l'Ancien Testament dans le Nouveau
Testament," *Dictionnaire de la Bible,* Supplément II (1934).

Von Rad, Gerhard, *Old Testament Theology,* Vol. II, tr. by
D. M. Stalker. Harper & Row, Publishers, Inc., 1965.

Weiser, Artur, *The Psalms, A Commentary,* tr. by Herbert
Hartwell (The Old Testament Library). The Westminster
Press, 1962.

Westermann, Claus, *The Old Testament and Jesus Christ,* tr.
by O. Kaste. Augsburg Publishing House, 1968.

Subject Index

Bible Passages Index

I. OLD TESTAMENT [*with N.T. Parallels*]

II. NEW TESTAMENT [*with O.T. Parallels*]